Because It Didn't Stop When It Ended

Patricia M **Wennell**

Dear Valerie,

A beautiful light in the darkness!

Love

Tricia x .

GUTENBERG
Press

First Edition 2022

ISBN: 978-1-913822-34-7

About the Author

Patricia Wennell is married and lives with her partner in southeast London. She has three daughters, two stepchildren and six grandchildren, with a seventh on the way. She qualified as a social worker in 1994 and after 27 years in adult social care she took a career break before retiring from the profession in 2022.

Over the years Patricia has been actively involved in supporting adult survivors of childhood abuse on a voluntary basis. This included speaking at conferences and with media in the UK and overseas, joining organised marches to raise awareness and providing one to one support to individual survivors. Since April 2021 Tricia has focused on writing, caring for older relatives and grandchildren, and spending time with family. This is her first book.

Acknowledgements

The impact of trauma in my childhood has remained with me because it didn't stop when it ended. If you have read this book, you will understand something of the impact that abuse in childhood can have on a person and how challenging it can be to work through it all in therapy. You may wonder how I survived it all. There will be theories about resilience, nature vs nurture and well-known quotes such as 'Give me a child until he is seven and I will give you the man'. I cannot answer how I survived when so many have taken their lives, have significant physical health problems through self-neglect or substance misuse or required medication to help manage depression. That is not my story. The love and support of many people not only helped me through my childhood but have provided me with a reason to want to live rather than merely exist. To achieve, to love, to be the best version of myself and to write this book. The impact of feeling loved and supported doesn't stop when it ends either and the warmth and colour from that love and care sustains me.

To my daughters Charlene, Tanya and Debbie: you are life's precious gift to me. I love the different and unique relationship I have with each of you and delight in you all. My love and thanks belong first to you, to the beautiful, kind, and generous children you were and the amazing young women you have become. Thank you for all your love and support, especially during the many years of my therapy and in writing this book.

To my partner, your capacity to love me despite your pain is a gift I will always cherish. Your courage and determination to make things right for us, for our children, our grandchildren and so many others are what I thank you for most. Thank you for your patience and generosity in giving me space during my many years of therapy and in writing this book. You also have an important story to tell, and I hope you find the strength to tell it.

To my sister and older brothers, we had each other for comfort as children and I believe it helped us during those harsh years of childhood and sustains us as adults. Your love for me throughout my life, especially from my sister, our ongoing relationship with each other, and your support in me writing this book is another gift I cherish. I thank each of you and have great respect for all you have achieved. To my younger brother, I have loved you from the moment I saw you, less than an hour after you were born. My hope is that you know how much you are loved and that you will find your way.

We don't get to choose the family we are born into and I wouldn't choose to be related to all those whom I share a name or DNA with. For the sake of wider family harmony, I will refrain from sharing more about that here but just to clarify; I am not referring to any of those mentioned above!

We can choose our friends and I have the gift of many who I have chosen as family and who have loved and supported me for many years. At different times and in different ways you have helped me withstand incredibly difficult challenges and shared in my joys. I thank you all. I mention first by name those who, in addition to the lovely friendship we share, have also contributed to helping me complete this book: Debbie Keane, Julie Brock, Clive Brock, Lynne and Ken Newell and Katie John. I thank you for agreeing to be critical friends, for proofreading and for all your comments. To Maureen Floyd, Gary Floyd, Eileen Evans, Tony Evans, Valerie Jay and many others who are in my life. I thank you for your friendship and encouragement.

Sezan M. Sansom is the artist responsible for many of the images in this book. Sez, I cannot begin to thank you for your generosity in sharing your art in this way or for the friendship we share.

To the artist Aileen Churchill, I thank you for your friendship and your generosity of your amazing artwork for my book.

Those who have supported me in a professional capacity over the years from childhood are the late John Robinson CBE and Valerie Foster from the Bromley Y. Even though I couldn't tell you about what was happening to me, I thank you for providing a safe place for me to be and for your continued support of me into my adult years. In my late 20s, Jane, a psychologist, helped me to function as a single mum of three small children during a time of immeasurable pain. Thank you for being that person at that time.

From my mid-40s, Maggie Schaedel and Hilary from The Woman's Service gave me the courage to face the full extent of my childhood trauma and to accept the abused little girl within me. Without them I would not be the woman I have become, and this book could not have been written.

Maggie, I thank you for setting up The Woman's Service, for your ongoing support of me and for your contributions to this book. The opportunity for me to be involved in the documentary about The Woman's Service with Janthia Taylor in 2018 gave me the confidence to share my poetry beyond the pages of my journal and prompted me to think about how I might use them to help others. There is so much more to say about how you have helped me to move on but that is another story for another time.

Hilary, although our therapy sessions stopped in March 2016 my experience of you, our relationship, your absolute commitment to me, your skills, patience, sense of humour, your love and care didn't stop. I have learned so much about myself during, and since, therapy with you. One of the tools I now own as mine is how to be curious about my feelings. It continues to help me in many situations but especially in moments when my fragile sense of self is triggered by the occasional visits of unwelcome memories and feelings from trauma in my childhood. You have been so willing to read my manuscript and share your thoughts. You have offered me significant encouragement five years after you retired. I continue to draw strength from our relationship and believe I always will. Thank you.

Finally, to everyone at Fortis Publishing, thank you for your advice and support in the process of getting Because It Didn't Stop When It Ended to readers.

Patricia M Wennell
July 2022

Instagram contact for Sezan: _sezan_m_sansom

To all those who were abused as children who are no longer here and to all those who are.

Preface

At the turn of the century, I was asked by Oxleas NHS Foundation Trust to develop a specialist psychotherapy service for women survivors of historic child sexual abuse (HCSA).

Our pilot project had shown promising results and funding was agreed for a new NHS-based substantive service for survivors of HCSA. As a collaboration involving the Department of Health, the NHS, MIND and various University-based psychotherapy training departments in the Southeast, we named this project 'The Woman's Service'. We understood that for survivors of HCSA, psychoanalytic psychotherapy may be a phase-based journey, that individual bespoke programmes of care are needed and that no one size would fit all. Our approach embraced a fundamental NHS principle: psychotherapy would be offered according to need in a service which is free at the point of use.

Our first years were fuelled with adequate funding and optimistic collegial generosity and support from many quarters. As psychotherapist witnesses, we helped contain and transform the traumatic impact of HCSA in unique resonances with our patients. The challenge, to commit to thinking the unthinkable and bearing the unbearable, is no easy option. Child sexual abuse is a crime often committed in plain sight yet neither recognised nor witnessed. Helplessness and despair may become overwhelming and sometimes leave long-lasting emotional and psychological scars.

For more than two decades we have listened carefully to our patients and understood how the transformational personal and collective processes of psychotherapy are imagined as a journey in which meaning, agency, purpose, and the re-establishment of levels of trust may develop.

We have understood that the service has another important and privileged function, which is to act as witness. Many survivors with the courage to speak about what has happened to them also learn new forms of resilience and in turn may help others to move from isolation and fear. We have also learned that despair may be survived creatively when given voice.

Every story is unique and complex. For many, remembering early trauma may be accompanied by a terror similar to that experienced in the original attacks. It was during this first decade of the history of The Woman's Service that I met Tricia and came to know of her desire and determination to write and then to bring her experience to share with others.

In a unique and life-affirming way Tricia's poetry and writing bridge past and present. She is not only a brave witness to the violent atrocity that is child sexual abuse. Her poetry and art are also testimony to the power of creativity and the revitalising impact of an important psychotherapeutic relationship.

Maggie Schaedel
Consultant Lead Adult Psychoanalytic Psychotherapist
Oxleas NHS Foundation Trust

Introduction

This book is dedicated to a woman and a little girl. I am the woman, and the little girl is me as a child. There are two other extremely important women without whom I would not be the person I am today. They are Maggie Schaedel and Hilary, the psychotherapists who enabled me to reconnect with the little girl that I was, to work on the damaging and long-lasting impact caused by the abuse I experienced as a child, abuse that traumatised me into becoming disconnected with myself. Without them I would have continued to be governed by the feelings of shame, guilt, worthlessness, and, worst of all, an all-consuming self-hatred. Feelings that I carried for over 40 years because it didn't stop when it ended. Feelings that belonged to those who didn't know how to manage or own their damaged selves and who used me as an outlet for their hurt and sexual gratification. Without them I would not have known how to find and accept the little girl within or to become my adult self, how to move from merely existing to living. I would not have known how it felt to find emotional connections to myself and others.

Why *Because it didn't stop when it ended*? I hope this will become clear as I take you through the narrative, poetry and art that tell the story of how the commitment and dedication of my – whole – self, of Hilary, of Maggie and The Woman's Service helped me move from existing to living. How I learned to reconnect with the little girl who had been lost to me, 'to bear witness…' to her pain – buried deep within me – and to love all of me through building trusting relationships with skilled and dedicated therapists. You will read graphic and difficult material as you experience the journey with me as I experienced it.

I do not include everything that happened in my childhood, and I do not go into detail about some painful and difficult aspects of my adult life that impacted on me and my children. I continue to work through these issues in therapy, but they will not be shared in this book. My first and most important reason for not including all the detail is to ensure sensitivity, respect, and the right to confidentiality for those involved who were hurt by the despicable actions of 'others'. The second is to minimise the risk of those 'others' who are still alive being identifiable and having any opportunity to cause more hurt.

My desire is that what I do share will serve to provide hope to those who are in a similar place, regardless of the type of abuse they experienced and to raise awareness about the devastation caused by abuse in childhood. I also wish it to be a learning tool for those intending to train in this area of work or who are working in this area and would benefit from learning more. Finally, it is a request to those who hold the purse strings, those with political power, to see the need for this longer-term therapeutic support and ensure it is funded so more adults – both men and women – who were abused as children, are offered a service of the type and quality provided by The Woman's Service. Free on point of delivery and available across the country.

An overview of my childhood

My dad was from a working class background and met my mum through his friendship with her first husband, whom he met whilst doing National Service. His friend died suddenly, which left my mum widowed at 19, with a toddler and six months pregnant. She and Dad married and had my sister and me within three years, so by the time they were 23 and 24 years old they had four children – two sons and two daughters. Mum was from a middle class background and was fortunate in that my maternal grandparents owned the house we lived in. We were one of the few families in our area to own a car.

I would describe my early childhood as being loving and fun with some shouting, the threat of a smack, the belt or the cane if we stepped out of line, and a mum whose moods were unpredictable but who managed to provide good enough parenting. Dad tended to be more predictable but would react to Mum's frustration and anger and use physical punishment at her behest rather than stand up to her. My maternal grandparents had significant influence over my mother and how she behaved in their presence. At home her guard was down, and life was quite different.

I felt loved by my parents, and although not perfect, if that had been my experience throughout my childhood I would probably have been OK.

Me as a new-born baby with my siblings in our grandparents' garden.

*A photo of us as a family in better times in our grandparents' garden;
I am aged 3 years.*

My mum gradually changed as she became gripped by mental illness. I recall a difference in how she treated me from around six or seven years old. She had her first 'breakdown' when I was seven, resulting in her being away from us for two weeks.

On her return her ability to cope didn't improve, and I continued to experience violence and cruelty at her hands. Dad worked away during the week, so she was at home with us four children, cleaning houses, selling Avon products, and not coping. With Dad's absence and her mental health deteriorating she became increasingly violent and cruel, and when he was home both she and Dad spent more and more time at the local pub. This was hidden from my grandparents.

For much of the time I was left without the supervision of my parents and spent time with other children who, like me, were extremely vulnerable. On one occasion when out unsupervised, some of those children met Ernest, who soon groomed us all and introduced himself to my parents and befriended the family. In their ignorance and neglect we were all defenceless, and he was free to take me and others away for weekends and school holidays. Over a period of two years, he abused us, exposing us to things no child should ever have to endure.

Mum continued to deteriorate mentally, followed by Dad. This resulted in our maternal grandparents taking me and two of my siblings to live with them when I was 10 years old. They ran their own business and were in their late fifties and mid-sixties, so it cannot have been easy for them to care for us during that year. Our auntie and great-grandmother also lived with our grandparents. Although I was well cared for by them physically, and my auntie was lots of fun, I didn't want to be there. My grandparents were Victorian in their values and held strict boundaries on bedtimes, homework and who we socialised with. This meant I didn't stay overnight with Ernest – but he was allowed to take me out for days with other children. It didn't prevent him abusing me or them, but it reduced the frequency. We had to be on our best behaviour all the time at our grandparents, which for us was extremely tough, especially as we had become accustomed to fending for ourselves and had few boundaries at home.

Our grandparents decided the distance from their house to my school was too far for such a young child to travel by bus in the mornings, so my grandmother drove me to school every day. It meant I couldn't skip school, which I also didn't like.

Soon after my return home my parents separated at my mum's behest, and Dad reluctantly left the family home. The violence at the hands of my mother had mostly stopped, but she continued to neglect us all, leaving us to fend for ourselves. Money was extremely tight even though she worked two jobs to try and manage financially. I didn't see my dad for several months after their break-up, but once my parents reached some sort of agreement I saw him regularly. Dad didn't raise his voice or use any form of physical punishment once he left the family home.

Ernest died in September 1973, so the sexual abuse ended. Mum met my stepdad during this time, and over the following couple of years I began to recognise some aspects of the mum I had known as a small child. I was 13 or 14 the last time she was violent towards me. She married my stepdad when I was 14, and although difficulties continued in the household, particularly for my older brothers, things improved for me. Mum had another son, my younger brother, when I was 16. By this time I felt like I had a mum who loved me and cared about me again. I didn't forget what my mum and Ernest did to me, but I didn't think about it. I didn't talk about it, I tucked it away and somehow existed.

Not thinking about it didn't mean I was OK. I wasn't OK. Like many I tried my best to make a life for myself, but I remained disconnected and lost, at odds with myself and the world. I was not responsible for what happened to me as a child, no child is, but I, like many, continue to suffer the consequences of it.

I am of the view that, because it doesn't stop when it ends, long-term therapy must be an option for all, not just a few, to reduce the devastating and long-lasting impact of abuse in childhood

Before I talk about my experience of therapy, I will say something about Sezan M. Sansom, the talented artist responsible for much of the art in this book. She has her own unique story of what she calls 'self-discovery and recovery' to tell.

Sezan describes herself as a second-generation British citizen born to Muslim immigrant parents. She says she knows little of her heritage and in craving an identity uses imagery from historical paintings to give her presence and a place in society. Sezan uses escapism and imagination to create meaningful interactions with the great painters from the past as a means to re-write her difficult life experiences of neglect, abandonment and emotional abuse, which left her confused and unsure of the extent and breadth of that abuse. She says, 'I meet with ghosts from the past like Frida Kahlo and John William Waterhouse who allow me to feel acceptance, belonging and self-worth through my interpretation of their work.' She describes us as 'two women with different experiences and from very different walks of life, who connect and re-enforce the belief that abuse in any context or form can bring people together, no matter who they are or where they are going in their journeys of self-discovery and recovery'.

However we choose to do it, when we share our abusive experiences, our childhood trauma, we are connecting with each other in what I believe to be a universal language of pain.

Sezan M. Sansom, after Thomas Gainsborough's The Painter's Daughters Chasing a Butterfly.

The assessment with Maggie

I first met Maggie early in 2007 when my partner and I attended an assessment appointment for couple therapy at The Woman's Service. We are both survivors of sexual abuse and are each on our second marriage. It was clear to us that we needed help if our relationship was to succeed rather than become another sad statistic. We had tried Relate in the recent past, which was helpful, but both knew the difficulties we faced went so much deeper and a more specialist approach on a longer-term basis was needed. With five young adult children, one grandchild and very little spare cash this wasn't something we could pay for. To our amazement The Woman's Service was provided free of charge through Oxleas NHS Foundation Trust. Sadly, it was, and remains, the only service of its kind in the UK. In my view, if it were to lose its funding this would equal the crime that caused us to need the service in the first place.

The Woman's Service was based in a fairly new purpose-built building near the town centre. The reception area was furnished with comfortable chairs and was a clean and pleasant environment with off-white painted walls hung with colourful framed prints. There was a high counter behind which sat two women busily answering phones and working on their computers. After a moment, one of them noticed us standing there. She took our names, told us that Maggie wouldn't be long and asked us to take a seat.

We both felt a little apprehensive, but that quickly left us when Maggie came into the waiting area and with a warm welcome invited us into a consulting room. The room was much like the reception area, only smaller, and the chairs were placed in a more intimate way, allowing us to have eye contact.

Maggie had a warmth about her and a relaxed body language; I felt reassured by her gentle confidence and knew she was interested in what we had to say. We both felt safe enough to be honest with her from the start, and after sharing some of our life experiences and the difficulties we were facing in our marriage Maggie offered us the couple therapy service.

The couple sessions with Hilary

We were introduced to Hilary a few weeks later. We were both unsure what to expect, but Hilary greeted us with an assertive but kind voice and showed us into one of the consulting rooms, a room that was similar to the one Maggie used and felt familiar and comfortable.

I felt a little wary of Hilary initially; she appeared outwardly confident, with a glint in her eyes that suggested a mixture of being fun-loving but someone who would take no nonsense. We began a relationship that would help us as a couple and as individuals in ways I never thought possible. We both found the couple sessions very helpful and liked that Hilary encouraged and challenged us to share how we felt and explore our reactions with each other.

Interestingly, over the months the process of couple therapy highlighted that my partner wasn't ready to work through his feelings as part of a couple; he found it too difficult to be honest about his feelings and actions, let alone embark on exploring how his and my pain played out in our relationship. It wasn't working for him, so we decided to work towards an ending. I had learned enough in my lifetime and in the months with Hilary to know that I needed support as an individual, and I also knew that I was ready to face my pain. To my partner's obvious relief, he stopped attending, and apprehensively I began seeing Hilary on a one-to-one basis.

From the early days of my individual therapy with Hilary I kept a journal. I had learned, from previous experiences of therapy, my few attempts at self-help and the couple sessions, that I would at times feel restless with the feelings that stirred within me. Writing them down helped me to process them. I also knew I was embarking on a journey, one that I knew would cause me to think about the memories and pain that had been left behind in what felt like an unreachable place, a place I had disconnected from and wasn't sure I wanted to visit. I feared that if I connected with that part of my life I would completely break down and no longer be able to function, that I would lose everything I had built over the years. Writing down how I felt and reading it back as I worked through the thoughts and feelings arising from my sessions helped me to survive for a second time and then to connect with myself and to begin to live.

So, why embark on this journey, you may ask?

Well, I had survived my childhood, had raised my children, had become a grandmother, had a professional career and was outwardly successful – but inwardly I knew there was something wrong, I remained at odds with myself, I didn't feel like I belonged. I never felt good enough, regardless of how much I did for others or how much I achieved. I felt uncomfortable with myself, worthless, and worst of all I experienced feelings of self-hatred. I knew it didn't have to be that way, and I felt ready to work on me.

Year One

My first few individual sessions with Hilary felt a little odd, given that there had been three of us for the first 19 months. I had felt invisible at times in our couple sessions, and although I had resented that I had also been relieved because I felt less vulnerable that way. I hadn't given much thought to the significance of how feeling invisible in my relationship with my partner was being played out in our couple sessions, nor had I spoken about it during those sessions – yet another consequence of abuse. My voice had been taken away from me by those who should have protected me in my child years, and consequently my needs were hidden from myself and from the outside world. I was disconnected.

I used my journal to write what Hilary and I talked about, how I was feeling and what I had learned. After a few weeks of therapy I told her about my journal, what I had been writing and how I felt. She focused on me, on the child in me. I found it hard but told her my innermost secrets, things I felt ashamed of.

Hilary focused on me as a little girl and asked me what I saw when I thought about me at the age when I was being abused. I tried but I couldn't see little me. It really surprised me. I had not realised that I could only see myself as an adult; it was as though the child had never existed. Hilary asked if I had photographs of me as a child and suggested I look at them and maybe at some photos of my children.

I wanted to find that little girl and I wanted to stop being afraid and stop feeling ashamed of her. That night I looked for photos of me. I found some and I thought about the little me and how she felt. I knew she was very unhappy; I knew she felt bad and dirty, and I knew she didn't feel as though she belonged, she often felt misunderstood.

I said to myself, 'Why would I want to get in touch with her again when there was only unhappiness?' I felt afraid of what or whom I would find!

I looked at photos of my daughters and compared them to photos of me at the ages that matched the years when I had been abused. I tried to think of me as a child, but I still couldn't feel the little me or see her in my mind's eye. I looked at the many photos of my girls and could see their beauty. I felt a rush of love for them, I knew I adored them. They were unquestionably loveable.

During my photo search I came across the transcript of some published research I had taken part in several years earlier, where I had given a detailed account of my childhood trauma. As I read through the pages, I realised that I had told my story as if it were about someone else. I also realised that as a child I did not understand what was happening to me and I didn't have a chance of stopping it. I was just a child.

I looked at the photo of me and was amazed at how little I was. Just a little girl, small for my age. I tried to feel something, to feel what it was like to be that little girl as I was then, not through my adult eyes. I couldn't feel her vulnerability; I didn't see her as the little girl that she was. A vulnerable child and free of blame! I couldn't see her the way I saw my girls. I knew that what was done to her was so wrong and I knew she wasn't responsible for it, but I could not feel it.

I realised that day that I didn't like 'Little Me'. I looked at the photo of me again and again but had no feelings of compassion for her at all. I questioned why I couldn't feel anything positive towards Little Me. Is she dirty? Yes, I felt she was, but I didn't think that was right … how can she have been? She was just a little girl. I wondered, how was I going to embrace her and love her? I battled with myself and questioned myself, how I could feel so negatively towards a little child? A small and vulnerable girl, who was just trying to survive in a world where adults hurt her. I was a little girl, just a little girl.

Photo of me at age 10, in my grandparents' garden, wearing a bridesmaid's dress for an uncle's wedding that I didn't attend.

I remember the relief I felt when it was time for my next appointment with Hilary. It was only a week later, but it felt like forever.

We looked at some photos of my girls and I talked about them with such joy and affection. When Hilary asked me about the photo of me, however, I told her that I didn't like the girl in the picture. We talked about it all and about some of the things I did and felt at that age. I told her that I would chew my food for ages but still couldn't swallow it, and that I was fearful of crossing roads and in a panic would run out in front of a car. I told her that I wet the bed, bullied other kids and wouldn't go to school. Hilary reassured me that none of it was surprising given what had been done to me.

We talked about my inability to love Little Me. Hilary followed my lead and talked about Little Me as a third person in the same way I was doing. She asked me to think about how she (Little Me) might be feeling and went on to say that my mother had abused that little girl and I was also abusing her, rejecting her; she couldn't get away from me, she was stuck with me, and I wasn't taking care of her. I found that hard to hear. I knew I cared about her, and I didn't want her to have been through all that. Did I hate her or hate what happened to her? Hilary viewed her as a brave girl and really quite wonderful. I knew I didn't feel the same way. I initially felt angry that Hilary was saying something that I thought was not true, and then I felt indifferent.

Little did I know what would emerge within me from those sessions, from the relationship that would grow between Hilary and me. Hilary helped me to focus on Little Me, and I was hungry for what I saw as self-discovery, healing, and wholeness. I was totally absorbed

14

by the process I was going through. I had tried different ways of helping myself over the years and had read self-help books such as *The Courage to Heal* by Ellen Bass and Laura Davis, *Homecoming: Reclaiming and Championing Your Inner Child* by John Bradshaw and, in more recent years, *Recovery of Your Inner Child* by Lucia Capacchione. I had written to my inner child and tried to connect with her from time to time, but with limited success. My life was so full of the needs of my children, which included me studying to build a career so that I could provide us with a better life. I therefore couldn't focus on myself.

Now, with my children grown, Hilary and Maggie by my side and bringing the needs of the little girl within me to the fore, I wrote to Little Me. I found a renewed courage to begin to enter her space and tell her I knew what had happened to her wasn't her fault.

I developed a way of communicating with Little Me, asking her questions and writing whatever came to mind, then asking her more until I could no longer get a sense of an answer. The questions that no one asked when I was little and vulnerable. I responded to her pain not because I could physically see her but because I could physically feel her, a feeling so strong that I could begin to see her in my mind's eye.

It wasn't an easy thing to do and starting was the hardest part, but from this early connection, this relationship with Hilary, I began to connect with Little Me. I sat with my laptop, fingers in position, and pressed the keys without thinking about what I was typing. It was as if another part of me, that I didn't know existed, was asking the questions and hearing the answers, and I would be completely lost in the experience. At times I felt like my fingers were just the mechanical means of transferring the message. I would read what I had written and be surprised by the words and how I expressed them.

This is the first of many poems that emerged from this way of talking to Little Me.

> I don't know what to say to you
> How to love you, hold and protect you
> I want to save you from the hurt
> If I could go back in time
> If I could reach you before it started
> I would, if only I could.
> How do I rescue you, how do I?

More sessions with Hilary followed and I gradually became more in touch with myself, more connected. I was in touch with a sense that I had never grieved for Little Me. I had never seen Little Me properly. I was beginning to feel delight in Little Me and started to see myself differently and told her how I felt.

> When I look at you, I see you.
> I see wonder, innocence, beauty.
> A small child who deserved so much
> From the adults responsible for your care.
> You needed to just 'be'
> To become a confident grown up me.
> None of it was your fault
> Beautiful little girl, none of it.

I felt fearful of what would happen – but somehow I knew that I needed to get out of my adult mind and enter that of my inner child if I was going to make this work. I had to move from the one with the power and control and give Little Me a chance to have a voice. I had Hilary there as my safety net, backed up by Maggie and The Woman's Service. More importantly, Little Me had them there too, so I embarked on dialogues with her.

I continued to type without thinking about what I was saying. I went with my feelings, asking Little Me how she was feeling and listening to her answers. I encouraged her and told her how beautiful she was. I let her know I could see her, I could hear her, feel her, see her pain.

Now that I see you
I am drawn to you
I feel your joy and pain
There is no one like you
I feel such love when I see you
You are beautiful wonderful unique

For so long you have waited
So alone so isolated
Not being seen invisible to me
When you tried to reach me
I didn't like what I saw
Your wonder I chose to ignore

How wrong I was to lay the blame
On the little girl that you are
Hate disgust guilt and shame
Is with you and I no more
It belongs out there with them
And not with you my beautiful wonderful child within

I know you couldn't shed a tear
For you had nowhere to go
No safe place to take your fears
No one to protect you. Stop the hurt.
Now you can cry. Now you are safe.
Through me you can shed your tears

I will hold you. I will love you.
No matter how ugly it all feels
Nothing you say nothing you express
Will stop me loving you through your pain
It's okay to hurt for all that has happened
It wasn't you it wasn't your fault.

The more time I spent reassuring Little Me, the more of her fear I could feel. It was as though the power of the suffering experienced by Little Me was so strong that nothing helped. Learning to be patient and love her, no matter how ugly it all felt or whatever she expressed, was challenging. I remembered what Hilary said about Little Me being stuck with me – and although at times I felt like the one who was stuck with Little Me, I knew I had to care for her and love her through it all.

Be free little girl, release the pain
Don't be afraid, it can't happen again
You are safe, I am here, I see you
Now that I see you, I won't leave you
I am delighted you are within me
I will protect you, set you free

As the weeks rolled into months, I began to struggle with the intensity of the feelings. I often couldn't name the feelings but noticed physical sensations in my gut. They felt familiar and I thought it was how I felt when I was small. Like dread or something?

Hilary was aware that I was finding therapy very difficult, especially during the week when I consciously and unconsciously worked on myself, feeling very alone and isolated. She arranged for me to have a second session by telephone to start after the Christmas break, to help me through it all.

I knew I needed to cry but I just couldn't release the pain. I needed to 'just be' and to 'just cry'! Cry with the freedom of a little child. Was it me who couldn't cry or was it the little girl within me?

Let it go little girl, let it go
You don't have to be brave you know
There's nothing for you to do
No one for you to protect
Just the little, wonderful you
To be held and loved all through
The deluge of deep searing pain
That you fight to keep contained
Forcing it down, keeping it where
You believe it's under control
It's not yours to hold down
It's not your burden to carry
It's causing you to be tense and worried
You don't need it for your survival
You are safe, I see you, I won't leave you
You are not ugly
Your pain is not snivelling
You are not a selfish little bitch
Who should be grateful

And think yourself lucky worse hasn't happened.
You are safe, I see you, I won't leave you.

With the ongoing inner dialogue, 1 began to connect with her and let her know I was trying to get it right; I began to feel as though we were in this together and I could be honest with her.

> I am used to forcing away the pain
> I did it to survive again and again
> But I want to learn a different way
> Of being, of living not just to survive
> We don't need to just survive anymore
> We can be free to live and to love
> To be loved and have Joy
> We will keep working to understand
> And to learn how to just be
> With us both, you and me.

My therapy sessions felt like a mixture of success and failure; at times I would feel good about me, and other times I would feel disappointed with myself. I so wanted to cry but at times felt silenced. I didn't like that feeling. When it was time for each session to end, I would feel angry that I had to go, had to wait all week before seeing Hilary again. The extra session agreed for after Christmas felt like a lifetime away. How hard and painful it all was. I so wanted to just 'be' and cry for all that Little Me had been through and what I was still going through. Sometimes I felt able to read my poems to Hilary, and she would acknowledge my pain, but I felt so angry that I couldn't cry. I so wanted to cry for the little child that I was. To feel for her and to help her let go of all that hurt and pain. Why couldn't I let go?

I felt desperate that Little Me would feel let down by me. I told her I was sorry that I didn't know how to cry. I knew Hilary was a safe person so it would be safe to cry and sob and let her see the pain and vulnerability I was feeling. I knew it was okay to trust her. I knew she would cope with it and hoped she wouldn't be hurt by it. I told myself and Little Me that I could cope with it too, but I still couldn't cry.

Hilary would say I needed to give myself time and trust in the process, but I couldn't. I feared I would never be able to cry. But within a few days of feeling this frustration and more pain, I was able to cry. Hilary was right.

I held Little Me in mind, so close. Some detail of the abuse came to mind, but with feelings this time, and it was very painful. I was in touch with what I went through and pieced some information together. It was so emotional and so, so powerful. I felt the deep searing pain that I experienced as a child and felt so distressed for the suffering of me as a little girl. I knew it had all happened but could hardly believe I suffered it all silently. I could not tell, just kept silent. How incredible I was to have lived through such things. I could do nothing, say nothing. I had carried the secret, kept it hidden. I believed it was my doing, my fault.

I remembered in vivid detail what the family friend Ernest did to me, that he would ask me if I wanted him to touch me, he would ask me if I wanted to touch him. I didn't have the power to say no.

I remembered my throat felt numb after Ernest had finished orally raping me. As I relived the memory, nearly

40 years later, I felt sick, and my gag reflexes were working as if it was happening to me in that moment. I was just a little girl and he violated me. My throat muscles were holding on to a memory that my mind struggled to piece together. He gave me all the responsibility, he took none, he left me with the trauma.

In those few short months, I had become dependent on Hilary and needed my sessions with her. I felt as though my very survival depended on her. When I learned from Hilary in the last session before Christmas that I wouldn't be seeing her for a month, I felt so angry about it. She hadn't told me it would be so long, and even though I knew from when we had the couple sessions that she took long breaks, I hadn't remembered. I hadn't felt that level of dependency on her before. I was so pissed off with her. I had to do so much work in between sessions on my own. I was so angry and felt I might not bother going back after the break; she wasn't going to be there when I needed her. I felt Hilary was mirroring my whole life and my childhood. I didn't tell her how desperate I was feeling, I was too afraid! I hid how I felt.

I felt abandoned and alone. I cried out to God, I told Him that I felt really angry because when I was a child I asked him to stop me from wetting the bed, but he didn't do it for me. It was so horrible being hit, my skin being twisted and pinched and being screamed at by my mum because she was so angry that my bed was wet. It was so horrible being violated by Ernest, my mum happy to let him take me away whilst she was having fun with her friends, free of responsibility for me. She was having a good time whilst I was being abused. I felt abandoned and unloved, and she didn't even see. She didn't see me. I felt alone without anyone seeing me and I felt broken by it. It was good that I was starting to cry, but so painful to be doing it alone. It was just me. Little Me had to go it alone, and so did big me. I hated Hilary for going away and in that moment, I never wanted to see her again.

The Christmas break was not a break for me. The process Hilary talked about didn't stop, and I couldn't leave any of it alone. I was experiencing feelings. I had feelings that I had not known before, and I was desperate to work them out and to stop hurting. I was fuelled by the desperation to understand what those feelings were and feared I would run out of time to work through them all with Hilary. I remembered existing in a sense of being bad, alone and very sad, but trying to be okay.

Seeing Hilary and working on Little Me had been the right thing for me. But being left with a feeling of rejection and neglect when I realised how long it would be before I would see her again was so hard. Instead of telling her how hurt I felt, I protected her feelings, but was left feeling rejected. I didn't stick up for Little Me and I felt I had betrayed her. I knew I needed to stay in touch with Little Me if I was to heal and be whole. I couldn't continue with a hurting, neglected child within me. I so wanted her to be free. I had made her a promise that I knew I needed to keep.

My life outside my therapy sessions continued to happen around me. I knew my feelings were not just in relation to the gaping wounds arising from my childhood trauma. They were also in relation to my partner and all the struggles we were having as two adults with all the skip-load of undealt with damage we carried between us. Most of the time I didn't feel I could share my rawness with him. I knew he didn't cope well when I showed vulnerability; he knew me as strong and as the rescuer, and

I couldn't be that person for him whilst feeling such intense pain.

> Behind those eyes
> Who could have known
> The pain behind those eyes
> Who could have looked
> Into the windows of your soul
>
> It was you who wore the mask of pretence
> Carried the burden, were silenced
> No voice, no words, no speech.

As the days became weeks I continued to work on my feelings and found some peace within myself. I understood more about my feelings and, interestingly, drew on my faith to help me get through it all, even though I also felt let down by God. I was aware that in my internal world I felt overwhelmed, lacking in confidence and feeling unsure, and my persona of being confident and able was not easy to maintain. I reminded myself that I was no longer that vulnerable child who was hurt by others. I was able to think through what was being said and form my own opinions.

Despite that, I struggled with making my point and continued to be unsure of myself. I thought about what the Bible said about the furnace and how the flame didn't scorch the men when Nebuchadnezzar threw them in to burn. God did not let them be harmed, but the fire burned me when abuse was my furnace. I was burned and scorched. Wounded. I carried the scars and there was nobody to protect me – not even God.

By the new year, there had been so much processing and so much pain over the weeks since I had seen Hilary. I didn't know if I would go to the next session – and if I did, I didn't know if I would have the courage to tell Hilary how angry I had felt. I felt like I was risking everything. I hated her for going away for what felt like a lifetime, but I needed her.

I did find the courage to tell her how I had felt. She accepted my feelings! She told me it was a normal feeling! I found comfort in being told my feelings were normal. We explored my inability to protect Little Me and how I wanted to learn to do that in the moment. She heard me and gave some help with linking in my choices and decisions and what I settled for. She listened to me when I told her how angry I felt towards her, that she left me with so much pain, that she left me with these feelings of hurting and not having a way to contact her when I felt desperate. There was a number for The Woman's Service, but it was Hilary I wanted.

Hilary worked with my negative feelings, exploring what might work for us both, and gave me a phone number to call her when I needed to. I didn't feel I deserved it. I was so angry with her, and yet she offered me additional support. She had already extended our sessions, and in response to my distress found a way that would give me more. I was suspicious of that. I thought about how I had learned to hide my feelings, how I felt ashamed for feeling so angry with Hilary. I felt guilty that she was giving me more when I thought I had been ungrateful for what she was already giving me.

I continued to dread breaks – but, having learned how hard they were for me, Hilary worked with me to prepare for them. In one of the sessions before another break I experienced physical trembling, my body shook, and I couldn't stop it. I hadn't experienced it quite like that before. I so wished I could have let go of my pain with tears, but I couldn't. My tears were stubbornly remaining hidden, but my body could not contain the trauma. Little Me was determined to be seen even if big me was still too afraid. I felt frustrated that I could get in touch with anger but not release tears. Hilary asked me to be patient with myself, particularly given that it had only been a few months since I had been angry with her for not being with me over Christmas and we were facing another break. I told her I wished she could press a button and do the work for me, and she said she wished she could too. I knew in that moment we were in this together.

I had the phone number that I could call Hilary on if it all got too much. I felt anxious and restless, almost as if I was trying to breathe oxygen when there was no air. But I didn't have to be alone in this pain, and for the first time since being given the phone number I found the courage to call her. I feared she would be negative towards me, I feared she would say I had intruded on her space. I told her about being afraid. Told her I knew I was safe with her but didn't feel it and that I was afraid.

Hilary recalled a situation I shared with her when, as a child, I was faced with a medical examination that I feared would reveal I had been abused – I had been so afraid, I scrubbed myself until I was sore, as I was so scared of what the doctor would see. Hilary said she could link my fear to this incident and she wondered if I was afraid of what she or I might see if I allowed her to be part of my pain and fear. I could understand what she was saying. I wished she could have taken me home with her. Hilary said she was glad I had phoned her. I felt cared for.

I didn't understand why Hilary was so willing to be available, why she cared so much.

Why do you care Hilary?
Why do you care
What's in it for you Hilary
What's in it for you

I want to trust you
Let you see my pain
But what will you do Hilary?
What will you do?

In the weeks that followed I had more dialogues with Little Me. I still didn't think about it, I just typed. It continued to be an amazing experience and gave me insight into myself. I learned of the reasons why I couldn't trust Hilary even though each time I tested her she responded in a very caring way.

I couldn't trust her because of how others had let me down when I was a child. I also felt conflicted because I had some fond memories of my childhood. My family nickname was Boo, given because my mum called me beautiful and would say to me, 'What are you?', and eventually, as I began to form words, I would say, 'Boo'. I knew an early childhood that felt so much safer and was warmer and loving, with fun and laughter and with adults who protected and cared for me. I had felt loved; I had felt 'seen' for my first five or six years of life.

Early childhood – 'Boo'.

I also knew a childhood that was unsafe, with neglect, coldness, pain, physical violence, mental cruelty, and sexual abuse where adults didn't protect or care for me. For my survival I learned to hide my feelings. The sanity of my choice to communicate with Little Me, to write and speak to the little girl of so long ago, was something I often questioned, but it worked. I could feel the little girl within during those dialogues.

On one occasion, while relating to Little Me in this way, without thinking about it, I took a pencil in my left hand, even though I am right-handed, and I sketched how Little Me felt. She felt completely alone; I felt completely alone and trapped.

My drawing of Little Me. My artwork.

There were times when I felt like there was just me facing the enormity of the therapy and all it entailed. I felt so alone. I wanted to be seen, I needed to be seen, but I was afraid of what it would mean. When Hilary was on holiday, even though she gave me her number and said I could call her or text her, I couldn't quite believe her. I couldn't quite believe that she meant it even though I had previously called her, and she had been kind, caring and patient. I agonised over whether to call her or not. I felt I had to manage because she couldn't be there as much as I needed her to be. I was so afraid. If I needed her too much, she wouldn't be able to cope with me or she would leave me, and I would have nothing again. It was safer not to need her, so I continued to deny myself and Little Me the comfort of Hilary and remained alone in my pain. I hated Hilary for caring – it left me in such inner turmoil, conflict and confusion.

Painting by Sezan M. Sansom (confusion, woman in thorns).

The feelings of uncertainty, the sense of myself as dirty and feelings of shame were with me, and I felt stuck. Not phoning Hilary was depriving myself of comfort and I didn't understand why I was doing it. I entered into a dialogue with Little Me and I knew she needed somewhere safe to cry. Yet I stubbornly stayed with the pain and didn't listen to that little voice, even though I had promised I would!

The last part of Revelations about God's perfect kingdom came to mind; I thought about the comfort of there being no more tears. But I wasn't in God's perfect kingdom. I had to live in the moment with needing the tears. I needed them so I could heal. I couldn't cry. I felt alone. Hilary was offering to be there for me, but I hated her for caring. I wanted her to stop.

I was comfortable with having to fend for myself; I knew where I stood with that. I wondered what Hilary would do with so many tears and such deep pain if I were to cry. I wondered what she would do if I needed softness and tenderness. I wondered how I would look if I expressed so much pain; what Hilary would think of me?

I questioned why Hilary cared so much when my own mother didn't or couldn't.

Why do you care, Hilary? Why do you care?
Who am I to you, Hilary? Who am I to you?

Painting by Sezan M. Sansom (little girl).

Over the next day or two the following feelings spilled from my deepest self and flowed effortlessly.

Just me.
Facing the work alone in my pain
Just me.
Trying to make sense of it all
Just me.
Wanting something better than this
Just me.
Doing it, living it, surviving it alone
Just me.
Hiding, hoping I won't be seen
Just me.
Living behind a pretence, a screen
Just me.
Reaching out, hoping, but missing out
Just me.
Yearning to find a way to turn around
Just me.
Not wanting to do it alone
Just me.

Alone
No one to turn to who understands
Alone and afraid all the time
Wanting it to stop, when will it end?
Not knowing what it is, but knowing I feel bad.

I didn't know what to do with the intensity of the feelings and entered into more dialogues with Little Me. I knew from them that Little Me needed to know she was loved unconditionally; I knew I needed to know that too!

I found it difficult to manage what was happening to me emotionally. Within a day of feeling good I would have a day of intense pain, sometimes I would feel I could contact Hilary and other times I would feel I couldn't. The pit of my stomach ached as I entered this internal debate, questioning whether Hilary really cared. I thought I was ready to be vulnerable but found it too much. On this occasion, after expelling so much energy procrastinating, I called Hilary and we explored my vulnerability and issues of trust.

Again, I couldn't cry, and I told her I felt frustration at myself. Hilary described me as a person who seemed driven. I knew she was right. I was exhausted and needed to work on myself less intensively. I decided I would take a break. Unless I really needed to write, I wouldn't; instead I would try and play. I wanted to see if I could. I made a promise to Little Me that I wouldn't drive her so hard!

I thought about the sketch of Little Me sitting in the corner, looking so alone. I felt I kept Little Me in the corner because when I was little I hurt other kids who were smaller than me and then I cuddled them better. I bullied them and I felt guilty and ashamed of myself. I was punishing Little Me.

I told Hilary I didn't want to carry this intense pain around – that it was like torturing myself, abusing myself and I couldn't handle the intensity of it. I told Hilary I needed her to help me stop working so hard and to find a way to be gentler with myself. Hilary asked me what I meant by that, and I said I wanted to play, so we explored ways I could do that. I felt so good after talking with her. Nurtured, heard and understood in that moment. My good sense of self was fragile; the following day I thought about all those who self-harm and felt an empathy with them because there were times when I felt I would do *anything* to stop the pain I was feeling.

Learning how to nurture myself was so hard. During one of the sessions Hilary asked me if I could give Little Me a blanket because the sketch of me in the corner was of an afraid and alone little girl who needed to be comforted. As a little girl I needed someone safe to hold me. I needed someone to see. Nobody did and I was left so alone, so isolated. I had no one to trust. Nowhere to turn. But I couldn't give Little Me a blanket; I just didn't know how to.

> When will someone notice?
> When will someone see?
> The little tiny vulnerable me.
> Grown up now but still in pain
> I'm not strong, it's just a game
> A pretence so I can hide the shame
> The little me sits and trembles
> The experience of such deep hurt
> I fear its intensity to express.
> Can't reach the little me, who sits
> In a corner afraid to show
> The depth of pain and all I know.

My emotions felt as though they were all powerful and the master of their own destiny and I couldn't seem to slow them down. I had more dialogue with Little Me, but the awkwardness and embarrassment I felt about bringing a blanket to my sessions remained. I wasn't sure if I was ready to nurture myself in that way, but I knew I needed to. I thought about making sure there was a safety mechanism in place in case my inability to nurture became an unstoppable desire to hurt myself. I knew I might not be able to get hold of Hilary immediately in the moment, and that felt scary. I didn't want to be alone with such deep, unexplored pain.

I felt that Hilary had suggested a blanket to help Little Me feel safe and I had started to explore how to ensure I would be physically safe, able to contact her when I needed her. I was beginning to see Little Me within me, rather than in the corner of the room, on her own.

You're not alone little girl
I am here to take your hand
To hold you close and protect you
You're not alone little girl
I am here to take your hand
To hold you close and protect you

I was battered, bruised and abused
With nowhere to go and no one to tell
No point in crying, no point in feeling
Better to just exist somehow
Sometimes I would hurt others
Sometimes I would help others
No sense in any of it, just existing

So needed someone to hold me
And to see my pain
No one did, no one came
Left alone, I buried it all
Locked it away, pushed down deep
Not so now, ready to deal with it
To find a way to hold little me
To let her out, to help her cry
What do I need to do for you?

I had struggled with fears of throwing up with the intensity of pain during one of the sessions but hadn't told Hilary at the time. I found it difficult to say how I was feeling, especially when I hadn't processed it sufficiently. I finally managed to tell Hilary about fearing I would spew up all the rot and dirt. Hilary responded with total calmness as if it would be a normal thing to do and said, 'There is a bin in the room.' That evening I spent time looking for other photos and found one of me at about the age of 10. I didn't like the photo; I remembered feeling stupid and ugly in the dress I had been given to wear. I saw Little Me and chose to ignore the dress and told her I loved her and that it was OK to cry out those tears. I cried and felt so much better. I knew it was only the beginning, but it was such a good start.

Photo of me in the checked dress; I was about 11 years old here.

Another break was coming up and this time it was longer, because I had an unexpected offer to visit New York the week before Hilary was going away. I was so torn because it meant more time away from her. In the week or so that followed, the hurt at the prospect of such a long break had been too much for me. When I called Hilary I was so distressed I couldn't speak straight away. She was patient and reassuring until I was able to tell her I felt I had been silenced and I talked about me never being able to tell, having no one to tell and nowhere safe to go. I told her I hated the breaks, and she reassured me that it was OK to tell her. I felt safer and told Hilary about the deep pain in my gut that left me feeling I couldn't breathe. Hilary suggested she give me something to hold so I would know she was still holding me in mind when we didn't see each other. She said I had the courage to give Little Me a voice by phoning and telling her how I felt. I had found a voice to tell. As we talked, she asked me if I still had the pain and I realised it had gone. It was such a powerful moment.

Hilary kept her promise and gave me a card, and in it she wrote that she would be thinking of me. I welcomed it as something to hold on to during the break. She asked me to consider times when I feel frustrated with myself, and she shared with me that when I expressed so much anger towards myself, it made her wince and she wanted me to stop being so hard on myself, on Little Me. She said she wanted me to walk beautifully in my own skin, all of me, and wouldn't take no for an answer!

I was amused by her instructions and appreciated her attempts to help me feel held, but even with the card and kind words I felt I wouldn't be able to survive being separated from her. However, she knew me well and arranged that we could speak part-way through the break to help me manage. Yet, although I felt it was amazing that she would do that for me, I knew the break would still be an enormous challenge for me.

As I left the session and in the following days, I had so much pain inside, and even the card from Hilary didn't feel like it was helping. I wondered if Little Me needed to write from her perspective – was I giving her a voice? I decided to ask her what it was like to be Little Me.

From my dialogue with Little Me I felt a deep sense of there being no warmth, it was cold, I didn't feel safe. The physical pain from the attacks by my mother left me distraught, and from Ernest I felt dirty and ashamed. I was so unhappy. There was such loneliness and sadness. I reassured Little Me that things were different now because we had Hilary.

My reassurance to Little Me helped in the moment, but within a few days I was hurting and struggling to tolerate the feelings I was experiencing. I couldn't sleep. The pain of the beautiful Little Me was wrenching at my gut and I felt sick. I needed Hilary more than ever. I thought about what I would say to her and how I would say it. I played it over and over, not willingly but because I had to.

It occurred to me, amidst an overwhelming sense of pain and breathless agony where I wished I could die, that the times when I was totally dependent and attached to the adults around me was also a time when I was at my most vulnerable and they both hurt me, abused me, and the trauma was still lodged within me. My mum started off loving me and cuddling me, but in her poor mental state became wicked, hateful and violent. Ernest started off kind and loving and then, once he had groomed me, he forced his erect penis down my throat until I thought I would die. I feared that if I didn't understand what I did to make them change, then Hilary would change too! I felt I would eventually become such a burden to her that she would stop caring and then I would cause her to hurt me. I would lose the caring Hilary. I felt I needed to know why she cared so I could stop myself causing her to hate me or to want to hurt me. I wished I could tell her. I wished I didn't have to wait.

I thought about my young age of nine when Ernest hurt me – but when my mum hurt me I was even smaller, even more vulnerable, and she was my mum. She wasn't some random man who found me for the purpose of his own sexual gratification. She grew me inside her and felt me kick and grow. She gave birth to me, and I am alive because during complications at my birth she stopped pushing so that I wasn't strangled by my own cord. Yet she vented her frustration and lost control. Hilary had pointed out that my mum's behaviour was about her inability to deal with her own stuff. I knew that, but it felt like it was because of something I did, someone I was. From the little six-year-old point of view it was because I was a bad girl. A naughty girl who didn't deserve to be loved.

My first school photo, at age five.

I was struck by how my emotions and my feelings were so behind my knowledge. How no matter what I understood about mental illness and grooming, it didn't seem to help, didn't seem to bring comfort. I knew Hilary was there for me, that she cared and that she would be thinking of me, but I feared she wouldn't be. I just couldn't trust that she would be there for me.

I feared that if my own mother could allow herself to hurt me so much, what's to stop Hilary? The struggle to tolerate the feelings was too challenging for me, so with Hilary away and not contactable on the number we would usually talk on, I used the option of calling The Woman's Service for support. I felt terrible for feeling so needy, I felt I had been given so much already, but Maggie and the service were there. They understood how difficult life could be for adults who had suffered childhood trauma, how hard trusting in the process of therapy could be.

The missing intensified and again I felt like nothing was helping me. I so wanted to talk to Hilary. I just wanted to talk to her; the missing was unbearable. I wondered if some of this missing was for my mum. She died of cancer in 2007, but this missing felt like it belonged to losing her to mental illness when I was a child. Such difficult feelings within, I felt her hatred, yet I knew her love for me. A love I felt from her as a young child, a love I was reminded of when I was 16 as she held my younger brother in her arms, and a love I saw in her eyes and in the way she enveloped my daughters into that familiar snuggly way whenever she held them. Then there was my love for her, and I so wanted her to be my mummy who was warm and smelt nice. I wanted someone to rescue me, someone to hold me and protect me.

Hilary was the person I felt I needed in the moment, but she wasn't available. I felt like I needed her all the time. Needed her to hold me, cuddle me, tell me everything would be OK and that I was OK. I so wished she hadn't gone away. I so wished I could talk to her. I needed to find a way to manage my pain for the next 13 days until I could talk to Hilary. I didn't know what I could do. I prayed, I repeatedly held and read Hilary's card, but I could find no comfort. I thought perhaps I just needed to sit with the pain and feel it instead of trying to fight it, push it away or reject it. I was trying not to get angry with myself for feeling how I felt. I knew I needed to accept that, 'If I can't cry, I can't cry, if I'm stuck, I'm stuck.' I was trying to be OK with it, it was me and where I was at. I thought, 'It's OK to be where I am.' I was still missing Hilary. Wanted to talk to her. Wanted to hear her voice.

Bible verses and prayers helped, and I thought of the psalm where God lifted David from the slimy pit, set his feet firmly on the rock and put a new song on his heart. I sang in the Worship Group in Church and I felt lifted by praising God in song. There were times when I felt God had put a new song on my heart and I felt it was sort of what Hilary was saying when she wanted me to walk beautifully in my own skin. Yet I needed more than prayer and worship offered me. I needed more than what family and friends offered me. I felt so raw without Hilary.

I continued to hurt; there was no relief from the dread and the sick feeling I had. I didn't know what to do with myself or what to do with the pain. It occurred to me again that Hilary wasn't really who I wanted. I really wanted my mum to know how I was feeling. I wished I could have told her how it felt when she hit and shouted and when her physical and verbal cruelty caused me so much pain. I wished I could have told her what Ernest was doing to me. I will never know how she would have reacted. I couldn't tell. It wasn't safe. He said I would be taken away from my mum. I remembered dreams of being taken away by an unknown person in a strange vehicle and my mum looking at me with such anger, her arms folded. She didn't reach for me; she didn't try and stop me being taken away from her. I believed him.

The pain reached a level I had never known before. I began to sob, I wanted to howl. I held myself, not knowing whether to sit or stand. I cradled myself, rocking back and forth, feeling like I would spew. Tears fell, I couldn't breathe properly. Pain was so intense. Didn't know where to put myself. I cried out to God. How could he have just watched as a vulnerable child was being abused by a grown man? How could God not intervene? How could my mum allow herself to hurt me? Why didn't she stop herself? How come she didn't walk away when she was angry? I didn't feel cried out. I felt alone. I sat over the toilet, so sure I would throw up all the shit. I felt exhausted, drained. The experience was so raw. I understood why it felt so hard to let go of it all with Hilary or with anyone. The tears dropping from my eyes, the snot dripping from my nose, the sound of such pain coming from so deep within me. Would have to feel very safe to let it all go in front of another. The therapy room didn't feel a safe enough place for that. No warm covers and too many people around. I needed a place to go without others seeing me or hearing me.

As the days went on, the pain was less intense. I looked at the sketch I drew of me in the corner. I knew she wasn't there anymore. I couldn't help but wonder where she was. I needed to ask Little Me.

I felt lighter. I could breathe again. I was still missing Hilary, but I was also angry that I had to wait so long for her to come back, to be accessible to me by phone. The pain I had gone through had left me exhausted and she wasn't there when I needed her the most. At a time when all I wanted to do was call her, hear her voice, she just wasn't there. I had to go through all that alone. I wanted to know how Little Me was feeling and seeing things.

Spending time thinking about how I felt as a child and entering that space was the only way to give Little Me a voice, the voice she didn't have at the time. I had an overwhelming feeling of being sorry for not being a good girl, for making my mum angry, for wetting the bed. I so wished I could have told my mum what Ernest was doing to me. I could feel what had become the familiar sadness and unhappiness, the feelings of being dirty and ashamed. When I reassured Little Me that it wasn't her fault, I genuinely believed it. I knew and I felt it wasn't her fault, wasn't my fault. I knew and felt that it wasn't my fault I was abused, and I felt Little Me as part of me, brave and wonderful, not dirty and bad. I felt I knew what Hilary meant about Little Me being a heroine. I knew what she meant about me walking beautifully in my own skin.

The process I had been through in those first seven months of therapy had unlocked something profound within me. I had a deep understanding, from a feeling and knowing point of view, that the adults around me should have kept me safe. I should have been protected. The adults in my life could never have a good enough reason for their actions. Never. The little girl should have been treated well. She should have been and still should be treated with a genuine love and respect. There is nothing more and nothing else. Just that she didn't deserve to be abused and hurt. She was just a lovely little girl and she should have been nurtured. She should have been loved and treasured. It was the fault of the adults around her that caused the problem, not Little Me. It wasn't me; it wasn't my fault. I was just a little girl. A beautiful, trusting little girl.

I felt devastated and traumatised by what I had been through. It felt as though I had connected with what Little Me had lived through, how she felt, and I knew the devastation of abuse. I feared I wouldn't survive more pain. I felt the power of the child within and knew she needed me to manage this. I reassured Little Me that I would take responsibility for how she felt. I would test Hilary and make sure Little Me was safe, make sure I was safe.

What I want to know Hilary is
What do you see?
How much hurt, pain do you see when looking at me?
If I asked you to summarise me, what would you say
How do you determine whether I am okay?
If I am safe enough to wait another day

The level of pain I am able to express
It's nothing compared to my level of distress
I can't begin to show my depth of raw
How desperately I wish I could claw
Out the pain, ripping open my chest
To stop it all, to give me rest

If I hurt myself then maybe you'll see
The level of pain that's hidden in me
If I scream at you, call you names

44

Call your number several times a day
If I don't turn up, refuse to speak
Keep away ignore you for weeks

Then will you see and understand
My deep unending merciless pain
The misery I feel, the sadness the loss
Of child years robbed of everything
I'm not as strong as you think.

I often found it helpful talking to Hilary as if she were with me in the moment, in a similar way to how I spoke to Little Me. Not really a prayer like speaking to God, but still a conversation indicating a living relationship.

The relationship with Hilary was alive and real. In my inner conversation with her I told her, 'Hilary, when we speak either over the phone or face to face, I am aware that my fear of letting you see the extent and depth of my pain is present. I don't know what you will do with it or me. What will you think of me? How long until you tire of me and all this? I so want to cry for all that was taken from me, all I suffered, for the loss of my child years and all that went wrong in my adult years because of it. I want to cry out the cry of fear and loneliness, the raw screams of the traumatic things, and I want to speak out the words I could never say. I want to do that whilst I am with you and not the next day when I am alone. So, what's the point if all I can do is sit and talk with you whilst I hurt, unable to release the pain until you're not there?'

In the same way I continued to converse with Little Me. I couldn't always respond and didn't always know what to say to Little Me, but I began to understand that both Little Me and adult me feared the loss of Hilary.

Feared that if I were to let Hilary see the true rawness of the pain, the extent of it all, she would be tainted with my dirt, I would lose so much. I would be alone again. Abused again. There was too much at stake for me to let her witness the vulnerable me who makes people loathe her, who causes others to treat her as a non-person. I couldn't let it happen. I felt I had to let Hilary believe that I was OK and only let her in so far then she would keep seeing 'the me' who she liked, who she approved of and admired. I wondered how I could move on from that place and take the risk. I felt like I was on a painful fisherman's hook. I was writhing and wriggling but couldn't get free because I was caught, and the pain was ripping me apart. I knew the pain of Little Me so well, the shivering and shaking in the night, the stomach pains, feeling cold, unable to breathe, the loneliness, the fear.

It felt so hard to keep going, and I desperately searched for something to help me. As I searched for some peace, 'don't hang up your harp' from Psalm 137 came to mind and helped me to hold on. I knew I wouldn't give up!

There was no respite from this process. I was so tired and felt powerless to stop the memory of the abuse that played like a video with no off switch, over and over in my head. I felt so angry. I thought about the things he did to me and how his actions were so totally disgusting. I hated what he did to me. All I could think of was the beautiful little girl whose heart was breaking behind the face of obedience. I felt so angry for all that I went through as a little girl. I had no chance. I couldn't get this stuff out of my head and I was burning with rage. As each slow painful hour went by, I could do no more than live through the memories; they robbed me of rest and sleep.

I phoned Hilary, feeling desperate, and she suggested, amongst many other things, that I get some cushions from a charity shop and whenever Ernest came into my mind and took control of my memories, I should tell him to 'fuck off' and throw the cushion out of the window. I loved the sentiment. Hilary also asked me to call her and let her know if I couldn't sleep the next night. I felt so supported by her. I wished I had her around me when I was a child. It was great to talk to Hilary, and I was and still am so grateful for her. Looking back on those days and the intensity of the pain I suffered, it could not have been easy for Hilary. I knew she cared about me, and I knew she was angry about what had happened to me.

The following day I sent her a text to tell her how she had helped me. I had woken in the early hours again, and the unwelcome video was playing. I could not handle another night like that. I prayed it away and finally fell asleep around six-ish and didn't wake until late morning. Brilliant. I told her I'd used the PPP approach – Punched the Perv' with Prayer – and it worked for me. I wanted her to know I was OK.

I also needed to talk to Little Me. It was too easy to get carried away with my determination to 'deal' with my hurts, but I reminded myself that the adult me must remember to listen to Little Me. I felt the need to cuddle her and protect her. I had promised to hold her and love her, and I knew I was doing that.

More than three years after meeting Hilary and eight months into individual therapy with her, I cried freely as I told her I felt embarrassed, humiliated, and awkward, and battled with myself before calling her. I had fleetingly felt safe before being overwhelmed with fear. Hilary talked about me not having a safe place as a child and said, 'Trusting that feeling of safety is going to take time.'

I was glad to be able to cry with Hilary, and she was so good and gentle. She spent time re-enforcing the message to me, with her assertive voice, that whenever I needed her, I was to 'pick up the phone'. I acknowledged with Hilary that she had told me this lots of times but that it wasn't going in. I told her that I didn't understand any of it. I didn't understand why Ernest abused me; in the same way I didn't understand why Hilary was so willing to be there for me. She talked about us nurturing Little Me together. We also talked about how much moving on had occurred in me, and how amazing Little Me had been to have come this far. She asked me to remember to pray because she knew I found it helpful. Feeling sadness, feeling fear, feeling safe, feelings generally weren't yet all that familiar to me. At the end of our talk, Hilary asked how I felt, and I was aware that I felt sad. Appropriately sad, not scary sad. Hilary helped me so much. I really appreciated her.

The sadness stayed with me. There was a heaviness within, and I felt a weight in my chest. My heart ached for Little Me to feel OK again, but I also knew I was feeling the benefit of having Hilary in my life and the benefit of her nurturing. I told Hilary I wanted to say sorry to her. I said I was sorry, I told her I was sorry but that I didn't know why. Hilary said I didn't need to say sorry to her, but she wondered if I needed to say sorry to Little Me for refusing to acknowledge her and for finding her disgusting. I felt sorry for keeping my little hurt girl away for so long. I felt so sorry for not hearing or seeing her and for blaming her for the terrible things that were done to her. I set some quiet time aside and I told Little Me that I was sorry for being so hard on her and not listening to her, for blaming her. I thanked her for being the strength within me that made survival possible.

After that I had a couple of days' respite from the pain, but by the time I saw Hilary again I was feeling terrible. I didn't want her to look at me, my stomach was wrenching, and I felt sick. It was a helpful session in terms of me understanding the enormity of what I went through, that it was too big for me to deal with. I felt an overwhelming sense of not being integrated with Little Me. I felt I didn't like her all over again. I cried out, asking myself, 'How can I learn to accept what happened to me when I was small, how can I integrate and feel OK about Little Me when life was so terrible and I had no safe place to go?' I felt like I was rejecting the little girl I was because I couldn't deal with the reality and enormity of the pain she lived with. I didn't want that pain; I didn't want that life. I couldn't leave her in there. I couldn't leave her behind.

Hilary understood about guilt and shame. She agreed that I couldn't yet accept Little Me and suggested I didn't want her to be part of me. I told her I felt I was back to square one, that I was pissed off with dealing with it and was tired of the wrenching and burning in my gut. I'd had enough and I wanted to give up. Hilary said, 'So that little girl had to live with all that pain and put up with it, but you can't?'

I told Hilary I wanted to rip it all out of me because I didn't want to feel it anymore. I told her I didn't understand why I couldn't just cry it all out. I had been seeing Hilary for what felt like ages yet still couldn't let go of it all.

These conversations were such an important part of the process and the relationship. I questioned why I couldn't tell Hilary how I felt in the moment and we linked it back to being asked by Ernest if I wanted him to touch me. I had no power to say no. It was disabling! I was starting to trust that I could tell Hilary how I felt in the moment, it felt like a small step, but it was a start. I felt contained by her and I knew I needed more of what she provided, she offered me the 'more' that I needed. Hilary had said to me many times, sometimes with clear frustration in her voice, 'Pick up the phone, if you need to talk pick up the phone.'

There were times when I felt like something horrible would crawl out of me, like there was something evil and nasty in there that had to be controlled. If Hilary really saw me, she would see it. Then what? Hilary was able to work with what I said about the evil, nasty thing coming out. She spoke about me being very in touch with the child. My desire to hide was what a child would do. Hilary very helpfully said that she thought it was because the abuse had left me feeling bad, so bad, and that's what I am left with. We explored ideas and I suggested that I try and let her know when Little Me is active, so she knows how I am feeling in the moment. I also shared with Hilary my deepest fears about letting go of all the pain because I might crumble, might feel like I had during the break. I had said I was afraid Hilary would find me so horrible that she would walk away, and I would be left there. In her voice that meant there was no arguing, Hilary said, 'With Woman's Service you would be cared for and not left alone.'

I feared that I would have a complete mental breakdown. Hilary talked about my mum's mental ill health, and I could see where my fear stemmed from.

The feelings continued and I had a picture of ripped decaying flesh, welts all over the body, with the stench penetrating the air forcing itself into the lungs of anyone near it, causing them to vomit. If my inner self could be seen externally, that's what it would look like. If Hilary couldn't stomach that, she couldn't stomach my inner badness. Or my inner feelings of badness. It felt so big. No wonder it was burning into my gut. I had to know – was that how Little Me really felt? I had an overwhelming sense that Little Me felt she was that bad!

I reassured Little Me with Hilary's words and was in touch with how I carried the scars and burdens of the abuse. If the hurt of the abuse could be seen externally, then you would see open wounds and scars on my skin. Some would be chronic, some healed but fragile and easily becoming sore, others raw but not smelling and not infectious.

The intensity of what I was feeling and how exhausted it left me was difficult to hide. I was adept at hiding my pain but was aware the process was tough and at times hard for my partner. He was also living with the cruel, long-lasting impact of abuse from his childhood, and I knew it was hard for him to witness my distress, especially as much of the time I couldn't share how I was feeling, leaving him on the outside. I was so aware of the damage caused by abuse, for the person abused and for those around them. I will never know about my mum's level of choice to be cruel given she was suffering from mental illness and seemed to completely lose control, but I absolutely believe Ernest, and others like him, could – then and now – make a choice not to hurt, not to abuse.

> Deep within my soul
> There's an unwritten rule
> Don't Pass It On

I feel I am full of toxic waste,
I am not sure if I feel toxic but I feel it is in me.
Like in the garden of Eden
Eve blamed the serpent
Adam blamed Eve
They knew guilt and shame
It caused them to hide
They made a choice and got it wrong
They chose to pass it on

Deep within my soul
There's an unwritten rule
Whatever was done
You don't pass it on.

After several months of intense feelings, I noticed I was feeling lighter. Hilary said she thought I had been reliving how traumatised I was as a child. I completely agreed with her. I felt as though I had lived through the trauma of the abuse I had suffered as a child but couldn't feel at the time. No wonder I disconnected from myself. Would I have managed to exist at all had I felt it all at the time, or would I have been one of the many who self-harmed by cutting their skin or who took their life to escape from the pain? I had self-harmed regularly by pushing myself too hard and occasionally by hitting myself and pulling my hair when I felt overwhelmed, but it wasn't something I recognised as self-harm until being in therapy.

I developed a sense of being OK, of being contained. I experienced myself in a way I hadn't before. I laughed in a different way. I felt the laughter. Felt lighter and free. I had carried all that pain; it was a heavy burden. Hilary helped me to understand that my ability to express and heal was because I felt safe. At the end of the sessions I never wanted to leave, and on one particular occasion I was able to tell Hilary in the moment as I felt it. She reassured me by saying, 'That little girl had no one and now she has someone she doesn't want to let her go.' She added, 'She needs more and can have more.'

I often felt I wanted to cry when with Hilary. I laughed with her sometimes and I loved that. My fear was that I would never be able to reach in and collect Little Me. Would never be able to go in and get her, rescue her from the pit of abuse. I will always have been abused. The little girl that I was will always have been abused. Nothing could change that, but I was healing from it. I was learning to love and accept Little Me. I felt so much freer. I wanted to be with Hilary most of the time. I just wanted to be in her presence, around her. At those times I would send her a text saying I needed to know she was there, and she would send back each time, 'I'm here.' That short message kept me going, it was enough to reassure me, and I knew in those moments she was thinking of me.

We had continued with an additional telephone session, and I realised that I wanted to bring the telephone and face to face together. Feeling safer over the phone related to Hilary not being able to see me; face to face needed more courage. I wanted to become one. The me who was hurt, the me who got it right, the me who got it wrong, the me who failed, the me who felt like I wish I'd never been born. The me who worked hard, achieved and made Hilary laugh. The me who no one wanted to be friends with, the me who isolated herself and felt hateful and dirty and the me who valued herself and knew she's OK. I began to understand, 'I am me.'

Everything about my life was relevant in my therapy sessions, and there were times when I felt OK enough to share those things. I told Hilary about the fun I'd had with my girls at a spa weekend. I told her that I wished she could have joined us for afternoon tea, and she told me she was touched by the sentiment. Being able to say that to Hilary was an in-the-moment thing. I was feeling more integrated, and I realised I could tolerate a sense of belonging; I was feeling safe enough to be connected to her.

In response to one of my times of feeling frustrated and powerless, Hilary talked about 'the emotional high street' and explained it as a useful concept of managing difficult emotions. She went on to say that some 'shops of emotion' are ones you mean to visit, and others you find yourself in but you can walk out of them. You don't have to stay in them if you don't want to. I said I wanted to bring all of me to our sessions, but that I was so aware that I phoned her when I'm hurting and that's when I need her. That my face-to-face sessions were a set time when I didn't necessarily feel vulnerable. I so wanted to bring all of me together in the one place. Using her metaphor, I told her that I felt my real vulnerability was in a side street, not the high street. Hilary agreed and understood. She always understood. I told her that I really appreciated what she gave me. I felt Hilary kept on giving and that I was starting to feel entitled. Hilary agreed. I also spoke about an iceberg and fearing what was below the surface. I liked feeling together, and I was also feeling OK. A bit wary of it not lasting or of the iceberg revealing something deep and painful. A break was coming up; I was going away, and I desperately didn't want to miss Hilary so much or be so needy of her or ache because I was away from her.

I went on holiday to the Atlantic side of Barbados, where its rugged beauty moved me. Whilst there I realised I had reached a place within myself where I had grown to accept an imperfect or rugged beauty inside and out. The ruggedness was the scars of my life, and the beauty was who I was becoming in the process of developing a relationship with Hilary and Little Me. Connecting with her and Little Me was enabling me to grow into who I was and loving her would enable me to be who I will become.

The rollercoaster of emotions continued, and I moved from feeling lighter to struggling. I used Hilary's high street of emotion and the power of it allowed me to move from emotional store to emotional store by choice to help me as I experienced angry feelings for what was done to me. No one paid for what they did to me. I hated the injustice of it, and I wanted to hurt back. I wanted to ask Hilary to help me move from fearing I would be a 'snivelling wreck' to being comfortable with the wracking sobs that needed to be released. I knew she wouldn't like me saying I was a snivelling wreck, she would say, 'That old chestnut,' but I didn't care. It was how I felt. I hadn't spoken to her for several days because we could only communicate by text whilst I was so far away.

I wanted to be free to grieve. I so wanted to let go of the deep pain of loss, the searing pain that cut deep within, out of reach. I needed Hilary to hold me but if she were to move towards me to cradle me, I would withdraw in fear of her touch. I would hide and not want her to look at me for fear that I would see pity, understanding, love or acceptance in her eyes; or a judgement of loathing and disgust at my snivelling ugliness – either would cause me to crumble. Both would be intense, both a trigger of what I most needed but most feared. I still wanted all of me to be with Hilary when I saw her next. Whatever all of me was and whatever emotional store I was in. I wanted to be there.

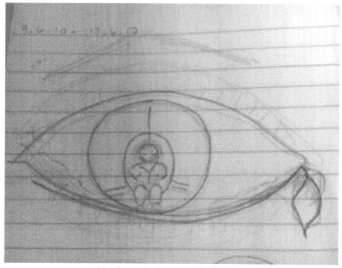

Me through the eye. My artwork.

I became very aware of that iceberg I had mentioned to Hilary. Ironic, given I was in the Caribbean! I felt as though it was so cold and huge, it burned into me. I wanted to tell Hilary. It was so solid that it lodged itself within me and I didn't know how to get it to melt, to dissolve so that I could reach the deep pain of loss that sat within me. I wanted to let go of the pain, to be free of the hurt. I knew Hilary would understand. I felt like she was giving me the parenting I never had.

> What is the depth of the iceberg
> What will it reveal to me
> More hurt than I can bear?

More memories buried.
Who knows except God himself?
He knows, He was there
Lord it all feels so unfair.

I remembered some of the things my mum used to say when she was hitting me for wetting the bed. I stopped crying when she did it because she would work herself up more and more into a frenzy of violence until she was slapping, twisting and breaking my skin with every angry word before hitting me with kitchen utensils, telling me she would beat the piss out of me. I had always remembered some of this but not all. It hurt so much to remember that she told me I was ugly when I cried, saying I was snivelling and would tell me she'd give me something to cry for if I didn't stop.

How was I going to move from feeling I was an 'ugly, snivelling, dirty, nasty little girl' who would be 'given something to really cry for', whose very existence was responsible for my mum's misery? How was I to move from there to crying for the tiny little girl who grew up with self-loathing, self-hate, believing she deserved nothing and expected nothing? How was I to reach that tiny little girl who needed to be cried for, whose pain, suffering and abuse was not her fault? Could Hilary really enable me to get there? Did she really care, did she want my healing enough to hold me when I am ugly?

I felt like I was fast losing my sense of the comfort of Hilary within me. That I was struggling to keep hold of my part of her. I sent her a text, and she sent one back saying, 'Your part of me is safe with you.' She told me, 'I am thinking of you in the beautiful country and looking forward to seeing you next week.' She knew what I needed, and my sense of her was restored in that moment.

The iceberg within me. My artwork.

I managed to feel in the moment when I next saw Hilary and was able to tell her about my mum rubbing wet bed sheets around my face, her pinching and twisting my skin and her hurting me until I stopped crying. Hilary said it was no wonder I couldn't cry. In that moment I stopped feeling like I was doing something wrong. I became aware of Hilary looking at me. I told her I couldn't look at her and felt like I was wriggling painfully like a fish on a hook, that I was so uncomfortable. Hilary asked me what I thought she would see in me or me in her. I feared that if she looked at me, she might see me as tearful, see vulnerability. If I looked at her, I might see hate or disapproval. She asked me to tell her when I had seen that in her eyes. I told her I couldn't tell her a time when it had happened. She said she knew that but wanted me to recognise it for myself and that the discomfort belonged to me feeling ashamed, rather than to her disapproving of me. I could feel the emotional connection between us.

During my struggles to understand more about the abuse I experienced, I looked online for definitions of what was done to me. Everything that happened to me was described generically as physical, emotional or sexual abuse. There was no clear single definition that would describe the horror of it all. Hilary asked me not to look when I told her about it, saying I wouldn't find anything that would help me feel for Little Me and I had to accept it was within me, not out there. I was in touch with so much anger for the hurt inflicted on me. No one was paying for it except me. I was angry that Hilary was going away again and felt abandoned, and I added another week by going away myself. I was left with the shit of what others had done, and because my mum and Ernest are dead, I couldn't make them answer for it. Hilary asked me what I thought making them answer would achieve. I was clear about that and told her, 'It would allow me to tell them I remembered what they did.'

Hilary suggested I wanted to get it off my chest, but she didn't think it would help because the feelings were with me and putting them outside wouldn't help me, just like having a name for what was done to me won't help me. At the end of the session I no longer felt angry but left with a block in my chest, I didn't know what it was. Hilary talked about the reality of the mess in my childhood and called me 'a miracle'. I winced when she said that, but I couldn't say why when she asked. Hilary also said she expected to hear from me during the break and talked positively about me and my strength. I was struck by how much Hilary cared and by her commitment to me. She was working so hard to help me. I continued to wonder: Why?

Over time, I gradually learned that I could turn to Hilary in moments of distress. I so loved working with her. She showed me, by her willingness and efforts to reassure me, of her care and commitment to me. I felt taken care of, not something I was used to in my life. She spoke of my experience in childhood where I was forced to deny my pain by being hit for 'snivelling'. I felt the ugliness wasn't me but that the abuse was ugly, and it felt better. It felt freer and lighter. I felt I was pushing away the pain. Hilary asked me if I felt any benefit from all the pain. I spoke of the awful cry of wracking pain and anger that had left me feeling terrible. That I had not been able to ring her and leave a message in the moment. I didn't want her to hear me like that. She said that I was not able to believe that she would hold me if I was hurting like that because of what had happened in the past when I cried. I remembered how my mum mimicked me when I cried or showed distress. She would exaggerate my expression and distort her face and voice, tell me how ugly I looked when I cried and then hit me or threaten to if I didn't stop 'snivelling'. Hilary was there for me, and I knew I was safe with her. She nurtured me and parented me and reassured me that it will take time but 'bit by bit' it will feel better. I didn't want bit by bit; I wanted it all sorted!

As my confidence grew in my relationship with Hilary, I was more able to tell her how I felt in the moment, even to say that I wanted her to hold me. I felt 'clean' enough to risk telling her that! Hilary talked about my mum and whether I could know more about her life to help me understand why she was the way she was. She wanted me to understand that none of what my mum did was anything to do with me, that it wasn't helpful for me to see my mum and Ernest as the same. She asked if I thought my mum intentionally hurt me. I didn't think that. She asked me about Ernest, and I believed he did.

Hilary saying that I was a miracle the previous week got me wondering how and where I got kindness from. Where did I get the capacity to love out of a childhood of abuse? I told Hilary there was a very kind lady in my life, Barbara, whom I loved spending time with. I lived with my grandmother for some of my childhood, and Hilary asked me how my grandmother reacted when I wet the bed. I remembered that she didn't punish me but told me to strip the bed and put the sheets in the bath. Hilary then asked if I remembered what the bed there felt like. I remembered and found it so hard to answer with the pain of realising there was such a contrast between the two homes I lived in. I hadn't thought of how clean, fresh and comfy I was in bed at my gran's. I remembered lying awake and being afraid even though I knew I was safe. My grandmother was quite matter of fact, a practical person and at times abrupt, but she was also affectionate and didn't punish me for wetting the bed. I began to understand that my mother's abuse of me and that of Ernest wasn't to do with me, it wasn't anything to do with me. Just as it wasn't anything to do with me that Hilary would be away for six sessions. But it was me who was hurt by it. Me, who was lost and alone with nowhere to go.

Hilary was the last person I wanted to feel angry with, but I did feel angry with her. I wanted to ask her not to go. In thinking about planning for the long break, Hilary offered to find an affordable way to receive text messages or arrange some phone time which was so kind, but it didn't feel enough. I wanted a safe house. I wanted to be with Hilary and just be around her. Then when I was hurting, she would be ready to hold me, see my pain and help me in the moment. A part of me wanted to cry out to Hilary, 'Help me – please help me.' I wanted to tell Hilary that I needed her and that I couldn't handle her going away for so long. I messaged her and she messaged me back to say she could be with me in mind, knowing my anger and accepting it, and that it was another way of me being held. It helped me, and when we next spoke, I told her that I was hurting because I didn't want to feel angry with her. She asked why, saying that she would if she were me. I told her it felt like an injustice, and I cried. Hilary was gentle and tender with me and I felt contained by her.

I often didn't call Hilary when I needed her, and after exploring that in more depth, she suggested I was depriving myself. I told her I had to get used to being without her for six weeks, that she won't always be there, so I might as well get used to it sooner and when it was my choice. We talked about my level of vulnerability, and I was in touch with a new feeling that I couldn't name. I wondered how distressed or vulnerable I would allow myself to be before I would call, even though in the moment I didn't feel it was a choice. I couldn't describe the feeling – and then I managed to show her, using my hands, that I felt small and fragile as though I might break, exposed, almost naked. Hilary questioned whether it related to me being seen. She was right. Seen, exposed? I felt so disappointed that I couldn't cry. Could never cry!

That night felt so raw, and through texts we arranged to speak the following day, when I told Hilary I couldn't see how I was going to manage so many weeks without her. She said, 'We will find a way,' and together, we did. I felt so comforted and supported by her kind offers to be there for me.

I thought about Little Me and knew my feelings of desperation were hers. I was determined to listen and give Little Me a voice. I bought a set of Russian dolls and put photos of me on them, at the ages when the abuse by my mother and by Ernest started. I gave it to Hilary, feeling very embarrassed, but she said she liked it. She was confident I would manage the break and reassured me she would be with me in thought. I knew what she meant, and she had hurting Little Me in the layers of the Russian dolls, but I was in such agony and told her it felt too horrible. She offered to be around again if I needed her and I thanked her, telling her I cared for her and was aware that she needed a break. She said that she did and that she knew she would function better with one. I wanted to be able to have the break too.

The thoughts of the dolls and of me really being seen were on my mind when I awoke the next day. It occurred to me that Little Me had found a new safe level with Hilary. To show her how tiny and vulnerable I was, to expose that tiny girl's fragility was putting my life, my very existence into her hands. To trust her with my very being. I had a need and a dependency on Hilary, I was reliant on her for what felt like my breath, my survival. The way a baby or small child is dependent on its mother.

I could feel the tiny little girl who had been lost, left behind, afraid. The rest of me carried on without her and eventually I stopped feeling her. She couldn't be heard, and it was very scary for her to be lost for so long. She was too afraid to trust and didn't know safety when it was there. I thought she was gone, then I thought she knew safe, but I learned that she didn't. She knew safer before the age of seven, but she didn't know safe again until Hilary came into my life. The layers had started to peel back and there was a glimpse of this beautiful, delicate little girl like the bud of a new rose. A scent so sweet and petals so delicate that anything but the gentle brush of a touch would bruise her. So afraid, so vulnerable and I didn't feel I had been able to prepare her to emerge and show herself. I was trying and I needed to keep trying.

Communicating and connecting with Little Me was an essential ongoing part of the process for me.

Hello you, tiny little girl
So delicate, so beautiful
Such a gift to this world
So long ago in that secret place
We were one with each other, loved our self
A force came in so harsh
That it fragmented our very being
Split us apart, and the you part of me was left behind
I was catapulted into growing up, knowing
Over the years your form, our being
Was hidden from me.
Your smallness, your delicate beauty, lost.
The search for you started when I understood
That something so profound was missing
My being, my soul, the very essence of my inner self

To become whole, I needed you
To find you, I had to work through the layers
Of distress that hid you from me

I have found you so deep within me
So delicate, fragile and beautiful

To find you is to become whole
Is to dissolve the divide, the barrier
To become one again.

Painting by Sezan M. Sansom

With this connection, with this gradual process of learning to trust, came uncertainty and fear. The needing, the realisation of the enormity of what had happened. Was Hilary really safe, was Hilary really going to stay?

65

Will I ever stop needing you
Will this pain ever go away
I can't get enough of you
I never had enough, was dry
Like a desert, no moisture
Prevented me from growing
Prevented me from blossoming
I was small, I was frightened
I was hurting, left behind

My little self – small, shrivelled
Neglected, dirty, smelling, dishevelled
Pinched and punched when I snivelled
Threatened with worse so I stifled
My cries, silenced my hurting, didn't tell
Couldn't tell, there was no one to tell
Nowhere to go, no sweet smell
Nowhere soft to snuggle
No one to give me a cuddle ´

Now you are there, I hate needing you
I hate the fear of knowing safe
When will you be taken away
When will you stop being there
When will you stop the care?
You say you won't, but it's not true
You say you'll always find a way
That you are signed up to this
You're committed to seeing it through
I so wish I could believe you.

I was searching for someone to love me
And he stepped in
Gave me attention, nice things, was kind
Filled the gap
I was so grateful that he cared for me
He spent time
Then he asked me for something back
He gave first
I owed him so much, he was kind
He started to take
I couldn't say no, he might go away
Then I would be alone
Who would love me, who would care
If he went away
I became confused, didn't belong anywhere
He needed me
I knew how to please him, make him happy
I no longer existed
There was no me, just an empty shell
I didn't matter
So, I had no needs only to please
I was so alone.

I am there again. I feel there again

I was searching for someone to help me
You stepped in
I wasn't sure if I could trust you
You seemed okay
I didn't think you liked me much
Didn't know why
I couldn't trust my own judgement
So, gave you a try

Building a relationship, a bond
Feeling grateful
You are so kind, give me time
Feeling hateful
Can't handle these bad feelings
I'm being ungrateful
I have to protect you, keep you safe
It's what I know
It's that familiar place
If I put me first, it feels so wrong
Makes me feel all alone.

Spoke to Hilary as planned. Described feeling embarrassed about my pictures of the dolls and told her that when I had held the dolls I had cried. I had realised there was an even smaller, tiny, delicate me within. I didn't think I was prepared to care for her, she was so small. Hilary said she wouldn't have shown herself if she didn't feel safe.

I talked about my level of safe with her and understood that prior to age seven my mum was kinder but still unpredictable and short-tempered, so I didn't know safe with her in the way Hilary made me feel safe. I told Hilary that I had woken that morning feeling safe and 'wrapped up' but didn't really know what it all meant. She asked how I was feeling about the break, and I said less afraid but still didn't know how I would handle things. We agreed to bring stones and dolls to the session. The fear of managing in the break left me wanting to curl in a ball and cry. I wished I could tell her, tell Hilary, how vulnerable I was feeling.

I wished she could hold me, and I wished I could feel her arms around me. I wished I could tell her I needed her and cry out to her, but I couldn't.

I wished I could ask her to hold me, to put her arms around me and hold me.

I couldn't tell her over the phone or face to face, but used my journal and wrote: *Hilary, please would you hold me, please put your arms around me. Hold my delicate and tiny self, take me in your arms and help me to breathe. Bring safety where there has been abuse, bring tenderness where there has been violence.*

I continued to struggle and sent a text to Hilary, which she didn't reply to until much later. I could find no comfort in Hilary's emotional 'high street', felt distant, and it hurt. I feared I had annoyed her, as though she was fed up with me. Didn't know why, but I so wanted to call out to her and ask her to help me. To be there and hold me, but I couldn't ask her – I felt as though she'd had enough. Feared I had pushed her to the limits of what she could hear, and she didn't like me anymore. Like she was pushing me away so she didn't have to think about me, and no way would she want to feel me near her. Like she hated me and wished she had never met me. Didn't want to be committed to me anymore. Like I had done something wrong to make her not care anymore – but I didn't know what. This was so hard. So painful. I really wanted it to be different. I so wished she could be there always. Cradle me, hold me, love me. Love me as I needed to be loved when I was that tiny little delicate girl. I knew these feelings were about me and my fears, but I had convinced myself she was different with me during our last phone call; I felt it painfully.

Our last session before the break was a real mixture of talking about our relationship and how we worked together. I told Hilary that I would miss her. She said she would miss me too and said she loved her work and she loved working with me. My fears that Hilary didn't like me, fears that she'd had enough of me melted away. I felt connected to her, felt important to her. As promised, Hilary put a set of rocks on the table with my dolls. I chose a rock that reminded me of the iceberg I had drawn with the little me tiny in the corner – it was so much like my drawing.

Hilary also gave me a card with the following words: *Please remember how brave you are especially when you are not feeling it, we're not seeing each other but we can text and we've both agreed that if you need to, give me a shout, text me and we will find a time to speak on my mobile. I'm not disappearing to Outer Mongolia – just France! This is just another part of the adventure of living your own life – sometimes scary, sometimes exciting and all stations in between, but with you in charge as best you can be and with people who care about you. Love, Hilary.*

During the following couple of weeks and what felt like a lifetime without seeing Hilary, I was in touch with how angry I felt about God. I didn't feel I could take the pain of my tiny little girl to God. I couldn't trust Him with her; as a child I prayed and asked for His help and He didn't protect me. I prayed in anger and I felt reminded that God lifted me from the slimy pit, from the mud and mire and set my feet firmly on the rock. He put a new song on my heart. I knew there was a new song in my heart from my relationship with Christ and with Hilary. I learned to love Little Me and see that what happened to her was not her fault and that she was not dirty, there was nothing for me to be ashamed of. As the layers continued to peel back, I could feel more of her deep within me, so delicate, so beautiful. How could I let God or Hilary really see her pain? God didn't stop the adults around me from cutting into my very soul, smashing her away from me. Hilary was helping me to find her and connect with her again.

Early waking returned; I couldn't sleep and was missing Hilary so much. I didn't believe she would ever really understand how much I missed her or needed her. It felt so, so hard. I wished she really understood how unhappy and alone I felt in the pain I was in. I remembered she had told me I was brave and that I could manage this. But I couldn't tolerate the intensity of the pain.

I worked longer hours to stop me feeling. I knew I was sinking into old ways of behaviour, which was not good for me. I knew Hilary was there for me, but I felt as though I was fending for myself just as I had done as a child. I was trying not to feel angry with myself for feeling this way. Hilary had asked me if I could be curious about how I felt. I used curiosity where I could, but it did 'kill the cat', as the saying goes, so I had some reservations!

I struggled with feeling the intensity of feelings. I couldn't believe Hilary really knew my pain and I felt desperate. I hated needing her and hated trusting her. I survived by not feeling and working hard until I reached exhaustion so that I was too tired to feel. That no longer worked for me. I was angry that our unconscious allows us to forget and blank things out for good reason, but I could no longer switch off or disconnect like I used to. There was no department called 'storeroom' in the 'high street' that I could wander into for a break!

The tools I had been given and worked on to develop with Hilary weren't enough for me, and I knew I had to find a way of relieving myself of such overwhelming anger and hurt, so I wrote the following as if I was with Hilary, telling her how I felt.

71

I need to tell you how angry and hurt I am feeling so I hope you meant it when you said your being there for me isn't dependent on anything! It is so hard to say this, but I need to.

I can't believe you started all this work with me, bringing up all this pain and taking away my usual methods of coping then pissed off for six weeks leaving me to hurt alone. It feels so abusive and painful. You made me believe I could trust you and then you left me to struggle with all this pain alone. I know you said we could text and talk if I really needed to but that requires me to overcome my difficult feelings of burdening you and I am not there yet. Texting you, short calls or even long calls or one face to face session a week when you are here just isn't enough. How can it be? There was absolutely no one to protect me from being beaten and abused both physically and emotionally by my fucking mother, the caregiver! Absolutely no one there to protect me from having his penis forced into my mouth till I thought I would die by choking on his disgusting spunk vomiting out of his penis down my throat. How else was I going to survive any of that had I not used methods to shut it out? Now I can't shut it out and you are not there now or when I awake at 3 a.m., feeling what he did to me as if it were now and I were only 10. You tell me I am strong and that you believe I can get through this. Well, I can't. I can't hold it and be a miracle.

I am not a miracle, I'm an angry hurting woman who feels like a little child with no power and I want all this bollocks to stop. You can't help *me 'cos you can't change what happened to me. Your tenderness and acceptance your understanding and your kindness will not change anything. I still will have been an abused little girl who had a shit life with a mother who was completely incapable of protecting me and giving me any kind of safe parenting; and a fucking bastard pervert who saw how vulnerable and needy I was and like a wolf in a chicken run greedily devoured me, taking what he wanted, leaving behind devastation, licking his lips as he went. No one cared, no one saw, and I found ways of surviving it. Somehow, I got to be an adult. I learned not to need.*

Now I need you like never before, and I hate it. I don't want to need anyone 'cos it is too painful. I want to live in blissful ignorance of emotional pain. Don't want to be self-aware and in touch with my pain. I don't want to be rewarding to work with. I want to resist and fight you all the way and give you sleepless nights wondering what the bloody hell you can do next to get me to engage. I want you to worry about me and be left wondering whether I am staying safe. All the things I wanted to protect you from before.

Your text telling me that you being there for me isn't dependent on anything was before a conversation we had where you said even if I was horrible to you, you would still be there for me. Another time I cried with you over the phone when I felt angry with you because it felt so wrong and you told me you would feel angry if you were me. Well, this is raw anger and I don't feel it is wrong.

73

I feel justified in feeling it and telling you what I feel. If I let myself care if it hurts you or makes you feel uncomfortable I won't tell you. I didn't know all this was there before you went away but I knew deep hurt was there. All of me had this hurt but couldn't express it to you. If I had the words before you went, I wouldn't have told you. I wanted to protect you, wanted you to have a good break. I still hope you had a good break but I need you to know how terrible my pain is so I can't protect you from these angry feelings.

I couldn't do this alone anymore and didn't feel I could, or wanted to, put me last anymore. I edited down what I wrote, saying that I was feeling raw anger towards my mum and Ernest but also towards her for leaving me. I told Hilary nothing felt enough, and I couldn't do this. I was trying to be curious and reminded her that it had 'killed the cat' and I didn't want to die.

Hilary texted back suggesting we speak. We had half an hour together. Despite how angry I felt, I loved hearing her voice. She was tender and caring. I told her about my anger and that I had edited the feelings from the day before. Hilary knew and understood. I was all over the place emotionally and told her my feelings of being alone were 'cos I felt I couldn't contact her during the break, so she didn't feel available to me. That it just never felt enough.

Hilary listened and said, 'When you were small you never had enough and what you had was toxic. You are doing great and are going at a pace.' I told her I didn't think so, but she said, 'Take it from me professionally, you are. Some people take years to trust.' She also said that she thought I must have had something loving from my mum, because when she first met me, she could see I had the capacity to love and be loved. That I want that. She wanted me to see that my anger was OK, and she saw me as needing to find someone to vent it at to help me work through it. Hilary said she would be that person. Apart from me breaking a window with a chair or punching her, she could work with my anger. I told her I wouldn't hit her, and she said she didn't think I would but wanted me to understand that she will work with me. She said she signed up for it. She also said it was good to hear my voice and I should ring her before I feel I can't do this anymore. I was overwhelmed by her tenderness and care.

I felt the benefit of time with Hilary, the anger subsided, and sadness emerged. I felt seen and heard and a sense of safe, but I didn't know what it looked like. I asked Little Me and felt she was saying it felt like being cuddled, felt light and free like when the sun comes out after the cloud has gone.

I wondered when 'my wanting more' and 'feeling that I haven't enough' would stop. When will my yearning slow so that I can stand strong and happy in my own skin? When? I couldn't imagine not needing Hilary or not wanting her in my life and couldn't imagine sitting with her face to face and just being able to cry without fear. I wanted to sit with her and cry without inhibition and have her hold me like I should have been held, love me like I should have been loved, accept me like I should have been accepted. That's what all children need.

I thought about Hilary saying I must have got something from my mother because of my capacity to love and desire to be loved. Well, I absorbed what love she could give like a dying plant and held it there for as long as I could, but the tiny bit of love had to stretch too far, and it wasn't enough to help me grow well. Like a plant that is dry and damaged and will never produce beautiful and colourful moist fruit. My fruit will always be smaller, less colourful and less beautiful and it will never have had enough moisture. It will always show the evidence of neglect. It will always show that there was never enough. Hilary told me that I wanted more of her because I never had enough, and she said I could have that more until I don't need it anymore. Until I don't need her anymore. How can I not need it or her anymore? I will always need what I missed out on.

There wasn't a moment when I didn't want to text Hilary, and I finally found the courage to tell her I needed her. She offered a time the following weekend, and I knew with a time arranged I could keep going. I needed to talk to her, to hear her voice and to tell her how I was feeling. So much pain, so much hurt.

Will I ever stop needing you
Will this pain ever go away
I can't get enough of you
I never had enough, was dry
Like a desert, no moisture
Prevented me from growing
Prevented me from blossoming
I was small, I was frightened
I was hurting, left behind

My little self – small, shrivelled
Neglected, dirty, smelling, dishevelled
Pinched and punched when I snivelled
Threatened with worse so I stifled

My cries, silenced my hurting, didn't tell
Couldn't tell, there was no one to tell
Nowhere to go, no sweet smell
Nowhere soft to snuggle
No one to give me a cuddle

Now you are there, I hate needing you
I hate the fear of knowing safe
When will you be taken away
When will you stop being there
When will you stop the care
You say you won't, but it's not true
You say you'll always find a way
That you are signed up to this
You're committed to seeing it through
I so wish I could believe you.

Hilary was giving me time in her holiday, and I felt so bad about it. Felt I shouldn't call her. I felt so cared for that she was so willing to speak to me, but then I'd fear she didn't really want to and just said what I wanted to hear because she said she would. I still didn't trust her, and I hated saying that. I knew those feelings belonged to a different relationship at a different time, but the Little Me fear seemed to govern my adult feelings.

As the agreed day and time to speak with Hilary approached, I felt less like I needed to talk to her. It was such a strange thing. I did want to talk to her, but I didn't know what I would say. Hilary had sent me a postcard saying she had kept my dolls in the cool of the house and I felt touched that she had taken them with her. Felt cared for and thought about. Sort of looked after. Not something I was used to. I was forced to protect my mum and Ernest and left without my mum's love and care. Hilary would say that my mum was ill but it doesn't change the fact that she left me and didn't provide a safe place for me. Hilary being away got me in touch with being abandoned and being left without care and without safety. Before I knew Hilary, I didn't know this kind of safe.

My telephone conversation with Hilary was so helpful. I could never say everything about my feelings and struggles, but we focused on how I struggle to contact her, and we agreed it was a complex mixture of reasons. The feelings of never having enough came up, and Hilary told me that I needed to accept I never had enough as a little girl before I could move on. I wanted to cry for the suffering of Little Me, to take her with me. I knew I would never leave her behind again. She will never be left abandoned and alone to fend for herself. I will always protect her. I love her and love wanting to care for her. Still not sure how I will heal from all this stuff, but Hilary was right; I was doing the processing.

The feelings continued to emerge and overwhelm me. I began to accept that they would come, and I would hurt. I felt the devastation of how the adults who should have protected me didn't! How they hurt me and how no one rescued me and how impossible I found it to trust Hilary enough to sob, cry tears of fear and shame from when I was small. I hated needing her. I hated it that nothing ever felt enough, and I hated it that I couldn't cry away the pain and had to go through the agony of processing it all bit by bit. It felt too hard to continue having therapy.

I was searching for someone to love me
And he stepped in
Gave me attention, nice things, was kind

Filled the gap
I was so grateful that he cared for me
He spent time
Then he asked me for something back
He gave first
I owed him so much, he was kind
He started to take
I couldn't say no, he might go away
Then I would be alone
Who would love me, who would care
If he went away
I became confused, didn't belong anywhere
He needed me
I knew how to please him, make him happy
I no longer existed
There was no me, just an empty shell
I didn't matter
So I had no needs only to please
I was so alone.

I am there again. I feel there again

I was searching for someone to help me
You stepped in
I wasn't sure if I could trust you
You seemed okay
I didn't think you liked me much
Didn't know why
I couldn't trust my own judgement
So, gave you a try
Building a relationship, a bond
Feeling grateful
You are so kind, give me time

Feeling hateful
Can't handle these bad feelings
I'm being ungrateful
I have to protect you, keep you safe
It's what I know
It's that familiar place
If I put me first, it feels so wrong
Makes me feel all alone.

I knew that I wanted to stop the work of therapy, it felt too much, and I wanted to stop it before another break would arrive and I didn't feel I could cope with the pain that came with it. I felt I couldn't do it; I couldn't do it.

The long break was almost over. I would be seeing Hilary the following week and the fears that were never far away came to the fore, and I worried about being able to express my feelings, worried that she might be angry with me for needing her during the break, that she would think me ugly. That she would look at me and I wouldn't understand her language. I felt so governed by what I felt but understood my feelings were not how Hilary felt. I wondered: should I just not turn up, act out how I felt?

I would have many feelings and fears that I often didn't understand. On this occasion I was on holiday in Madeira with my sister. I woke with a sense of being totally violated but didn't know by whom. I pictured myself with such pain expressed in my face. The pain was from an erect penis being forced inside my vagina. It felt like a cold hard ache, like an iron rod, and felt as though my very soul was being violated, it was a sense of violation. I felt very distressed and sent Hilary a text saying I had a sense of being violated but didn't know by whom and asked her for help with it. She texted back to say that I shouldn't try and deal with that on my own, that I must acknowledge it, feel it and put it aside for when we are back from the break. I said I'd try.

I later dreamt that I hadn't turned up to my appointment with Hilary. There were several things stopping me, but I also didn't want to go. Hilary cut me off in my dream and told me she'd see me the following week with no contact in between. I felt devastated and completely let down. When Hilary said I should put the hurt aside, it kind of left me feeling like she'd had enough of me. Fed up with me even though she was also saying that I shouldn't try and deal with it on my own. I was troubled by the dream of being violated; I didn't recall it as an experience and was confused by it. Was there more to remember? I hoped not. I spent time with Little Me and realised that all of me felt that way. I reassured myself that Hilary had given good advice, I needed my holiday and wanted to enjoy it, so tried to set it aside.

I tried hard not to think about my dreams, but the unwelcome thoughts and feelings were stronger than my efforts. I lay awake most of the night. Could not make any sense of them.

I rehearsed telling Hilary that I couldn't do therapy anymore. I started to understand what I meant by that. I was totally vulnerable. I felt I was captured by Hilary and could only escape if I stopped seeing her. Then she couldn't get me. She couldn't hurt me; she couldn't overpower me. I would not sob with her and give her the ultimate power over me. She would not see my nakedness – if I did that, if I let go, I would be hiding nothing. Could I give over all I have and all I am and trust her to hold me? Could I trust me to allow her to hold me? It was so hard. My total vulnerability equalled abuse. I could trust me to at least stay. I didn't want to do it alone anymore. I feared Hilary didn't like me, blamed me, expected too much of me. I wanted to test her with a clear message of when her wisdom and my valiant attempts failed – what then? What happens when feelings force their might?

I texted her and she sent back that my feelings are inevitable and perhaps I'm apprehensive about Tuesday when we were to meet again. I sent back that I was and didn't know if I could make it. Hilary sent back saying she would be there and hoped to see me but would accept whatever happened. I wanted to tell her that I was feeling so vulnerable, that my guard was weak, and I wouldn't be able to protect myself anymore but that I feared I would find a way and then be disappointed or a disappointment.

> That guard that I wrapped around us
> Protected us and kept us safe
> It's been there for so long, impenetrable
> At least till you came along
> Bit by painful bit you chipped away
> Building up trust along the way
> Finally, I stand almost naked
> No cover, no guard, just me
> I am so afraid of what it will mean
> What will you do, what will you say

> I want to fight you
> I'm ready for battle
> To keep you out
> To keep you away.

Painting by Sezan M. Sansom

Year Two

In the days prior to my next session with Hilary, I really didn't know if I would turn up for the session. She had helped me so much by accepting me regardless of my decision. Yet I feared what she might do with my level of vulnerability; how would she respond if I were to sob or didn't talk?

My first session back after the summer break felt so good. The fears of what might happen, what I might do, what Hilary might do, didn't happen. Hilary had helped me so much whilst we were apart and as I thought back over those difficult weeks and over the first year of therapy, I knew I had processed so much, I knew I had moved on. My struggles to find an external answer to describe what happened to me were, as Hilary said, within me. Although it wasn't clear to me at the time, I realised that my dream gave me the description in just one word. Violation. I had been violated and that violation had penetrated my very soul.

I felt so sad for the little girl that was me. I told her I so wished I could go back and get her when she was seven. That if I could have taken her away from it, she would never have been hit and screamed at, no one would have rubbed wet bed sheets across her face or pinched and beaten her vagina until she bled, until the hurt and stinging took away her breath. No one would have forced their penis down her throat, bitten her clitoris or exposed her to bondage and torture. She would never have lived to believe she was worthless and unlovable, hateful and detestable, loathsome and abhorrent in the eyes of her mother. She would never have been an object of pleasure for a paedophile.

As hard as the process of working through all that pain was, I knew I was benefiting from it. I was starting to feel and starting to live, rather than exist. Hilary and The Woman's Service were providing me with the opportunity to live. Hilary told me that the Service had won a recognition award for their work, and I took the opportunity to write to Maggie and share my experience of the service. I wanted to give something back.

Letter to Maggie for The Woman's Service:

Dear Maggie,

As you know I have had the benefit of both the couple and individual therapy sessions offered by The Woman's Service and am writing to say that I am delighted to learn that the Service has won an award. I understand from the letter I received that any comments made will be kept anonymous and under those circumstances wanted to share my experience of the Service. I have made the following comments for you to use if you would like to.

For the past 41 years I have existed with the devastating effects of being physically, emotionally and sexually abused as a child. There are no easy words to describe that devastation, but it was a violation of my very being and caused self-loathing, forcing that part of me to exist in a non-place. A place so bleak and scary that I could never imagine finding the courage to visit what was locked inside and wouldn't have but for the support of The Woman's Service. I say this because finding a therapist who has the knowledge and skill to work with the complexities that come from being so violated as a child, and the money to pay for one, has been an impossible barrier for me to overcome. The Woman's Service provides me with a safe environment where, through building a relationship with my therapist, I am learning what it means to trust and bit by painful bit we are exploring that bleak and scary place. There are times when the depth of sadness I feel from it all takes away my breath and puts me on my knees, but I am starting to experience what it feels like to live rather than just exist. For the first time in my life I have felt the emotional freedom that comes from knowing at my very core that the burden of guilt and shame is not mine to carry. I am starting to know who I am and what I want from relationships. I am starting to recognise the strength within that enabled me to survive, to accept the little part of me who was so violated and to like who I am. My developing sense of self is fragile, and I struggle to keep hold of it, but with the ongoing relationship with my therapist through The Woman's Service I believe I will get there. Thank you.

I had never known such love and care, acceptance and validation. I felt held, contained, given to. I was working hard to recover and heal, and I was hungry for it, desperate to live more and exist less, but I didn't see that as me giving anything – I saw it as being given to. Hilary continued to support me during and between sessions. We had developed a good relationship and I was learning to trust. I sent her a fun message asking her if she would foster me and she sent back, 'What a privilege', which amused me, but also moved me. I texted back to say I had never considered that caring for me would be seen as a privilege! Certainly, it wasn't for my mother. Hilary sent back to say, 'It's called a relationship and we both give.' I found her comments so at odds with how I felt about myself and how I feared she felt about me.

Hilary shared with me how my letter had been received at the award ceremony and I thought little of it; I didn't trust that I could have given something good.

Then I received the following letter from Maggie thanking me for sharing my experience and sharing with me the impact of it at the award ceremony.

Dear Trish,

Thank you so much for your letter. I felt deeply moved and at the same time so impressed at your courage, your strength and your creativity.

I felt that you have spoken of your own experience but had also found a way of expressing and giving a voice to the suffering and despair that underpins so much of the experiences of our patients. However, yours was not a message of despair but one of hope for a future that can contain the possibility of moving on, the possibility of learning to begin to trust again and of believing in a self that needs and deserves to live rather than to merely exist.

That you have the generosity of spirit to give credit in part to a psychotherapeutic relationship is something that means so much to me and to my team and to any survivor of childhood sexual abuse who might hope to find a way forward within ours or other specialist services.

Trish I want to thank you also for giving me permission to use this and I have already done so. Yesterday the team of The Woman's Service attended the Annual Members Meeting and Award Ceremony at the O2 where, as you know, we were due to receive recognition from Oxleas for our work. This was a large meeting with some four hundred people present and I felt very proud to be able to allow the Chief Executive, Stephen Firn, to read that part of your letter which you gave me permission to use.

As we walked onto the stage to receive our award, he chose to read this out. Trish, you could have heard a pin drop – the audience were rapt. The applause which followed filled our hearts and I wanted to let you know this because it belonged firstly to you.

So you will be able to see that you have created something that is likely to have far reaching implications for everyone present, for our service, and for those in Oxleas who will now not claim that a specialist psychotherapy service for Survivors of Childhood Sexual Abuse is not essential.

Finally, while you write so beautifully and you have such a creative talent so clearly demonstrated, I also imagine it is not without cost

*to find such words or to remember and to risk
sharing that also and I want to thank you very
much for your generosity of spirit, for the role-
model and example you have set for other
survivors who may still be searching for a way
forward.*

*With all good wishes.
Yours Sincerely,
Maggie Schaedel*

Maggie's letter filled me with such pride; I felt so special.
I still found what Maggie said, Hilary's commitment to me
and our relationship difficult to accept. I felt angry that
trusting people and feeling safe had left me abused and
hurt, so how was I to really trust what Maggie had said and
what she and Hilary were saying and doing? Hilary and I
explored these difficult feelings and I was so in touch with
how much I gave as a child, but no matter how hard I tried,
how much I gave, how good I was, none of my efforts had
stopped my mum or Ernest from abusing me. I realised in
that moment, on another level, that I was not to blame for
what they did to me. I couldn't have done anything to stop
them abusing me. At that moment I also feared what
Hilary or Maggie might collect from me to pay the debt I
felt I owed them. Hilary talked about my 'generosity of
spirit' and asked if I could see how I had helped The
Woman's Service and said, 'What a gift you are to them
and others.' I knew what she meant but I couldn't attribute
it to me.

I felt like I wanted to run away – I felt fearful, and I
wanted to run. I remembered being at the home of Ernest
and, although I couldn't recall why, I was afraid and ran

out of his flat into a dark night. I was going to run home but encountered a man sitting on a wall wearing dirty clothes. He stared at me, and I was more afraid of passing him than the fear of whatever had caused me to run. I ran back to Ernest. Nowhere was safe and there was nowhere to run.

There seemed to be so many triggers to my pain, which was from such a young age. As an adult I was experiencing feeling safe with Hilary – probably why I asked her to foster me. Hilary suggested that I might need to be seen more often than twice each week and told me it was important that we acknowledge how I felt in between sessions. I had a double session with Hilary face to face, a single session over the phone if I needed it and text support in between, along with the option of leaving a message on her answerphone if I felt the need to hear her voice or tell her something late at night or in the early hours of the morning. Even with that I feared Hilary didn't like me and was only tolerating me because she had promised to!

The feeling of wanting to run continued, and early-morning waking in distress came like a powerful and unwelcome intruder. I had cried a little with my partner on occasions but could never really let go of my pain with him or anyone else. In the early hours I took myself downstairs to the dark, quiet and privacy of our sitting room and dropped to my knees breathless with the pain. The known battle with myself ensued, but I finally overcame my fears and at 1.30 a.m. I called Hilary's answerphone and left a message telling her what was happening to me, that I thought I was rubbish and didn't think I could see her again. I felt so calm in the knowledge that I had been able to tell Hilary in the moment on her answerphone and she would hear my distress; even though I didn't expect she would hear it until later that day, telling her answerphone in the moment helped me. Hilary sent me a text later that day saying I wasn't rubbish. 'Never was, never will be.' The comfort I felt from being able to leave that message and from Hilary's text message was indescribable; it held me when I feared I would fall.

Exploring my feelings and the physical impact I experienced from them always led to understanding myself. Not always straight away, though, and we often revisited fears, beliefs and feelings. Feeling safe enough to cry face to face was a particular challenge and I was impatient and angry about it. Hilary reminded me that I was able to cry alone and although that didn't feel like an achievement, there was a time when I couldn't cry at all. She picked up on my previous statements about me believing I was snivelling and ugly. She suggested that all the time I believed I am snivelling and ugly when I cry and that she will loathe me, I wouldn't be able to feel safe. I knew there was a feeling of an abyss within me. I felt like the abyss was all the shit. As I shared that with Hilary, she mentioned the little boy in the film *Slumdog Millionaire*, where he dropped into shit to get the photo that he wanted signed – but he wasn't disgusting, he brought out hope and compassion. I agreed and thought about Maggie's letter to me. I was pleased with what I had written and knew it was powerful, but I told Hilary I didn't expect the reaction. I didn't feel a reaction; I thought a reaction, as if it was by proxy, as if it didn't belong to me. 'It will take time,' she reminded me.

In earlier sessions Hilary had referred to a new baby as being delicious. I remembered feelings when my granddaughter was born where I was bursting with something that I couldn't name. I adored her but couldn't name a feeling, but I liked Hilary's description. I read some of my poems to Hilary and showed her some more photos of me throughout my childhood. I told her I didn't know I was delicious, and I didn't know my children were delicious and I felt so sad for that.

Another break was looming, but I didn't know about it until I was in the session. Hilary had not told me and apologised, saying, 'I bottled out 'cos I knew it would upset you.'

I struggled to know how to respond, but later had text exchanges with Hilary. She had sent me a text that I didn't respond to, so she phoned me. I didn't get the text and then shared the ongoing feelings I had of her not liking me. Hilary was firm and said, 'It is not me that doesn't like you.' I told her I knew it, but my healing is down to me, and I had to carry the burden, that no one came and got me. Hilary waited a moment and then said, 'I came and got you today,' and she was right – she did.

We agreed that our phone session in the week would be a fixed time, like the face to face, to see if that helped. At the end of that discussion, in that moment, I felt safe with Hilary and believed that I could trust her; it felt so good. Hilary also said she knew it was important to be straight with me even if it is hard, referring to her not telling me she would be going on a break.

I could feel that I was able to be more open with Hilary. I also continued to connect with Little Me and told her from my heart that she was delicious and always had been and that she was amazing. I could feel a strong sense of being cared for, but I still wondered why Hilary gave me so much. I missed her during that break as much as any other, but somehow felt more contained. I continued to struggle with trusting Hilary, I remained suspicious and fearful of her reasons for giving so much to me.

You keep giving
I believe you give so much
You say 'so do you'
I say thank you for your love and care
You thank me back
I tell you that I value you
You say you value me too
I try to tell you I'm sorry
You ask me for what
And say it's me who's owed sorry
I say I want you to stop caring
You tell me 'no, I ain't gonna stop'
I tell you it annoys me that you care
You tell me 'it's understandable'
I say I might not turn up for a session
You say, 'I'll be here'
How bloody annoying are you
When I say, you thank me?
You say, 'I thank you'
You tell me it's called a relationship
I know that but don't know why

Why do you care so much about me
It's not just a job, this you and me.
There is so much more to what we do
The relationship, the me and you
Our work together, learning and discovering
What lay beneath preventing me recovering
So patiently and generously you give
Help me to learn, how to trust and to live.

Spending time for myself and listening to Little Me always helped me to be more open. Helped me to express how I was feeling, allowed me to go with the process and bit by painful bit something would shift; it helped.

When I hurt in my gut
Felt sick, felt bad, was stuck
I wrote how I felt at the time
And it flowed, effortless words
Spilling out, pouring, not stopping
When I read my words now
I am amazed at the insight
Into how I felt yet I didn't know then

Now I can't write, I have no flow
I can tell you more than I could before
When we started this work, I couldn't see
The tiny, small little girl that was me
Now I see her, now I feel her
I need you Hilary more so now
I don't like feeling but it's better somehow
Than the numb existence I used to know

Now when I hurt, I wish I could die
Don't want to live, but do want to cry
I'm afraid of all that cos if I really feel
The hurt and pain that is so real
I might fall apart, be sick and tremble
Sob and cry and become unstable
So, I keep control of all my pain
Hide it from you and from me again.

Help me, help me to be
Help me, help me to see
Help me, help me be free
Help me, help me be me.

Unusual for me, I couldn't write in my journal for a while. The poems seemed to meet that need for a couple of weeks. That was long for me. I was aware of feeling so needy of Hilary even though she already gave so much. I told her how I felt, and she asked me what wouldn't be acceptable with me in terms of level of contact, and I couldn't say. She said, 'A call every day in a drunken state was not on.'

I thought about it and said, 'I just wanted to be around you and then if I needed to cry with you in the moment of hurt, I could.'

Hilary, always true to her word of 'we'll find a way', suggested we try it, but I said I was afraid that I would be too demanding.

In her strong, assertive voice Hilary said, 'You will just have to get over yourself.'

I laughed and asked her what therapeutic approach that came from, and Hilary laughed, knowing full well she didn't have a name for it. I loved those spontaneous moments – they felt safe and connected.

I would often move from feeling good to feeling low, and that often meant something was about to emerge and another part of the bit by painful bit process was going to demand more from me! It was sometimes an indication that I needed to set some time aside with Little Me. Years of ignoring her, denying her existence and hating her meant I needed to actively keep her in mind, and I did wonder whether those self-help books that warned the adult not to ignore the inner child had something more important to say than I had previously given them credit for. I thought about the importance of 'getting over myself' for Little Me.

I shared my thoughts and feelings with Little Me as though she were physically sharing my space:

> 'So, little girl. There is so much I want to tell you and so much I wish I could have stopped. There was nowhere to go when we were small, and you were too little to understand what was happening. When I think of you wishing you could die, not wanting to live and feeling so cold and alone I want to weep. I think of you crying because of the physical pain you were in and crying because you had no one who could hold you safely and make you feel okay. She never said she was sorry for what she did to you. She just blamed you more and you believed her. You didn't know any different and you suffered because you had no choice. I am so, so sorry for what you had to live through, and I am in awe of you because you somehow survived it and carried yourself through with a strength that is uniquely yours.'

I listened to what came back from Little Me and it was so clear:

> 'I need to know that I can cry, and you won't think I am ugly, or my cry is ugly. If I make embarrassing noises that you won't leave me to manage the pain behind that noise on my own. That you will care no matter what and no matter

how ugly it all feels like you said you would. You will let me cry and you will let me be who I am when I need to let go of it all. When I feel alone and afraid that you will call Hilary instead of making me hurt and stay with it.'

I apologised to Little Me. What could I say – she was right in everything she said. I called Hilary and left a message telling her I was feeling alone and afraid. It was how Little Me felt. After the call and some quiet time to myself I began to feel angry. I wanted to tell them to stop hurting me, but I couldn't say it. I couldn't tell anyone how I wanted the hurting to stop. As I cried, I said out loud, 'Stop, stop hurting me.'

I knew powerfully that time communicating with Little Me was an important part of the process, and I reassured her that, with Hilary's help, I would protect her.

It's called a relationship
This her you and me
That's what she tells us
Takes time, this building trust
But we are doing great
We work together well
You her and me or so she tells
Is that what we believe
Well, we know she sees
There's so much more
To you, to her, to me

Oh, and by the way
There is no ugly
No ungrateful, wicked little you

Words said in foul mood
By mum in her despair
She was wrong, it just isn't there
No bad, dirty girl hiding
Here, there or anywhere.

More memories, more like a flashback, came flooding in. I was back there in the living room with the heat of the gas fire on my legs, the stench of urine as it dried to a yellow stain on my vest and clung to my body, my mother in a frenzy of anger holding down my arms to stop me defending myself against her violent attacks on my vagina. I lost the fight and felt my skin reacting as the fish slice came to an abrupt halt sending sharp stinging pain, the pinching and twisting of the skin also on my vagina as my mother's white knuckled hands followed the rhythm of her angry words, 'That's where the piss comes from.'

Oh, how I stung, how it hurt and there was no one to stop her.

It was hard to relive this memory as an adult; how did I survive it actually happening as a little seven-year-old?

Therapy felt like my lifeline, and I moved between being the survivor in therapy, trying my best to nurture Little Me and my adult self, to being a wife, mother and grandmother. I shared all aspects of my life with Hilary although tended not to talk too much about my relationship with my partner, which had plenty of challenges. I didn't want to share much in my sessions of that aspect of my life; I felt the needs of my partner imposed on so much of my life, and I wanted to keep my therapy and Hilary for me.

I shared with Hilary that I was about to welcome another grandchild into our family. I was very aware I had been robbed of the freedom to feel; I existed in my thinking for most of my life, but that was changing. I messaged Hilary to let her know the baby was on his way and she asked me to keep her updated. I messaged her when things worried me, and she gave me some great tips and the confidence to challenge situations when they arose. With Hilary's help I was protecting my daughter, her partner and their son in the moment, making sure they had everything they needed. Hilary had told me she had been a midwife before becoming a therapist, and I loved it that she wanted to share in this with me. My daughter was amazing, and when her son arrived and was laying on his mum, I knew he was my very own delicious. I fell in love with him in that moment and knew that even though I had been robbed of the freedom to feel I understood that those powerful feelings had always been there. I'd instinctively cared for my children, nurtured them and knew I loved them, but I just couldn't feel it with such depth at the time.

I now knew it was how I felt when my granddaughter was born four years earlier. I knew it is how I would have felt when my babies were born but couldn't feel at the time. I was able to experience beautiful connections with my grandchildren at their births, I could feel it instead of thinking it. Therapy had enabled me to connect fully with my love for my daughters as young adults, and it felt as though all the love I knew, but couldn't feel, flooded in. The iceberg had melted, and I could feel my love for them all. I felt joy and sadness.

> I didn't know you, I couldn't know
> Not till Hilary helped to show
> The amazing you, there all along
> You are so beautiful and so strong

An inner strength solid and there
With a life of hurts I couldn't bear
I left you alone, isolated, denied
Rejected, ignored and despised
It took so long for me to see
The beauty, the joy of little me
I know our work with Hilary
Is why I am now able to see
And feel the little you,
I am in awe of you little girl.

I shared my joy and sadness with Hilary. I was in touch with loving Hilary the way a child loves its mother. I loved the way she cared for me, the way she knew me. I felt as though she was giving me what my mother couldn't. She was helping me to nurture Little Me. I continued to feel fearful of needing Hilary.

I know that I need her
The care that she gives
The love that she shows
To the me that she knows
Big me, little me, all of me.

Those wonderful feelings of being connected and knowing how much I loved my children and grandchildren were followed by negative feelings. I felt like I was rubbish and worked on trying to be curious about how I was feeling rather than allowing myself to be consumed with self-hate. Expressing feelings was fuel to my mother's anger when I was a child, and I couldn't seem to help feeling I was bad or wrong and I didn't like my dependency on Hilary. I was so tired and wanted Hilary to do it all for me, but I didn't really know what 'it all' was.

Hilary hadn't responded so I phoned her – and instead of getting the answerphone as I had expected, a young woman answered and offered to get Hilary for me. Hilary came on the call and laughed when I said I didn't know what to say to the person, and we laughed together about her telling me she was shovelling snow from her driveway and admitting she was finding it a pleasure. Hilary said she thought my message was about containment and I told her I thought I was starting to do that a bit for myself. She encouraged me and said she thought I was doing it well. I couldn't help thinking she might want to add 'at last' to that statement which amused me. I wanted to be in her life more than someone who received therapy from her; I felt sad that I couldn't be.

On the same day I felt a haunting sadness. I had a sense that something was wrong, so wrong. I wanted to cry. I was stuck and I hated it. I so wished I knew what I needed to express. I asked myself and Little Me what it was. I felt like I did when there was no one to tell. I reminded myself and Little Me that there was someone to tell now. I had to accept that I couldn't work out what it was but that I was feeling uncomfortable and hurting. Bad things were done to me, but I knew in that moment that I wasn't bad, I knew it wasn't my fault, that I was just a little girl who had learned to push away the pain and tell myself I didn't need anyone. I reassured my little self that she was safe and that no one could hurt her, that there was no debt to pay and it was OK to cry.

I felt like there was an arrow in my heart and my gut was aching. I wanted to rip the pain out of me. I wanted Hilary to take away the pain, the pain that haunted me and caused me to feel stuck. I wanted her to give me something to release the restrictions in my throat, and comfort to take away the feeling in my chest and my gut. I didn't know what it was, but it was hurting me.

I didn't call Hilary, but I spent time with Little Me.

> You know what is happening
> What is happening to me
> You can see what is sticking
> In my throat and choking me
> Please take it away I want to be free
> You can sort it quickly
> Free me from captivity
> Don't leave me to work it out
> Don't make me do it all
> Please show me what it's about
> I'm afraid I'm going to fall.

The process of therapy was feeling particularly tough. I couldn't describe the feeling to Hilary but told her that during the previous therapy session I felt a powerful urge for my body to rise and pace the floor. It was like an energy within that was trying to get away from the pain. I felt as though I was the child my mother saw through her eyes and that Hilary was seeing me that way. I wasn't seeing myself through truth but through lies, through the eyes of an adult who hated herself and projected that on to the little girl that I was.

Hilary said, 'You are so clever.' I knew she meant it and that I had reached an understanding. I felt bruised, numb, and shocked, and felt like I had returned to how I had felt the previous week and told her I wanted to talk to her but didn't call. Hilary said I had betrayed Little Me by making her carry hurt and not responding to her. I felt angry with Hilary for her comments but said nothing.

The following day I had a memory of me begging my mum not to hurt me; she had me across her lap, forcing one of my arms behind her back so that I couldn't fight her off. I was being pinned down with a weight across my chest and I couldn't move.

Hilary said she thought I was starting to allow myself to be really vulnerable. I told her that although I had experienced some therapy several years ago when divorcing my first husband, which I found challenging and helpful;. I had no idea how hard working through this pain could be. I hadn't realised how much I had separated myself from my feelings. My memories of my mother pinning me down, and her angry, hateful face with eyes of madness staring at my vagina. I remembered feeling distressed; my begging didn't stop her. Her spiteful hands and nails pinching and digging in my skin. If I reacted in any way, looked at her or said anything she would hurt me more. I was only safe if I stayed unfeeling and paralysed, cold and completely separate from everything that was being done to me.

I told Hilary I was drained by it all and she asked me if I wanted her to look after Little Me for a while. I agreed. I knew I could trust Hilary with Little Me.

Hilary could tell I was finding the process extremely difficult, and she checked out how I felt about the benefits of therapy and how I felt when I came through a difficult time. She reminded me that weeks ago I had told her I knew something difficult was on its way. I thought about it and told her that when I come through a difficult time the freedom and awareness is amazing and I feel so self-aware and strong. Hilary agreed we could keep going.

Within days of me agreeing to give Little Me to Hilary, I messaged her to say that I could see how small she was and that she was clean and not dirty or bad, and although I wasn't sure how it worked, it worked. Hilary sent back a message to me saying, 'Trish she's absolutely lovely and thank you for trusting me with her.' I wanted to cry when I read that text. Her words were so moving, and I felt Little Me was safe and that even if my mum or Ernest were alive they couldn't hurt her because we were both there to protect her. I had an image of my littleness and could see me when my milk teeth were just starting to fall out. I was so little. I could see me as a little girl.

The fears when I didn't get a text back from Hilary within a few hours continued to challenge me. The snow had been too heavy for Hilary to drive to The Woman's Service, so we hadn't had a face-to-face session for a couple of weeks. I didn't like any interruption to me seeing Hilary. Even though we had phone sessions instead, I didn't like it. I began to regret giving Little Me to her and wanted her back. I didn't like what I felt had become the 'lovey-dovey' relationship I had with her.

I felt angry but didn't know why and wasn't sure I would go to the face-to-face session the following week. I wondered what Hilary would do if I were to test her; would she really be OK with me wasting her time, leaving her to hang around waiting for me not to turn up?

I didn't test her; I went to the session, but I hated it. I felt Hilary was challenging me, but I didn't understand what she was trying to show me. When I told her she didn't know either, but she wondered if perhaps we were in a bit of a rut. I told her I was angry with her regarding her reaction when I told her I believe my mum and Ernest had a choice and that they could have chosen not to abuse me. Hilary talked about my parenting and referred to me attacking my children when I had smacked them and that was a choice. I felt devasted that Hilary would connect my parenting decisions to smack my children to what my mum did to me. I responded with hurt and anger saying, 'There is no way my mum's parenting of me was anywhere near good enough and nowhere near my parenting of my kids.' I felt Hilary was attacking me and said, 'I don't need reminding that I failed my kids or that choices I made had hurt them.'

Hilary said she had succeeded in making me angry with her. We were at the end of the session and there was no time left for me to express the pain I was in. Hilary asked me how I was feeling. I told her I felt angry with her, but she said nothing to console me.

I texted Hilary the following day to tell her that I was left confused and angry and didn't know where she was taking me with it all. I told her I didn't want to talk the next day but that I wanted to understand, that it was really hard, and I felt alone. I didn't hear from Hilary but wanted to phone her and tell her I really did not want anger to be the conduit for my tears because that was the way I had always expressed myself. I wanted to tell her that I was lost and so sad, didn't feel we were in this together, that although she said she was signed up for this it didn't feel that way.

I awoke the following day, still angry, and I cried. I had to go to work so did what I always did and wiped away the tears and got on with my day.

Hilary didn't text me back and the feelings didn't lift. I felt the rules of our relationship had changed. But I thought about it and decided that she didn't say they had. Me not asking her for a response or calling her was about me, not about her, so I left her a message on her answerphone; unless she said otherwise this was still one of our established and agreed ways for me to communicate with her. I told her I didn't know what the rules were, that I felt terrible and didn't expect to feel so vulnerable when I am experiencing such powerful feelings as anger. I cried when I spoke and continued through the tears, saying it was all so hard and I didn't know where I was, that I had to force myself to call her. She later texted back saying, 'Let's see what we can understand when we speak tonight. I know it's so hard and that you feel confused and angry with me – I know how hard you are working to keep in there with us. Love Hilary.'

Her text made all the difference to me. I felt that although this was really hard, she did still want to work with me.

The next session felt really awkward to start with, but I told Hilary that her text had helped. She asked me what had helped, and I told her that before she responded I felt like she had gone back on everything and wasn't signed up for the long haul after all. We talked about my confusion and Hilary checked with me at what point I had felt confused. I reiterated what I had angrily said before about my parenting being nothing like my mother's, and not needing to be reminded of my failures as a parent. I asked Hilary what she saw in me that day because I felt so attacked by her. She said she thought my mother was around in the session. I wasn't sure what she meant but talked about how my mother would speak in a vindictive, angry manner and criticise me.

Hilary said she thought perhaps the little part of me was afraid because she and I were 'fighting' as though it was me and my mother. I told her I found it so hard to be angry with her and I knew I could never be angry with my mum or Ernest. Hilary said I needed them both and loved them both, and that she didn't think Little Me had ever felt the trauma she went through, she wouldn't have survived, and that she believed I was feeling it all for the first time. She suggested that if she thinks my mum is around or sees her in me, she will say, 'So we can examine what it is about.'

It was tough and I didn't understand it all, but I knew I needed to keep on processing it.

> What do you see Hilary, what do you see?
> Not the little girl but my mum in me
> Angry, abusive, judgmental, vindictive
> That what you see Hilary, is that what you see?
>
> You asked me how it felt to not have little me
> But I didn't know if she was with you or with me
> I still can't feel her, she isn't there
> I think she is gone because of fear
> Withdrawn and hidden, deep within
> Afraid to be visible, she's safer unseen
> It's what she knows.

As mentioned earlier, I didn't like to talk much about my partner with Hilary, but there were times when I needed her help in how I responded to him. He and I were experiencing turbulent times and I felt such anger towards him. I noticed a pattern in how I had reacted to him and what harm my anger may have caused. I had gradually learned not to be physically violent to myself and worried about how I presented in my anger towards my partner and others. Hilary amused me when I shared these feelings with her in one of my sessions. She referred to my 'perfectionism in not being angry in a certain way.' My angry feelings towards Hilary lessened but didn't go away, and I was struggling with trying to understand all that had happened between us. She had talked about me remaining a victim and said I could move on, but it just served to fuel my anger. She said trust takes time, but when I was feeling so vulnerable, I felt there was a time limit on me, and I didn't know if I had done enough work to hold and love Little Me. When would I know that I have done enough for Little Me, so she knows she is loved and nurtured? If I felt the loss of my mum, would I be betraying Little Me because of the horrible things she did?

It was Christmas and another break had arrived. I became determined not to call Hilary, determined not to need her. I felt let down by her reaction to me and I didn't think I could trust her; I felt it at my core.

> I thought you were different
> But how wrong was I
> What have I learned – only
> To be fooled and live a lie
> Who are you to me now
> I really don't know
> So, I feel very hurt and sad
> All lost and alone
> I won't let myself need you
> No, not ever again
> What does it mean?

I continued to not like the breaks, but to my relief my need for Hilary began to feel less intense. I was tearful and the process of therapy was no respecter of situations. Christmas and all its so-called joy didn't lessen how I was feeling; if anything, it made it more intense. I felt tearful; I couldn't feel Little Me and feared she had gone away. I yearned for Little Me to feel part of my whole self.

I felt dumped by Hilary, that she wasn't there for the long haul, that I was all too much for her. I wanted to talk to her, but also didn't know what I would say to her. I wondered if I would I be able to tell her that I am not OK, that I am lost and hurting, feeling as though I don't have what I thought I had with her. Would I tell her that I don't understand my feelings, or about what has happened to our relationship? I didn't want to carry all the hurts of my life of abuse with me; I wanted to be free of the pain that held me down like a heavy weight on my chest. I wondered if I should stop seeing Hilary and revert to my old ways of pretending that I am not hurting by not thinking about the situation. I'd survived by separating in that way. I could tell Hilary I have done enough for now and thank her for helping me. I questioned if that would work for me.

I knew I needed to connect with Little Me. I asked her how she was and felt that she was abandoned by me when I gave her to Hilary – I had sent her away when it got too hard. I read my first poem to Little Me:

> Now that I see you
> I am drawn to you
> I feel your joy and pain
> There is no one like you
> I feel such love when I see you
> You are beautiful, wonderful, unique
>
> For so long you have waited
> So alone, so isolated
> Not being seen, invisible to me

When you tried to reach me
I didn't like what I saw
Your wonder I chose to ignore

How wrong I was to lay the blame
On the little girl that you are
Hate, disgust, guilt and shame
Is with you and I No More
It belongs out there with them
And not with you, my beautiful, wonderful
child within

I know you couldn't shed a tear
For you had nowhere to go
No safe place to take your fears
No one to protect you. Stop the hurt
Now you can cry. Now you are safe
Through me you can shed your tears

I will hold you. I will love you
No matter how ugly it all feels
Nothing you say, nothing you express
Will stop me loving you through your pain
It's okay to hurt for all that has happened
It wasn't you, it wasn't your fault

Be free little girl, release the pain
Don't be afraid, it can't happen again
You are safe, I am here, I see you
Now that I see you, I won't leave you
I am delighted you are within me
I will protect you, set you free.

I then reassured her that I needed to separate the abuse from her and from me and that Hilary was the only person who I knew she would be safe with. I thought about how vulnerable Little Me was and how as an adult I still felt that way, but she didn't have to anymore. I told her that she had amazing courage to allow those horrific memories to come so that I could experience the pain of it for her. I told her that God promised to give back what the locusts had stolen, and we are being given back safety and love for her as a little girl. The other gift is our voice. I remember how beautifully Little Me could sing, but she stopped singing – abuse was the locust that took her voice away, caused her to be invisible.

This all came at a time when I had arranged for voice coaching lessons. I was still singing in a worship group in church and when I prayed, I would sing it in worship to God. It felt wonderful, but I knew there was more within me that I couldn't access. I wanted to reclaim my voice and nurture it back to health, and I knew little Little Me had to be part of that. She needed to know that I loved her and would keep my promise.

You are everything to me
My joy, my fun, my creativity
Lost to me for so long
You were there but not known
At times of hurt you didn't know
What to do or how to show
The pain you knew all too well
You hid it deep, afraid of it all
But you got through, found a way
To survive, to exist until today

From now little one, we start to live
So much to have and more to give
We can be true, we can be real
No more denying how we feel
Look out world, prepare yourself
For the free, whole little girl who
Bit by bit is being released
No longer in that scary place
With no feelings without a face
She is here, I feel her, I know her.

At last, I had a few days' rest from processing all the feelings. Spending time with Little Me had helped me to settle. Having an arranged time to talk to Hilary always helped me during the breaks, but sometimes brought up other feelings I hadn't expected. New Year's Day 2011 had arrived, and I woke in the early hours with a huge pain, something vast that stole my rest from me. I was feeling wakeful and watchful. As I cried, I wanted to hit myself and scream out, but I didn't know why or what it was in connection with. Was it grief, I wondered? I wanted to kick and scream and wished I was with Hilary in that moment so she could see my pain and help me to understand what was happening. The energy I felt from it made me want to pace the floor, but the pain left me breathless, drained and weak. I knew I could call Hilary and leave her an answerphone message – but for some reason that I didn't understand, I didn't want her worrying about me.

I waited for the telephone session I had pre-arranged with her before we were due back at the Service. I was able to tell her what had happened over the past few days and about knowing I was angry with my mum and Ernest, not wanting to be angry with them forever, but not knowing when I would have done enough to hear Little Me so she could be a part of me. Hilary talked about the abuse I experienced and how it was more complicated where it involved my mum. I told Hilary that I didn't call her because I didn't want her to see my vulnerability since our session when she had talked about me staying a victim. I said I could never show my tears to my mum and that I wouldn't show Hilary my vulnerability and was feeling separate from her and it was hard.

I read her my poem 'What do you see Hilary?' and realised that it was me who didn't want to be seen, because that is how it felt when I didn't feel accepted.

Hilary suggested we look at that in relation to how I behave in relationships and in that moment, I realised I was keeping Hilary at arm's length. She shared her thoughts about me protecting myself by delaying my emotional response and I knew that I had hidden my hurt from her. She told me I had to do that when I was a child because it wasn't safe with my mum, but Little Me was safe with big me and with Hilary. I told Hilary that I had felt compelled to hurt myself when I was in distress over the past few days, but that I was determined to manage my anger and pain differently so had not given in to it.

I was moving on slowly, but I was moving in the right direction. It meant at times I would return to old fears and insecurities.

I continued feeling insecure and fearful of what Hilary saw in me and wrote about it.

So, this is the truth the honesty
I believe when you look
You see in me

113

The filth of abuse inflicted on me
Spilling out and infecting those around me.

My distress was clear to Hilary even though I believed I couldn't show it to her. She generously gave me a double session and I was able to explore feelings of anger and feelings of the distance I felt between us. It had felt so hard when I needed her so much and I felt we had lost something. I was able to tell her that I didn't want her to know how much I needed her. She suggested there was some testing occurring in that I could tell her in a text how I felt, but not directly. I told her I missed the feeling of closeness with her. She said it does sometimes happen, where both feel it, but she didn't feel that way, so it indicated the experience only belonged to me. I felt tearful in that moment; I felt Hilary was accepting of me. I told her I didn't want her to see the unprocessed raw me, and she told me I needed to show her so that I could understand myself better. She acknowledged that was scary for me because it wasn't something I could be when I was a child.

There were times when I didn't feel the need to write in my journal, and after the intensity of the last few weeks it was a welcome break. I had shared the above poem with Hilary and the heaviness of feeling guilty for what had happened to me and for the mistakes I had made, and that I felt I was no good. Hilary said she didn't recognise me in the poem but thought it related to my mother. In a text she wrote, 'Well – you're not 'no good' for a start! My guess is that it's old protective mechanisms in play – it's a patience thing again – waiting to "know" it's safe.'

I responded, 'Me being patient with me is a challenge as you know, helps when you remind me but want this feeling to go away.' I felt the defence mechanism was destructive, but Hilary reminded me that the defence mechanism was a friend. I agreed, saying, 'It isn't my enemy.'

'No, it's not your enemy and you need to go gently.'

I began to feel a freer sense of self and talked to Hilary about how hard I had found it to tell her how much I appreciated her. I couldn't find the words to express how good it felt and that I hated it when I couldn't find the words to express myself. Hilary said, 'Perhaps you didn't have the words when you were younger?'

I told her I was overwhelmed with how much she cares for me, that she is so careful with me and it felt good. We talked about me not having anyone safe to tell.

I felt tearful in the session but didn't cry until later that evening when I was home alone. I wished I could have cried when I was with Hilary. I felt such sadness that the connection I could feel in that moment wasn't how I could feel when my children were small. I wanted to hold them in that moment. Hilary has helped me get to this place. Without her I wouldn't be free and I love the freedom – it's hard but it's real and free.

How did you do it, how?
You've given me freedom, somehow?
Shown me acceptance, cared about me
So much lighter now, I feel so free
The darkness, confusion, guilt and shame
Are going away, I don't feel the same
The non-place is no longer there
With your help I'm more self-aware
I'm still learning and sometimes fragile
But I no longer believe that I am vile

Those words my mother screamed at me
Were wrong, you helped me to see
By giving me time, by being you
This freedom, unknown, feels so new
I really feel that I am on my way
Thanking you just doesn't say
How much I appreciate who you are
What you do, the time you give.

I became aware of knowing what happiness felt like. I used to think happy, but I was learning how be it, to feel it. For most of my life when anyone asked if I'd had a good weekend or whether I enjoyed a holiday, I didn't ever know what to say because I didn't know. I would say, 'Yes thank you' out of politeness but wondered what it felt like to know how it felt. In that moment I realised I knew what it felt like to have a good time. I thought about my day and I'd had a good time with my sister and enjoyed my singing lesson, I had a fun evening with my partner teasing him about singing and getting him to join in with songs, making him laugh at the sounds we made. I was doing many of the things I had always done but I never knew how to feel, and I hadn't felt free like that before, I felt whole and it felt good.

Hilary had helped me so much. I didn't know how much longer she would be able to see me, how long The Woman's Service would be able to offer me the support, and I feared what I would do without her.

What will I do without you in my life
One day I won't see you anymore
And I don't like the idea of that.
Will I always know you, will I?

The joy of my newfound awareness was mixed with sadness, but I was determined to hold on to it. I had lost enough and suffered enough.

Life was always busy with children, grandchildren, other relationships, work, travelling, therapy, social interests and at times I went into overload and found myself shutting down. I had been learning new ways of managing my emotions and mostly managed to live rather than exist, but there were times when I had to stop myself from going back to old familiar ways. My new sense of self remained fragile, and my new learned ability to feel tenderness for Little Me and for myself was at risk of being lost.

I experienced such frustration with myself when I realised that I couldn't keep hold of feeling like I was living for long. I would default to existing by shutting down. It would happen all too easily, even after so much hard work trying to give myself in adulthood what I didn't have as a child. I believed through my relationship with Hilary I could recover and feel whole, but it was so hard.

I shared these feelings with her, and she talked about me needing to feel safe. I felt more frustrated at myself – how much more would I need before I could feel safe? Hilary reminded me that I was able to cry when I was alone and asked me why I thought it was that I couldn't cry with her. I told her that I felt ugly, ashamed and a snivelling wreck and I didn't want her to see me like that. She asked me what it felt like when I cried alone and, in that moment, I realised that although I could cry, I would be watchful and listen for signs of anyone coming and would silence my sobs until I knew I was alone again. Hilary reiterated her point. 'You are not yet safe enough.'

She went on, 'I believe Little Me needs to know that I wouldn't see her that way.'

It occurred to me that Hilary wasn't keen on the harshness she saw in me, which I knew she referred to as 'your mum is around. 'I could feel my lack of empathy for myself at those times. I feared that if Hilary didn't like that harshness, how would she see the sobbing, snivelling wreck whose ugliness is vile? A feeling which I felt at my core and one I knew was my mother's own self-hate that she could not tolerate and externalised, inflicting hurt on her children. I feared Hilary would get fed up with me and I texted her to tell her how I felt. She replied, 'It is the "fed up" bit that you need to discard.' It was enough to help me feel contained in that moment.

An opportunity to travel to Florida connected to my partner's work materialised – but I knew if I took it I would be missing a session with Hilary, something I continued to find incredibly difficult. The excitement of going away felt good; still a new feeling for me! The memories and hurts would surface whether I wanted them to or not and they were no respecter of where I was. On this occasion they came as dreams. I dreamt that I was beating Little Me, blaming her for my self-hate and belief that I was rubbish and deserved to be treated like shit. I didn't want to have been abused and I hated her being a part of me. I felt terrible for feeling that way and I feared if I told Hilary she would hate me for feeling that way. I thought about my need of Hilary and wondered if my need for her was to stop me hurting Little Me, stop me destroying her, of trying to get rid of her. I needed to talk to Hilary.

Hilary had previously shared her view that Little Me was afraid of big me. I thought about times when I had hit myself; I wondered if I was hitting Little Me and knew that I wanted to hurt the little girl, didn't want to accept she was part of me. After all I had learned I couldn't understand how I could want to hurt Little Me; it made no sense to me at all. I had a memory of a time when Ernest had taken photographs of me, of graphic poses of my genitals. The memory distressed me and disgusted me, I didn't want to believe that had happened to me, I was so small, so vulnerable. I felt so exposed with that memory. I then had an image of my face with a fist punching into it with tiny fragments of me being sent to oblivion. I knew that was not a memory and wondered how Little Me was feeling. I couldn't bear to ask her. I imagined she was feeling like shit and would be devastated with how I felt towards her. I feared that Hilary would tell me off and disapprove of me for not defending Little Me from the cruelty of my thoughts and feelings, but I didn't want her to. Even though I knew it was wrong I didn't care, and I didn't want to accept her as vulnerable.

The mixed feelings of sadness and distress were overshadowed by the more intense feelings of anger and hate. I knew I needed Hilary to help me. We arranged some time through text messages, and although I was 4,000 miles away and there was a time difference to manage, we were able to talk.

Hilary's promise that, 'we will find a way,' held true. I found the courage to tell her of the dream and feelings of such violent hate towards Little Me and shared with her that I had stubbornly held on to that feeling. Hilary wasn't fazed by any of it and asked me how I felt in that moment. I told her I couldn't accept that I could hate that part of me with such violence and feared that I might hurt myself. Hilary talked about me hurting myself for a long time before anyone knew but that I didn't harm myself or try and kill myself. She went on to say that now I was talking about it, I was far less likely to hurt myself even if I feared that I would. Those words helped so much but I told her that I felt I had taken a step backwards.

When I told Hilary that I didn't want to ask Little Me how she was feeling and that I didn't care, which felt so hard, she told me it wasn't Little Me I hated with such violence, it was what was done to Little Me that I hated. I wasn't taking a step backwards – it was all part of the process.

It helped to talk to Hilary; thirty minutes of her time and I was feeling different. I knew I could manage how I was feeling. I felt so much more contained. I allowed myself to ask Little Me how she was feeling.

I believed I was rejecting that little part of me at best and wanted to destroy her at worst, and I knew it would be difficult to connect with her. I knew Hilary was right and believed that my anger didn't belong to her – it belonged to those who had hurt me when I was little. I sensed there was more to remember and knew Little Me was unlikely to feel safe enough to show me what was so hidden whilst I was so angry. I wasn't sure how to communicate with Little Me, so I wrote how I felt.

> Where do we go from here?
> You believe the stench of abuse
> Too vile, too ugly to be seen
> You fear rejection from me
> A reaction of disgust from Hilary
>
> If I hate you for what I know
> What will I do if more you show?

You cannot risk being pushed away
Hated, despised, rejected, denied
So, you lay low, and memories you hide

How do I show you I mean to hold you?
Love you no matter how ugly it feels
What do you need from me, what can I do?
We have to face this thing me and you
It was you who suffered at the time
That terrible, cruel, evil crime

But we are one and in it together
I will not leave you now not ever
So little one, reveal what is there
No more secrets – it's time to share.

When I next saw Hilary, I felt raw, I felt sick and feared I would vomit. I needed to cry but couldn't. When Hilary asked me what I thought the barriers were, I talked about the stench of abuse, and I needed to protect her or me from it. I was stuck, I was unable to cry and I realised I was afraid. Hilary suggested that if I faced the fear this might bring release. I felt so frustrated that I couldn't get the pain out, couldn't express it.

Our next session was a phone call and I cried, I cried! Hilary suggested it was easier for Little Me because she could hide a little over the phone. She asked me not to push things and to accept how I was. Hilary reassured me, saying, 'Me knowing what happened to you doesn't disgust me but those that did nothing to protect you do!' It helped to hear that, but my sadness and rawness remained.

My need for Hilary didn't wane and we continued with face-to-face and phone sessions, texts and me leaving messages on her answerphone in the early hours of the morning. I'd text her to say I needed to feel her with me and she would text back saying, 'I am very much with you.'

When we talked, Hilary reflected how there was no one to wash me and change my bed when I was small, that I had missed out in terms of comfort. Hilary had previously asked me how my grandparents responded when I wet the bed at theirs, and I felt tearful when I remembered the comfort I experienced in the way they dealt with it. On my return from school, I had a clean fresh bed to sleep in. I wasn't punished, which was such a contrast to my life at home. Hilary talked about the comfort I should have had and talked about how she would have given it. That made me cry. As she spoke, I had a picture of an outer dirty shell, like a volcano, and inside I had a glimpse of comfort, silk and a sense of clean, soft. It didn't stay for long. It all felt so new to me, I couldn't hold on to it.

I felt more desperate to be with Hilary than ever before and feared she would reject me, but she continued to reassure me, and I began to feel safer. The feelings of comfort and the pleasure from that somehow led me down the path of remembering that I felt some nice body sensations from the abuse I experienced, and I felt so disgusted with myself.

Hilary talked about how our bodies are aroused, which is natural and essential for the survival of the human race, and although I knew that, I couldn't help feeling disgusted at myself. I then felt how horrible it all was and could feel in that moment that I wasn't infected with something horrible; it wasn't me. It was all extremely hard to feel but I felt safe with Hilary. She shared with me that we had covered some very difficult things but that we were both able to contain it all and hold each other through the experience and she was right. We had, and I felt held by her.

My trust in Hilary was fragile. I feared she would leave me. I felt angry but feared if I expressed it I would explode. Hilary said I didn't have to explode and suggested that if I felt angry with her, I could just tell her, and she wouldn't withdraw from me because of it. I felt a sense of fight or flight and of freezing and felt like I was in survival mode and in the trauma of reliving the feelings of being abused. I could feel how vulnerable I was as a little girl and thought about what I had survived. I had heard a talk about how a pearl starts out as grit, an irritant that becomes a thing of beauty and is the only precious gem that a life must be sacrificed for. The oyster dies to give it up. The pearl is my birthstone and is made from 'true grit', which I felt described me as a child and an adult.

In one session I shared the details of an argument I had with my partner where I felt judged and misunderstood by him. Hilary knew some of our struggles from our couple sessions and had challenged me from time to time on how I reacted to him. I jealously guarded my relationship with Hilary and didn't like it whenever she explored anything to do with him. I didn't see it as her exploring more about me and on this occasion, I felt bombarded by questions that I felt were about him. I felt she was taking away my feelings of comfort and safe. Hilary was accepting of my feelings and suggested that perhaps she had gone too fast. I could not describe the feeling, which I hated. Hilary reminded me that I had told her I had felt lost and small, felt bad and just wanted to feel safe. I then told her I had felt angry, I felt misunderstood and wanted to leave, that I didn't want to see her ever again. I told her I had considered not talking to her in our session later that week but knew she would say, 'Well, I will be here for you if you change your mind.'

I told her that really annoyed me, and we both laughed. She said she knew it would annoy me, but she would still do it because it was the right thing to do. I questioned whether she would keep being there for me if I were to continue not attending and she said she would. I questioned if she meant it and she told me, 'It takes time to trust.' Annoying!

Sleepless nights continued and my mind would race. I realised that I was feeling like the child in the corner when I couldn't describe how I felt. I gave up the fight to sleep and had a feeling of being dead inside. Hilary later asked me if I thought that was how I felt when I was little, when I had no power to fight back or stick up for myself. It occurred to me that no matter how hard I tried I was never good enough. I tried not to wet the bed, but I failed and then would suffer the onslaught of my mother who attacked me with such rage that even the desperate begging of her small child for her to stop fell on deafness. I tried so hard to get it right for Ernest to pleasure him perfectly and maybe he wouldn't want to do it again. I felt there had been something to aim for with my mum and with Ernest; if I tried hard to be what they wanted me to be, it might be all right. Hilary wouldn't tell me what she wanted from me or what she wanted me to be, and I couldn't work it out. My mum and Ernest blamed me when things didn't go right, and I felt like Hilary was blaming me for how I reacted to my partner.

I could feel Little Me and asked her how she was feeling. I knew if I didn't see Hilary then she couldn't have Hilary in her life either, she didn't have the power, she was dependent on my decisions, dependent on me being brave enough to be vulnerable otherwise Little Me would be staying in the that corner.

I am sitting here alone and afraid
I want you to see me, the efforts I've made
I want you to cuddle me, I can't do it myself
No part of me can hold and cuddle herself
Not physically wrap me in arms feeling safe
The warm, sweet-smelling, fun-loving mummy
Who cuddled me and played games tickling
my tummy

Where did she go and what did I do
To make her so angry and hurt me so badly
I tried so hard to be so good
I never knew or understood
Why she hit me, pinched me, bit me
Pulled my hair and screamed she hates me
You are different, kind and safe
But you have a similar soft face
Can I trust you to cuddle me
To be the way I need you to be.

Warm soft lovely snuggly mummy
Oh how I loved you and knew you loved me
I loved being snuggled and cuddled by you
Enveloped, dissolving, melting
In your arms feeling your softness and love
Enjoying the attention and fun-loving biting
of my nose.

It remained a mystery to me but somehow all the processing and pain led to a different level of connection between Hilary and me. I couldn't cry in the session and didn't share details of what I had recently written, but I didn't feel my usual disappointment or anger about it. I thought about the emotional 'high street' and was choosing not to enter a particular place of hurt in a given moment. It was empowering. I was aware of wanting to be in Hilary's arms and wanted to be part of her because I knew she was safe. I told her I struggled with our relationship because it was all about me and not her. She didn't agree and said, 'It is about us both, we are in this together and we know each other well within our relationship.'

I could accept what she was saying but it didn't feel enough for me. The connection was real and different, and it felt good. I felt more contained and stronger.

This was challenged by another break looming, and I talked about how I had known safe when I was small. That I felt safe with Hilary but also feared that she wouldn't be honest with me about the breaks because of what happened before. I knew The Woman's Service usually offered a set period of time and I feared she would avoid telling me if we had to stop working together. She told me she had 'dropped a clanger, got it wrong'; she told me that her discomfort about breaks because of how they affect me, are about her and not about me. I loved her honesty.

I was finally able to tell Hilary that I wanted to cry out for her to hold me and told her I couldn't hold myself physically and wanted to feel that safe lovely holding I had known as a child, where my lovely soft mummy cuddled me and laughed with me.

Hilary mentioned a different kind of therapy that focusses on touch, which is strictly not what her training allows. I told her that I didn't want her to pass me to someone else or for her to walk away from me or discard me. I felt like a dirty old rag and wanted to find one to take to my next session so she could see how I felt. She said I seemed to be saying I was a dirty old rag that could be thrown away, which amazed me because she was so in tune with me. She reassured me she didn't want to 'pass me over' but it was important that we looked at what we were doing to ensure my needs were met. I felt free of the burden I had been feeling and knew I was learning to be me.

I began to understand that my yearning was for my mum, the feelings of desperation are those of a small child who was left so confused by the loss of her mummy who moved from lovely, safe snuggly mummy to abusive angry mummy. I thought about the nursery rhyme: 'Sticks and stones may break my bones, but names will never hurt me.' It wasn't true!

Pinching, punching and pulling hair
Will bruise and break my skin
Names and insults screamed at me
I will absorb, own and take in.

I felt the loss of my mum so profoundly. I didn't want to be in the grown-up adult world thinking about why my mum hit and abused me. I just wanted to feel and be as that little six-year-old who knew a mummy with love in her eyes that sparkled with approval and love for me, the way Hilary's sparkled when she greeted me and when we laughed together. I was so confused as a child and didn't understand what was happening – how could I have, at such a young age? My mum attacked me emotionally and physically, devasting and destroying the relationship and the safety before giving up on me completely and leaving me in squalor sleeping in a wet bed, a dried out wet bed with no sheets and a crystallised mattress with no clean clothes to wear and no toothbrush or toiletries. I was a child with emotional injury, so exposed with gaping wounds but no one cared enough, no one chose to see and I was left with it all. No one to trust, nowhere to turn to and nowhere to go. Ernest came along and I felt there was hope for me but not for long. He took away any belief I had in being worthy of any love or care, and the nothingness had left me with a wall around me that hid me away from myself. The rawness of Little Me was being exposed because Hilary helped me to trust again and I was so afraid that if I took the risk, I might be hurt again.

I messaged Hilary with this revelation but hadn't heard back. I entered into one of my insecure battles about being too much for her but finally kept my promise to Little Me and left a message on her answerphone. I didn't have any private space to talk so decided to leave the conversation for our next session.

Hilary apologised for not seeing my message sooner. She asked me to phone her if I needed her and I owned up to how much I continued to struggle with that. She said she wasn't someone who often looked at her phone and I told her nor did I and if someone wants me, they ring me at home. I realised what I was saying, and Hilary said, 'Yes, people call me at home if they want me too.' We both laughed. Touché!

With another break came the familiar fears of losing Hilary. I was able to cry with her in the moment and tell her I felt angry with her. I told her I didn't really trust her not to stop giving and that if I hurt her feelings or made her angry that she would respond by leaving me. Hilary said she didn't think I understood about relationships and asked me why I thought she would go away. I told her if I annoyed her. She then asked why I thought she gave what she gave, and I said because she wants to but that if I was too much, she would change her mind and just take things away from me.

Hilary told me it didn't work like that and I was not her 'first child' in terms of her career in psychotherapy so she knew exactly what she was getting into. She added, 'Although you are unique, the process isn't, so I really do know what it takes and how long.'

I believed her and knew that I could feel angry with her and tell her. I also knew if I didn't tell her I would carry the pain of it myself.

Hilary said, 'I will be holding you in my heart and be thinking of you whilst I am away.' I knew she would.

We talked about me nurturing Little Me when I needed the comfort of being mothered, and although I felt angry that I had to nurture Little Me I told Hilary 'I could reassure her and tell her it's OK and she is safe.'

Hilary said that was exactly what Little Me needed.

Eighteen months into individual sessions with Hilary and I was connecting with my feelings. I was able to feel love for the abused little girl who sat within me and could express the angry feelings I felt towards Hilary. I continued to be stuck on feelings of abandonment during breaks, no matter how much Hilary reassured me! I messaged her to let her know that I didn't want to feel like crap every time there was a break, didn't want to carry the burning pain of her going away. I told her I would rather never go back and see her than feel that. She responded, 'I think it was very hard for a part of you to trust that someone you need would come back – nothing was alright when you were little and the feelings were more than you could bear – now you are trying so hard to process and manage those old unbearable feelings.' She added, 'I know it will be hard for you to come tonight because when you were little you had to withdraw into yourself to survive and coming tonight is our way of trying to find a new way to manage, at the risk of irritating you, that does take time.'

On reading Hilary's text all the pain of my hurt and rejection melted away. I called her at home and although she couldn't talk in that moment, she said, 'Well done for calling.' It didn't matter that she couldn't talk, it mattered that she was OK with me calling and that I had managed to call her.

In our last session before the break, I told Hilary that I didn't want to protect her feelings over mine, but it was all so painful. At the end of the session she gave me the number of where she would be staying so I could contact her, and a card for me to keep. It had a picture of a beautiful garden with a bench at the end of a flower-lined path. The flowers were different shades of pinks and bursting from their dark green stems with such vibrant colour and beauty. The bench had fewer flowers surrounding it but somehow seems to offer an invitation to sit and rest. Hilary said, 'The bench is where we can meet.' I felt so touched by her and had a feeling in my chest that I couldn't name but I felt light and held!

The card from Hilary, with the picture of the bench.

I was starting to believe that Hilary would come back but began to fear she would come back different. I feared the loving Hilary would come back abusive and I would be left bewildered and confused. A part of me knew this wasn't right and I thought about the little girl who knew all about such betrayal. I told her she was wonderful and beautiful and that I knew I was strong enough to protect her if Hilary did come back different.

I missed Hilary even though it was just two days since I had seen her and sent her a text to tell her how I felt. She sent back to say she was on the bench with me, 'and the same old Hilary would be coming back.' She reminded me of how beautiful the colours were for me when I was in Barbados and how beautiful the flowers were on the path leading up to the bench. I looked at the card she gave me and imagined being there with her, what we would talk about and how she would be with me and felt held.

I knew from other times that the Easter break would be several weeks, and I also knew I needed to find ways of taking my mind off missing Hilary and try and be in the moment. It was tough because although I was very busy with work, family, socialising and singing I didn't seem to be able to stop processing. I was so in touch with the little girl within.

In my singing lessons I so wanted to sing out beautiful, strong, joyful sounds as though I could sing out some of the beauty of the child inside of me. The one that felt so ugly for so long. The child that believed her inner self to be filth, so unclean that she couldn't allow herself to ever be seen. And yet she knew, there was something worth something inside. The little girl so pretty and fresh who would sing a sweet child song and be chosen to perform. That child so small and free for so little time before the cruelty. The violation of her soul that robbed all but the outer shell of herself. Leaving existence in place of living. So much sadness for that child, the little girl with the sweet child song. She was left flat without joy but a feeling, a coldness and death inside. She belonged nowhere, she didn't fit, she was no longer seen.

I knew she needed to find the lovely place with Hilary again so that she felt held and loved. The comfort she once knew from her mother who wrapped herself around her, snuggling her, a love beyond words communicated through the eyes of the mother, one where the child knows the look and understands she is completely safe. I told Little Me how sorry I was that it was snatched from her and that she didn't know it for long and reassured her that we didn't have to let that lovely place slip away from us. Hilary had told me that no one could take it from us, and we can spend time doing fun things and let others see who we are. We didn't have to hide anymore.

I so wished Hilary had been there when I was small. I thought about my mum and asked why she couldn't have learned to tolerate the distress she was in so that I wasn't hurt. As I spoke the words out loud, to a mother that was not there to hear them, hot tears fell, hot tears left my eyes, becoming cold as they ran down my face and hung from my chin. The release of sadness expressed in my short heavy breathing, so close was I to sobbing. I left a message on Hilary's answerphone that I knew she might not get for a couple of weeks but hearing her voice and knowing she would pick up the message and would understand was enough for me in the moment.

I texted Hilary over the weeks that followed when I needed to, and she reassured me, reiterating what had been said before. We also arranged a telephone session during that time. I had realised that I needed to listen to Little Me and reach out to Hilary when I needed to and she was there for me as and when she could be. I was starting to see and feel colour in our relationship and in my life.

I love the beauty of the colours
And the pleasure of that lovely place
I try so hard to keep it
To hold it all in my embrace

But the intensity of abuse in my childhood
The power of the cold cruelty, the pain
Overwhelms my fragile sense of self
The little girl I was who should
Have been loved, held and understood

133

Then the beauty of the colours
And the pleasure of that lovely place
Would have been there from my start
At the core of my very being
And not something for me to find
And learn to hold in heart and mind

You often say it takes time
To build trust through the relationship
To learn to trust and to feel safe
But each time you go away
The pain and trauma of those days
The confusion, bewilderment and isolation
Return and again and I feel dead inside

Every time you go away I am left behind
Managing the pain of abandonment and loss
The isolation of a little person at odds
With the world, looking but unable to find
A freedom and joy in heart and mind

I told you I was in a lovely place
But then it was slipping away
You told me no one can take it from me
From my point of view all I know
Is I love the beauty of the colours
And the pleasure of that lovely place
That I try so hard to keep within
And to hold in my embrace
The power and cold cruelty of abuse
The intensity of the pain
Overwhelms my little fragile sense of self
And I lose it all again

If I had been nurtured as I should
Cared for loved and understood
The beauty and pleasure of that lovely place
Would have been there from my start
At the very core of my little being
And not something for us to find
Or learn about holding in heart and mind

And yes, I know it all takes time
But it's me who hurts and has to face
The agony of finding then losing that lovely place
Sometimes I feel I'd be better off believing
As I did before, that I am a nothing
Dead inside with nobody caring, nobody seeing
Detached, invisible and without feeling.

I felt enlightened and sad all at once. I understood the impact of being so hurt as a child and having no one to tell. The importance of a safe nurturing relationship, like with Hilary. One where mistakes could be made and acknowledged, where challenges can take place, where acceptance of feelings, whether positive or negative, meant feeling like rubbish or feeling bad weren't part of it. I understood Little Me, I knew her life was nothing like it should have been and that I did nothing to deserve what was done to me.

My first session back after three weeks was hard and I was aware of feeling angry with Hilary, even though she had given me so much. I felt angry that I continued to fear how she might see Little Me if I really showed her. I asked her if she would really be able to cope with Little Me crying; would she be able to handle the ugly, snivelling, nasty dirty little girl'? Hilary said, 'Yes' in her strong assertive voice and then added, 'I don't see you through your mum's eyes, but you do and so there is your mum, you and me in the room.' She told me I had to stop seeing Little Me through my mum's eyes before Little Me would trust enough to come out.

I knew I had felt wary of Hilary in the session but didn't understand why and was feeling angry that she could make it all better but wasn't doing so. In a later conversation I was able to tell her how I felt. She talked about 'not forcing little me to come out', but she thought Little Me was wary of me and 'like a shy child hiding behind a sofa would just pop her head out and little by little and would come out when she was ready.' It was an emotional moment. I didn't know what 'normal' childhood fears were.-Hilary acknowledged that and said, 'We need to find out what would help little you to feel safe.'

Interestingly my fear of being ugly wasn't limited to my therapy. I found it very difficult to relax my face and jaw with the sounds my singing teacher had asked me to make during vocal exercises. I wondered why I felt so self-conscious and why my jaw would stay stubbornly tense no matter what my singing teacher did. Singing was so unrelated to my childhood trauma in my mind.

I decided to do some of the exercises at home in the mirror. I wanted to see what I looked like. I knew I was very conscious of how many fillings I had and hated having so many teeth looking like gravestones with the heaviness of the metal that sat between most of them due to neglect in my childhood. I found it so hard to look at myself and used a towel to block my view of my mouth. I sang freely when I could not see my mouth. I had an image of my mother with a pillow in her hands smothering my face as she growled, 'Shut your ugly fat mouth, do you know how ugly you look when you are whining and snivelling?'

I remembered her telling me she would kill me and smothering me, but I couldn't believe she did that. I phoned my sister and as I described the memory, she interrupted me and said, 'I know exactly what you are going to say. Mum tried to smother us and threatened to kill us when we were playing her up.' My singing teacher had asked me to 'cry the notes' when singing at the top of the scale so as not to strain my vocal cords, it felt like a big ask at the time and after that memory I understood why.

I struggled to accept what had happened to me and asked myself how I survived so much abuse, I was so young. When I started working with Hilary I couldn't feel or see Little Me but, in the moment, I felt overwhelmed with the pain of it. The intense feelings didn't pass and I wished I was dead. I messaged Hilary to tell her how I was feeling, and she told me it was important that Little Me knew she would come to no harm for telling me and that she knew I would hear her. She said, 'It's her way back to you!'

I trusted Hilary and knew I needed to make sure Little Me felt safe.

I couldn't describe how I felt beyond feeling overwhelmed, and realised I felt that way when Hilary was away over the summer and again when I was away earlier in the year. I didn't understand because Hilary wasn't away and nor was I. Hilary suggested that I was beginning to feel safe enough to feel with her in the moment and I cried. I felt it had taken me so long and so many sessions to achieve that. I knew the difference being able to leave a message at any time had made and told her it was a lifeline. I had someone to tell and somewhere to take my hurt and I thanked Hilary for being there for me, for the nurturing and comfort she gave.

Hilary's comfort extended to me as a mother and grandmother, and she often shared nurturing ideas when I told her what was happening in the lives of my daughters. During the last session I had told her that my daughter's baby, my third grandchild, was on his way and she asked questions and checked arrangements with me. A wisdom that any woman would want from a mother or someone who behaved like one. After a traumatic last few hours of her labour, which involved high-pitched screams, a very pale-faced dad to be, a calm and reassuring grandmother to be (even though I feared for the baby given he was stuck and given how many midwives responded to the emergency bell) and an assertive lead midwife who was able to talk in a firm voice despite all the noise and commotion, a very blue baby boy arrived at 5.30 a.m. the following morning – another little delicious! He slept peacefully after an initial cry and as my daughter held him, she said, 'He is worth every little contraction.' I didn't think my crushed hand from her ever-tightening grip or my eardrums from her screams, would agree there was anything little about those contractions! Neither was there anything little about her love for him, which was wonderful.

As often happened, I would all too easily lose the feelings of comfort I had gained from Hilary. I felt little six-year-old me was safely nurtured within, but the little girl of 10, the one who was sexually abused, wasn't there in the same way. I found this distressing. I had spent so much time and put in so much effort and thought when I reached the Little Me who had been traumatised by her mother that I was reaching Little Me in my entirety. When I thought about the photographs of me and pictured the 10-

year-old me, I knew that part of me was still lost, and I didn't accept her or love her in the same way. Hilary and I explored those feelings in the sessions and acknowledged that Little Me between the ages of nine and 11 needed to be seen and heard. I knew I didn't feel love for her, she was a part of me that I didn't love or nurture, and I felt she was angry and didn't give a shit, which scared me. I didn't want to communicate with her or ask her how she felt and told Hilary I wasn't sure I was ready to deal with this angry kid, so hoped she was!

I saw Little Me as a small child holding her arms out asking to be loved, but 10-year-old me was angry and I didn't feel she was asking to be loved.

My next session was over the phone, and there was an awkward silence on my part when I made the call. Hilary broke the silence by saying, 'Things are hard for you.' I shared how terrible I had been feeling and about 10-year-old me. Hilary told me that at 10 Little Me might want to hit out rather than admit she needed to be loved. I knew she was right and found it distressing when I thought about what she suffered.

As the days went by, I experienced so much rage, which changed from anger towards me at 10 to anger and hate for Hilary. I had left Hilary a message but hadn't heard from her as quickly as I wanted, but it felt like my 10-year-old was demanding a response, unprepared to wait. It felt so hard to feel hate towards Hilary; she had given me so much. I wrote a letter to her in my journal.

Dear Hilary,

I left you a message today but you haven't texted me or let me know you got it. I don't want to talk

139

to you and just feel hate towards you. I feel that
you are fed up with me and that you don't want to
be there for me. Bored with my shit and why
wouldn't you be? I have nothing to say that
doesn't have the same old shit attached to it and
no I still can't cry when I am with you. I told you
on Tuesday that I had never felt so vulnerable and
felt like you were emotionally holding me in your
arms but you didn't react and I feel you don't want
to get that close to me. I don't want to tell you all
this over the phone and I don't want to speak to
you on Friday. I want to test you. Find out if you
really do mean what you say. I told you the last
time I was bonded to an adult it was with my
mother and look what she did and then he came
along and look what he did. I will not bond with
you anymore and I don't want to see you again. I
want to stop all this me, me, me stuff 'cos it is all
shit. I don't want to think about his disgusting
penis down my throat and his stinking spunk all
over me. I was a child for fuck sake. Forced to
touch him, suck him and pretend I was enjoying it
because he told me that it was great, I was great.
Well it wasn't fucking great; it was the worst most
disgusting thing and I hated it. I hated him licking
and biting and sucking at me. It hurt and I wanted
him to stop, just to stop. AND BY THE TIME I
TELL YOU THIS IT WILL HAVE PASSED AND I
WOULD HAVE DONE IT ALL ALONE AGAIN.
ALONE WITH THIS HURT. I CAN'T JUST SEE
YOU ONCE A WEEK, IT ISN'T ENOUGH. I
NEED TO BE WITH YOU ALL THE TIME SO I
CAN BE HELD AND HEARD AND HAVE

140

SOMEWHERE TO GO WITH IT ALL. IT FEELS LIKE IT WANTS TO BURST OUT OF ME SO THAT I DON'T HAVE TO CARRY IT ANYMORE. IT ISN'T MINE TO CARRY IT IS HIS, IT IS HIS, IT WASN'T ME.

Although I wasn't communicating with Little Me and didn't want to ask how 10-year-old me was feeling, that part of me was making sure her voice was heard by how terrible I felt. I was struggling with everything; I didn't want to go to work, and that's how I felt about school when I was 10!

Telling Hilary about how I felt was hard, but she encouraged me to read what I had written to her. Reading it out loud, telling her I hated her and never wanted to see her again was one of the hardest things for me. She didn't seem fazed by it, which shocked me. She talked about the needs of 10-year-old me and how important it was that she felt safe enough to express herself and still be accepted. That both 10-year-old me and adult me hated what was done to me, and that she had a part in me feeling the pain of my childhood and I hated that.

I later told Hilary that I feared I would lose her love and acceptance and she said, 'Love and acceptance is part of our relationship and is part of us and it cannot go away!'

I said, 'I didn't know I could feel so held.' I felt as though Hilary's arms were physically around me. She asked me what part of me felt held and I realised it was all of me and I felt protective towards 10-year-old me. I felt accepted.

I put the photo of her in the checked dress, the one I had previously disliked, in a frame and put her next to the one of six-year-old me.

> I am full of and overwhelmed with pain
> The intensity of which I cannot explain
> All consuming, an all over body pain
> Feelings that I just cannot name
> Do I have to describe it for it to be real
> Or will you believe I'm not trying to conceal
> The enormity the intensity of what I feel
>
> After we spoke I began to know
> As the process unfolded and started to show
> The pain was lots of feelings, not just one
> A massive accumulation of what was done
> To me, a little girl a young child in need
> Of love and care a planting of the seed
> Where love like water enables growth
> And nurturing like breath, I needed both
> Neither was there, I somehow survived
> Existed for years and am still alive
> I grew, I breathed but it was a living hell
> With no one to turn to and no one to tell
>
> Now you are there and offering me
> The love and care that I needed to be
> Available and there when I was a child
> Holding me, protecting me from the vile
> Abuse from others who wanted to hurt
> If you were there, you'd have been alert
> And maybe just maybe I would have received
> The love and care you are now giving me

I don't know how to accept what you give
I know how to feel alive and how to live
I am not just existing and trying to survive
I am living and I am feeling so alive
Show me how to receive and how to know
The realness of our relationship, the love you show
I am so afraid that it is just pretend
That when I need you most it will all end
And alone again I will be and there'll be just me
With no one to turn to and no one to be
There for the child or for the grown up me

Knowing how to receive
Nurture love and care
Fear you would recoil
Would no longer be there.

The word 'recoil' came to mind, and in my next session I
told Hilary I feared she would recoil when I told her I felt
held by her. Hilary talked about what happened to me and
said that would make anyone want to recoil but not from
me. As we talked, I could feel myself tensing and
withdrawing in fear, but with my newfound trust I was
able to share that with Hilary in the moment. I experienced
such intense feelings but couldn't find the words to name
them. We talked about me feeling angry but that I didn't
want to hide from her anymore. Hilary shared her thoughts
about Little Me starting to put her head above the parapet
and letting Hilary see her. She went on to say that I was
able to express my feelings by writing in my journal and
through my poetry. We explored my difficulties in texting
or calling Hilary when I needed her, and I shared my fear
of her being fed up with me. As I said those words, I felt I

was the dirty little girl, the ungrateful little bitch, the ugly snivelling nasty little girl who caused my mum to have a breakdown, it was all my fault. I felt like the little girl who feared Ernest would be nasty or disapproving so I needed to do everything I could to make him happy. Hilary responded to that last part by saying, 'You kept going back to him because he was all you had.'

At the end of the session Hilary checked how I was feeling, and I told her I was OK but feared how I might feel later that day and might need to 'know you are there.' She said, 'Tricia, you must call me.'

We arranged a follow-up call before I left the session to make sure I would.

The process continued and I shared my fears of Hilary hurting me and our relationship going bad. I told her I would rather stop seeing her than continue with the risk of that happening. She acknowledged my fear and told me, 'It would be time and experience that would show you otherwise, you will just have to keep going and you will learn a different way.'

I experienced lovely feelings of safe and of warmth for a couple of days after the session, but then I started to feel it leave me. I checked in with Hilary by text to tell her how I had been feeling, didn't want it to go away and needed to know she was there. She messaged back, 'I am here' and it all felt OK.

I often didn't understand how things worked in the therapy process and this was one of those times. Within a few days of the loveliness of safety and warmth I was feeling such sadness. I thought about there being no 'sorry' from my mum or Ernest for what they did to me. I kept to my agreement with Hilary that I would message her or call her if I needed her. I had so much I wanted to say, so I called and left a message on her answerphone saying, 'I am really angry that my mum and Ernest would never say sorry, would never tell Little Me they were sorry for what they did to me or how what they did caused such damage throughout my life. They would never tell me how they regretted the hurt they caused me. That no matter how many times I tell Little Me that I am sorry, and I can do that until the day I die, it will never be them that is sorry. I also knew that in all the hurt I was feeling there were the feelings of safety and warmth in there somewhere.'

Somehow, I was holding on to the love and care from my early child years and from Hilary.

Just as there were other things in my life there were things in Hilary's, and we had to miss some sessions because she required an operation and had to attend a funeral. I expressed my concern for her, but she was more interested in how it would affect me. I knew that was why she mentioned it; she knew so well how hard breaks were for me. It was hard knowing this would be the last session for a couple of weeks, but acknowledging it helped. We talked about there being no 'sorry' for me and I talked about how painful I found it that no one saw the pain I was in as a child. Hilary had previously described my feelings of wishing I was dead as me feeling 'suicidal', and I agreed I was distressed, and a tear flowed down my cheek. I wiped it away and watched for a reaction in Hilary. She focused on me; she didn't draw attention to my tears, she just let me talk and I felt her love and her care for me. I told her how sorry I was that I had hated Little Me and sorry that I hadn't wanted her to be part of me. Hilary told me she thought I did the best I could and that I must get away from being sorry for something I didn't cause.

145

I felt the benefit of texting, leaving messages and speaking to Hilary rather than battle with myself over it. In a phone session before the break, I shared my worries about what was happening for Hilary particularly as she continued to give so much to me. She reassured me that they were life events that we needed to work around and that she was OK. As she always did, she brought the conversation back to me. We talked about my feelings of powerlessness when I felt distressed. Hilary suggested that perhaps I direct my anger towards my mum and Ernest in those moments because it was them and what they did to me that caused me to feel so bad at times. She suggested that when I felt bad I was to tell my mum and Ernest there is no place for them now and that I have a different relationship with someone who cares about me and who doesn't abuse me.

To help me manage in the break, I put the card Hilary had given me with the bench and beautiful flowers in a frame and put it on my dressing table near to the photos of me when I was six and 10. That night I dreamt that Hilary was holding out her arms to me, smiling at me with eyes that were warm and loving. I ran into her arms and felt warm and safe. I knew in that moment I had finally accepted that Hilary wants a relationship with me, and she is there because she wants to be. I sent her a text describing it all to her and she sent back to say, 'That's such a lovely place to be,' and I allowed myself to be in that place and enjoy it. I no longer felt she would recoil from me. Ring out the bells!

I felt stronger and more contained. I felt ready to write a letter to my mum expressing my hurt and disappointment and my anger at her. She would never read it, of course, but it helped to say all that I needed to. She had been dead for over three years, and I continued to have difficult and conflicting feelings about her and for her. The letter was possible because Hilary had accepted my letter to her; that experience felt like it settled me.

Dear Mum,

I have wanted to write to you for so long, but it is a hard thing to do. I haven't seen you for 3½ years and although I miss you at times I am also hurting and angry with you for all the unspoken hurts that I have carried from my childhood. It wasn't easy being your child and sometimes it was so hard that I wished I was dead. Other times it was OK and for a little while it was lovely.

I loved you being my mummy when I was really small. I loved your smell and how you snuggled me in your arms, I loved how you enjoyed my cheekiness and how we laughed together. I felt safe in your arms and I remember being excited when you came to collect me from school. I remember when I was very small and it was just me and you at home together and I remember how you nursed me when I was ill and made me nice food to encourage me to eat.

I didn't understand when that changed though. I was so afraid when you screamed and shouted at me and pinched me, punched me, pulled my hair, hit my vagina with a spatula and twisted my skin digging your nails in. You screwed up your face and contorted your features to mimic what you said I looked like when I cried. You called me ugly, a selfish little bitch, a dirty little girl and a hateful

147

child. You told me it was my fault you had been ill and threatened to give me something to cry for if I didn't stop crying after you had hit me, pulled my hair and smothered my face with wet sheets from my bed. You told me to stop snivelling and that I was an ungrateful little bitch. You said you hated me.

I don't know why you couldn't cope with your children and your life but it hurt me so much mum. You left me completely wounded and I survived in a living hell for years. I felt cold and alone with nowhere to go and I hated myself. Didn't you understand what you were doing? Didn't you know it was wrong to do those things? Do you remember when you came out of hospital and I couldn't cross the road and I couldn't breathe? You took me to the doctor and he said I was missing you and that is why I was in that state of anxiety. WRONG fucking so WRONG. I was in that state of anxiety mother because you hurt me and then left me in the care of a bastard paedophile and he was forcing his penis down my throat. You hit my vagina because I pissed the bed and he sucked and bit my vagina to get me to piss in his mouth. He spunked all over my body and made me kiss his disgusting wet slobbery mouth. That is why I was anxious – get it?

So then after a weekend with him I was back home to arguments between you and Dad. You pissing off up the pub every night and after you and Dad split, hearing you and seeing you having sex with blokes who took your fancy. I no longer existed. I became invisible to you. You stopped hitting me but you completely neglected me. Left me with no clean clothes. Oh and the launderette – do *you remember that one. I did the washing for six of us and didn't fold the clothes properly after I had tumble-dried them and you screamed at me and shouted at me 'cos I had made more work for you because of the creases. I was 10 mother, yes fucking 10. No deodorant either by the way. No sanitary towels. No toothbrush. NO FUCKING CHILDHOOD REALLY. So now do you remember?*

So, I grew up with absolutely no fucking idea of who I was. I hated myself and never knew how to just be. I lived to what I thought others expected me to be. I learned to watch for any sign of approval and then matched what others wanted because I had no identity of my own. I stopped growing emotionally and remained stuck there. I didn't know what I liked, I didn't know what made me laugh or cry because I didn't really laugh or cry. I thought laughter and I thought tears and I was like this for years and years. I missed out on the real deep feelings of love and how to feel them. How to know laughter and how to know feelings of happiness.

In my next session with Hilary, I felt both protective towards her because she'd had a difficult time and angry with her for missing my sessions. I was OK with those feelings, I understood them. We talked about the letter I wrote to my mum, and I shared how I felt I was discovering myself and learning how I appreciate the beauty of flowers. I knew none of this meant anything to me before other than 'thinking' they were beautiful. I could feel beauty and I cried as I told Hilary it felt so freeing. Hilary gave such gentle acceptance and I believed it was a thing of beauty that two people could just 'be' in quiet acceptance of the moment shared.

Although I had thought I had told my mum everything in the letter, as I explored feelings with Hilary, she checked that with me and I realised that I hadn't been able to tell my mum I wanted her to hold me in her arms, but if she was still alive I knew that after reacting angrily to being challenged by me, my mum would have held me. It was too late for me, but I didn't want it to be too late for my daughters.

I told Hilary I had asked them to write to me about the good things and hard things in their childhoods so we could work on the weeds in their gardens, some from me and some from themselves. Hilary asked me what I meant. I told her that in my childhood I had no flowers and many weeds, which almost destroyed me. Hilary agreed it was a bleak landscape. I told her I still had weeds, but I was starting to get rid of them and plant some beautiful flowers and I wanted to help my girls have their flowers. Hilary warned me that I was taking a risk in asking my girls to share how they felt about difficult times in their childhood. I knew it was, but I believed it was a risk worth taking. I didn't want them to be left with burdens, with pain from being my children. I didn't want anything I had passed on to go undealt with for them.

So much pain was locked inside me and with it a depth of love and joy that could not previously be reached. It takes one moment to hurt a child and that child is burdened with the hurt of that one moment for their whole life. I was beginning to know and understand how much that burden impacted on my life.

I was feeling at odds and sent messages to Hilary. I told her I felt I was taking a huge step back, and I was angry with her for bringing me comfort and then leaving me in a place of turmoil. She sent back to say, 'Going back and forth is part of the process and that perhaps you hate yourself and me for putting you in that situation.'

I cried when I read the text, and we arranged to talk. I told Hilary that I didn't hate her and I cried some more. We explored what might be happening and worked out that not only does Little Me want me to know she isn't yet OK and still needs me, but adult me also needs Hilary to know that, just because I was sometimes stronger and more healed, it didn't mean I was OK, and I still needed her. We talked some more about my letter to my mum, and I told her I wished her and Ernest were still alive so I could tell them what I wanted to tell them. Hilary explored with me how I might feel if they blamed me for what they did and I told her I didn't care, I just wanted them to know how much they hurt me and the impact of it on me.

I felt OK after therapy but knew I needed to write how I was feeling:

> What do I know about you and what do I care
> Whatever happened to you, it wasn't fair
> That you hurt me and you were so cruel
> Couldn't you see I was just a little girl
> Who loved you and needed you to be
> Loving and caring to the child that was me
> How could you do it, why didn't you try
> To be a better person instead of deny
> Me the right of a safe, secure childhood
> Where I could develop and grow as I should
> Didn't you know, didn't you understand
> The pain I was suffering at your hand
> Why did you do it, couldn't you see

The harm, the damage you were doing to me
Not just at 6,7,8,9 and 10
But all the years of a living hell since then
Now do you know, now do you care
How can you, you're dead and not aware
If I could have told you I know that I'd say
I missed you when you went away
But I hated what you were doing to me
And it's only now that I can see
The trauma, the pain and the enormity
Of the damage you did and the impact on me
I want you to know and to understand
The pain I am still suffering at your hand
Because it didn't stop when it ended
I got on with my life and just pretended
Nothing was wrong and this was instead
Of telling anyone I wish I was dead
I still feel that way some of the time
Such is the impact of your wicked crime.

The break from Hilary was longer than expected, and I didn't write much in my journal for those few weeks except for some poetry.

I often had dreams. Sometimes they would be comforting, but other times they would confuse me and leave me fearful. I dreamt I was down in a dark underground place and although there was a train, I couldn't see the way out. I had a baby with me that I comforted, but someone was missing. It felt like I was in a slimy pit.

I knew I needed Hilary. I messaged her and we arranged to talk. She didn't answer at our agreed time, and I experienced all sorts of fears about her having had enough of me, me not mattering to her anymore. I then examined my feelings and considered the evidence for them. I knew Hilary was always there when she said she would be, unless something unexpected cropped up. As I was procrastinating about what I should do my phone rang and it was Hilary apologising that she had been held up by a neighbour and some flooding. I didn't know what to say but she said, 'That must have been scary when you called and I wasn't there.'

I agreed it was and we examined my feelings of being unacceptable, and I told Hilary I believed my letter to my mum was like a letter to myself to help me understand how terrible it all was. That morning I felt a sadness that took away my breath and put me on my knees, but I couldn't cry and I hated being stuck in that way. I wanted Hilary to stop holding out her arms for me to run into and to come and get me instead.

I didn't write feelings for a couple of weeks and was dreading the long summer break that was looming. In our sessions Hilary and I explored that dread again, and she shared with me that she would feel sad when I didn't need her anymore. I knew she meant it. I knew she was telling me I was important to her and in that moment, I didn't feel like I was a burden to her or like someone she tolerated because she had to. I felt like I mattered to her and I cried.

I felt aware of the need I had had to care for my mum when she was dying, but I didn't understand why. Hilary wondered if I was showing my mum how to love and care for someone. I thought that was possible. I remembered the night in the hospice when I sat at my mum's bedside in her last days. I pulled a chair close to her bed and held her hand all night. I wanted to be close to her and feared I would lose my fight against sleep, which would leave her without human touch if she were to die in the night. I didn't want her to die alone. I stroked her hands, the hands that cared for me when I was a small child. They were also the hands and nails that so abused me, the same hands that I held and stroked to let my mum know I was there, that she wasn't alone in those moments of her hanging in whatever that place is between life and death. Such mixed emotions about her. I was so aware that I had existed in a non-place and felt so alone as a child because of what she did to me, but something instinctive within me knew that I didn't want her to feel alone.

I shared my distress with Hilary and found comfort in her knowing me the way she did. She knew I was in a dark place and said maybe we needed to be in there together. I was in so much intense pain that I could hardly talk, but knew Hilary was there and understood. I needed her, which felt so good.

> To go back into that slimy pit
> From where God lifted me, took true grit
> To visit that bleak and scary place
> And find little me, be in her space
> I needed to go there and know the pain
> That she suffered again and again
> To understand what she needs from me
> So that she can feel safe and be free
> I've begun to know, I've begun to feel
> How she felt, it feels so real
> As if I'm small and really there
> Feeling the gut-wrenching total despair
> Of how she felt, of what she survived
> I am so amazed she is still alive
> I can feel just how much she was deprived

154

Of basic love and of basic care
The soothing of a loving mother wasn't there

She was so alone with no one to tell
About her pain, her living hell
The fear of hoping, a big risk to take
If it went wrong her heart would break
Safer to stay in that bleak non-place
Where she could hide and have no face.

I didn't always feel connected to Hilary in a positive way, and that happened when I didn't understand something. I asked her to help me understand what I was doing that kept me feeling like I was in the slimy pit. She talked about choosing to go in there and commented on how we started working together. I had told her at the start of us working as a two that I didn't think she liked me much when she was providing couple sessions, yet I still wanted to work with her. In a later session Hilary mentioned that and laughed – but I didn't think it was funny and as was my usual way, I couldn't tell her in the session. I had a sleepless night and phoned Hilary's answerphone at 3 a.m. to tell her I was angry with her for laughing and that I was not choosing to stay in the slimy pit, I was trying to find my way out of it. I didn't hear from her so sent her a text to say I had left a message and didn't understand what she wanted me to do.

The next session didn't feel any better for me. Hilary suggested I provided a pillow or something of comfort for Little Me to sit on when in the slimy pit, and I told her I didn't know how to do that. She said, 'You go in there so there must be a way in.'

'I need you to be in there with me. You are the comfort.' I remained confused and I felt angry at the end of the session.

> Now I am in a place of confusion and pain
> I am so unsure if you accept all of me
> The small vulnerable child of innocence
> Is so easy to love and accept again and again
> Cos she was just a child with no responsibility
> For the cruel abuse, sexual, verbal violence
> That was inflicted on her by the adults
> Who should have kept her safe, free from harm
>
> I don't want to beat myself up anymore
> I don't ever want to hit myself as I did before
> When I think of the pain I inflicted on me
> It makes me cry because now I can see
> So much punishment and so much shame
> For what they did it was their choice
> To steal from me, silence me, take my voice
>
> Caused me to hide in that bleak non-place
> Preventing me from growing and having space.

I struggled with feeling so angry towards Hilary, but in spending time with Little Me an understanding seemed to emerge. I began to understand that I was choosing to stay in the slimy pit by not phoning Hilary and letting her be the cushion for me. I messaged Hilary to tell her and she messaged me back saying she knew how hard it was, and I felt held by her. Angry feelings were tough, but I knew Hilary cared about me. I wanted to invite her into my world as it was when I was a child, and for her to tell me what she would have done if she had walked in on my mum as she pinched and twisted my vagina, spitting out the venomous words of hate and loathing for the dirty, horrible, nasty little girl that I was for wetting the bed. What would she do if she walked in on Ernest with me on his bed with his erect penis in my mouth? Writing my fears helped me to have the courage to ask Hilary in my next session.

Hilary asked me what I thought she would do; I knew she would ask me that but I didn't know the answer. I feared she would think that I was the dirty, nasty, horrible little girl my mother said I was, but I knew I didn't deserve the abuse from her or Ernest. I told Hilary I thought she would be horrified at what was being done to me. Hilary asked me if I knew any child who deserved to be hurt, and I said I didn't. I told Hilary I needed her more than I needed my mum as a small child, and I feared she would hurt me or not be there for me in the way she says she will be. I was so aware that my mum had been loving and looked after me when I was very small, and I had to know what I did to make her hate me.

Hilary suggested that if her and my relationship wasn't working it would be gradual. That's not how I remembered the change in my mum, and with that I felt tears fall, which I tried to hide from Hilary.

I didn't want Hilary to be my therapist, I wanted her to be my mum. I felt worthless and wished I didn't exist and a part of me wanted to die and I wanted the comfort of Hilary. I knew she wouldn't be the perfect mother, no one is, but she would have loved me and cared for me and kept me safe. I messaged her and she let me know she had people visiting but could have a quick chat. I didn't want to take more from her so said I would be OK, which was true given her response was an offer and I knew she was there.

Late that night I sobbed as I felt the pain of the impact of the abuse inflicted on me. I knew the pain was too much for me, and the following morning I found the courage to phone Hilary at home! My heart raced as the phone rang, but Hilary sounded pleased to hear from me and she reiterated the importance of me phoning her when I needed to so that, 'The little part of you knows someone is there.'

We talked about choices in my next session, and about how as a child I didn't have the choice to leave situations where I was being hurt but as an adult I could choose. I understood that but I wasn't able to choose when another break would happen, and one was about to happen, or for her to be my mum. I shared that with Hilary and my feelings that if she had been my mum, I would have been OK. Hilary suggested if she had lived my mother's life, she may well have not been any better than my mum. I felt like she wasn't listening to me or understanding what I needed from her, and I felt rotten but couldn't tell her. I felt like she was sending me away as a grown-up and expecting me to be independent from her and it hurt. It didn't feel like the special moments usually did when we were having a break. Hilary gave me a card with words of comfort to help me through the long break ahead, but I felt like I just had to get on with it.

In our last phone session before the break, I was able to tell her that I felt she had resisted going with me into the place where I wanted to be hers. It was an emotional place. Hilary said she remembered thinking that she couldn't stay in the place where I had a longing for a different life or where I was staying in that level of pain. I shared my anger at having spent so much of my life not feeling for the pain of my childhood, not knowing I deserved anything. Hilary said, 'not being valued by another person.'

I agreed and said I was beginning to feel what it felt like and was still processing feelings of being abused. I felt I was wading through so much shit and although none of it was my shit, I was left to deal with it. Hilary asked me if I felt her resistance had been because she wouldn't have wanted me to be her child, and I didn't know but could tell her that I couldn't connect with her and felt alone. I didn't like her defending my mum. Hilary told me that her defence of my mum was in support of me, not against me, and on reflection she felt she was meeting her own needs of wanting me to be OK in the break and therefore didn't connect with my needs. She then went on to say that it was horrible that I was left feeling so alone. She added that she was sorry for not listening and for putting herself first.

I didn't know what to say, was silent and felt I couldn't bear it that she was apologising to me. I really couldn't believe what she was saying and said, 'Do you think that is was happened?'

In true Hilary style she said, 'What do you think?'

I was too overwhelmed in that moment. She gave me so much and then took responsibility for getting something wrong and said she was sorry? No one else did that for me.

This break felt different. I missed Hilary but felt more contained and realised that I believed she would be coming back as herself. I was visiting France that summer and Hilary had shared with me that she would also be in France. I liked it that we were in the same country. I was learning to enjoy the moments of comfort and not fret about how long they would last. My trip to France was a welcome break with close friends, and we enjoyed the beauty of the Alps and our drive to Saint Tropez to satisfy our curiosity of how the other half lives. We went on to Villefranche-sur-Mer, which Hilary knew and considered worth a visit.

Within days I felt such sadness; I missed Hilary and needed to know that I could be hers for a while, that she would welcome me as hers, that I would not be rejected by her, that I would not abhor her, that she wouldn't recoil at the thought of me being hers. If I had been her child, I would not have believed myself to be a dirty rag, worthless to all and only good enough when I was doing things for others. Like staying at home from school and cleaning my mum's house because I knew it would please her and because I couldn't bear to go to school and be with other kids. I didn't know how to play or how to act, I was at odds with myself and the world around me. I hated myself and felt dirty and bad, useless and a nothing. That's why I needed Hilary to stay with me in that place where I was hers, that she could bring me up emotionally in the way I should have been raised.

> Can you really be there for me? Can you
> really be there?
> Can you respond to me when I need your
> soothing care?
> It might be at midnight, it might be every day
> Are you really committed to this in every way?
> It could mean I hate you and scream at you in despair
> It could mean I need you when you don't
> want to be there
> I know that I need you and that makes me so afraid
> At times it makes me wish that I had stayed
> Separate from myself unable to know and feel
> The pain, the emotions of what our work reveals
> You have to be there I need you to stay with me.

The pain of the missing continued, and so did angry feelings that I was living with so much of it. I wanted to be with Hilary, I felt like I couldn't breathe without her, being separated from her was agony. Again, I felt I would rather stop seeing her than live with that pain every time there was a break. I gave myself some time and wrote a letter to Hilary in my journal to tell her how I was feeling. It helped me to manage for a few more days.

I trusted that I could contact Hilary and we used emails during this break. We talked about weeds in my garden, and I said they were offering up the bitter taste of abuse, which was such a contrast to the beautiful flowers that lined the path leading to the bench, our bench on the card she had given me. I asked Hilary to join me on the bench and she said she would. 'We could close our eyes and see the colours together.'

I felt so different with Hilary's love and care for me. I knew at my core that I felt different. There were many triggers and I still felt powerless to stop the videos of abuse playing and the surges of pain that followed. I fought back hard about accepting what happened to me and moved between fearing Hilary wouldn't be able to handle all my pain to knowing she would. I swung from fearing I would be too much for her, a burden and too demanding, to knowing she would cope with it all.

Year Three

I often didn't know how to start a conversation with Hilary, whether over the phone or face to face. Somehow I would manage to say something that would help, or Hilary would. It was always a bit harder coming back from a long break, even though I had lots of contact with her in between. In this next session I was in touch with feelings of shame when I talked about my deep hurts, the abuse I had suffered and a belief of being unlovable. Hilary said it was about my mum and Ernest and not about me. I had learned and grown enough over the past couple of years to know that to be true and I wanted to feel free of self-blame but didn't know how. Hilary said, 'Bit by bit.'

I knew she was right, but I hated hearing it. I hated that it meant more work, more pain. I knew I feared that if she saw me as hateful and unlovable then she might think I deserved to be hurt. She acknowledged how confusing it must all have been for me and said, 'You have had enough of being hurt.' I knew I had but it had a deeper meaning when she said it.

I continued to feel the frustration of not being able to cry in the session when I had wanted to. I believed I would die at the hands of my mother if I cried or made a demand when I was a child. As an adult I feared I would be gripped by death if I let out my pain and demanded what I needed from Hilary. I really did think that I would die when my mother threatened to kill me. I shared how I felt in the session and described the feeling of my mother squeezing my throat. I didn't have a word for how I felt, but when I wanted to cry in the session I felt a sensation in my throat as though it was being pinched and squeezed. I also felt feelings of shame for wanting to cry and when I showed her my pain, my sobs, my tears I wouldn't want Hilary to look at me. I was afraid of what she would see. My mum mimicked my distress after she attacked me, copying my sounds, and pulling faces to demonstrate what she thought I looked like. She looked so horrible and ugly, and I believed I was horrible and ugly and had nothing to cry for. Hilary reassured me, saying she wouldn't all of a sudden become someone different and would see it as my mother being around. 'There is no place in our relationship for her bullying and immature behaviour.'

I found some quiet time for Little Me and picked up the photo of me in the checked dress. I saw Little Me in that little girl for the first time. She was a young child and had the face of a young child. Instead of feeling she was bad and me having no sympathy for her, I saw a lost and hurting little girl. I cried for her, for the lost years of development and freedom that would have come naturally if she had a loving and nurturing parent. I saw what Hilary mentioned all those therapy sessions ago. I saw Boo, I felt like Boo felt.

As I thought about Boo I cried with a heaving in my chest and talked to her, telling her I loved her and that if I had been there with her as an adult, I would have held her when she wet the bed, I would have washed her and changed her clothes and tucked her up in a clean bed. I would have spent time with her reassuring her, asked her if there was anything worrying her, I would have played with her, gently brushed her hair, helped her with her homework and sat with her in school when she didn't want to be there. I was her, and everything she suffered I

163

suffered, but I wasn't big enough to keep me safe. I was her and I am her.

I shared this with Hilary and how frustrated I felt about the ongoing struggle with not being able to cry as often as I wanted to when in my sessions with her.

Hilary likened my process as contractions getting closer. We had talked about the experience of giving birth and I had told her how much I had hated the feeling of pressure when the baby's head is coming out. I felt like I was stuck in that place, afraid to push, and Hilary asked me why I didn't want to let go. I told her I needed her to come and get the baby out like in a caesarean.

Hilary said that midwives don't do the surgery and she isn't ready to hand me over because she thinks there is movement and we can achieve together. Something in what she said caused me to go quiet, and she called my name twice before I could respond to her.

I said, 'So you are not giving up on me?'

'If you are asking me if I am in this for the long haul then yes, I am.'

It is clear by now that I needed ongoing reassurance, and even though I was moving on and becoming more connected through the trust that was being built by this relationship, by Hilary's commitment to me, the original damage, the fears and the pain would revisit and revisit!

It opened us up to exploring more why I couldn't cry, and it related to me not being able to bear her looking at me. I could cry much more freely at home in my bed with my quilt cover. The room I saw Hilary in was formal, and neither she nor I were formal type of people. Hilary asked me to bring a blanket or pillow that would help me feel safe and cosy, and suggested we put the two chairs together to make it more comfortable. I felt embarrassed by her suggestion but didn't know why. We both acknowledged that we were physically changing position. I later felt like something had left me. It wasn't painful, it just fell away.

I became in touch with the familiar feeling of wanting to die and recognised it as how the little girl, who was so unhappy, felt. I couldn't reach her but knew I needed to.

I took a quilt to my next session with Hilary and she provided me with a pillow. She had set the room up for me, placing two chairs together, and I said I wasn't sure if I would use the quilt but used the pillow straight away. Hilary added another chair and placed herself so we weren't facing each other. I felt unsure but as we started to talk about how hard it was for me to cry, I could see the picture of my mum's face mimicking me and pulling the most ugly, horrible face. I had the most intense pain in my chest and felt so distressed. Hilary suggested I get the quilt out and lay down so we could 'work on that pain.' I was afraid and considered my choices – run or lay.

I decided to use the quilt and lay, and as I did Hilary put a box of tissues on my chest, a bin beside me and checked if I wanted the light off, which I did. I held my quilt around me and immediately cried. Hilary asked me what I wanted to say to my mum and as I talked, I could feel Boo, I wanted that time back. The time when my mum dressed me in clean clothes, made sure I was comfortable, and I felt safe. I remembered what it felt like to be Boo in a family where we played and laughed and Mum and Dad were our parents together. It wasn't perfect but it was much kinder and loving.

'You lost your mum,' said Hilary, and I cried again. She checked how I was at the end of the session and I told her I didn't expect to have been able to cry so comfortably.

She suggested I bring a second pillow and she would move the chairs around to make sure I could lay more comfortably in the next session.

I was amazed that it had worked. I felt tearful when I thought about how Hilary had been so loving and caring, how she set the room up for me and made sure I had what I needed. Two years into individual therapy with her, and I was able to cry with a comfort I had never known.

My relationship with Hilary had enabled me to find, start to accept and love Little Me. Life outside of the therapy room continued, and although it was tough to be working on so much pain, I was benefiting from living with feeling. I noticed how my grandchildren looked to me for reassurance when faced with something new, and how I could read to them and cuddle them – let them know they were safe. How much I loved it when my grandchildren wanted a cuddle and rested their heads on my shoulder and put their little faces against my cheek. I loved being able to feel the feelings and be connected with them. I loved that I could also feel that with my daughters and that I knew instinctively with feeling such love for them. I was becoming more sensitive to their needs and seemed to know what to do in the moment to support them in a way I couldn't before. I loved how I was beginning to laugh freely with them and my grandchildren. I was feeling, rather than just thinking, no longer robotic. I was getting back some of what I had lost so long ago.

I held on to the comfort of Hilary more and more but would be reminded of how fragile it was for me when an overwhelming pain would arrive. I would be revisited by that familiar fear that Hilary wouldn't stay. I messaged her about being in the horrible place and warned her, 'You would be wallowing in a shit pit of despair. Why would you elect to spend time in hell?'

I wanted to stop seeing Hilary for fear of what would happen if I stayed but I also wanted her to meet me at my core, to meet Boo, the little girl I had found who was afraid but also knew how to laugh. I was gripped by fear but also had a sense of feeling free. I somehow had managed to reach Boo.

I felt a raw anger towards my mum and Ernest. I hated them and I was glad that I hated them for what they did to me. I felt it was my right to hate them. Hilary responded by saying she could hear my pain. 'I think you know I am not afraid of the "shit pit of despair" and part of the reason for that is that we would be together – and we make a formidable team, you and I!'

She said that my feeling of wanting to run away was understandable but that because I knew she couldn't run away with me, I felt I would lose her. She said, 'But I wouldn't have gone – I'd still be there, waiting for you.'

I feared that spontaneity would bring negative reactions and criticism, I feared I would lose again – it is what I learned to expect as a child.

> When I'm laying down, I get that horrible pain.
> The cramp in my stomach makes me sit up again
> I am so afraid of being lost, alone with nowhere to go
> That I will lose the love and care you show.
> Will you come with me to the bleak and scary place
> It's that shit pit of despair, where I hid behind my face
> The pain of the hell of what I was going through
> A small vulnerable child, what else could I do.
> I'm an adult now but feel like that little girl
> Who was so afraid when she was in that living hell.

She needs to know you are strong enough
I need to know you will stay long enough
To bring me back from that bleakness
Won't let me get lost in a moment of weakness
I want to live through it so I can feel and see
The beauty of the colours you have shown me.

My insecurity about Hilary and whether she would stay continued. Over the weeks and months that followed, we worked on my feelings of being at odds with myself, feelings that Hilary wanted me to move on from where I was and was bored of me, which were my fears and not her requirements. She was interested in exploring why I felt the way I did and wasn't angry with me. I would fall into feeling we were not connected when I felt Hilary didn't understand me, and this would cause me so much distress.

Our written communication moved from text messages to emailing, where I could write in more detail about how I felt. That fragile sense of good would leave me and I would again feel like I was a worthless piece of shit. The difference was that I knew it wasn't true. It was how I felt about myself, but I knew it wasn't true.

Now we are grown in age at least
And having left behind the beast
Believed we could have a different life
Pushed down and buried all the strife
Thought we were free to love and to give
Free to make choices and to live
A life free of abuse, pleasant and good
Oh God, if only I could have understood
How all that shit rubbish and pain

Would manifest itself and cause hurt again
To me, to my children, when will it end?
How much more must I do to mend
The damage and destruction caused by abuse
The low self-esteem, the sense of no use
But worse than that, the knowledge that I
Made terrible choices and believed the lie
That I told myself thinking it was safe
To marry, not for love but for a place
In society to get rid of my identity have
another face
It didn't work, I didn't find that place
When I look inside, I see darkness, filth
I hate what I see, I hate myself.

Sleep continued to escape me at times and when Hilary
was away it would feel much harder. Having the option of
sending her emails was so helpful and hearing her voice on
her answerphone and leaving her a message and knowing
she would respond to me when she was able to, was an
absolute lifeline. Text messages continued to work in
moments when I needed Hilary to tell me she was there. I
continued to need these different ways of contact with her.

I was in touch with so much sadness, a sadness that
came from a knowing that the harshness, anger and
frustration I had aimed at myself for so long belonged
elsewhere. I was aware of a want or urge to scratch, pinch
and punch myself, but I fought it. My desire to want more
for myself was getting stronger. I was beginning to feel
entitled to want what Hilary would often say she wanted
for me, which was to 'stick up for myself' and for me to
'feel entitled'. She nurtured me and helped me to value
myself by valuing me first. She showed me a safe and

positive relationship with 'its ups and downs'. In a moment of me expressing so much frustration at myself and a fear of losing her, she said, 'We can all use help in understanding ourselves. Simply no need to be angry – we're all works in progress!' She added, 'And you are progressing so well.'

In response to me asking why she was there for me, Hilary would say, 'because I just am.' I couldn't fathom why she would want to be, and I would at times say, 'You are so annoying,' and we would laugh. We both knew she was giving me what I needed even if it wasn't always what I wanted!

I knew I had progressed; I felt more contained, and our relationship was solid – but holding on to it was such hard work for me. One moment I would feel contained; the next I would be struggling with believing it really was for me, that she wanted to be there, that she wasn't going anywhere, and that I was worth it.

> Yesterday was so far away
> From the beauty of the colours
> The despair and the aloneness
> All I could feel was anger
> I didn't want you near me
> I didn't want more time from you
> All I wanted was to see
> The beauty of the colours
>
> I don't know how to find that lovely place
> When the comfort of you is gone
> I don't like it when in your face
> I see the disapproval of my mum
> The words you use, the tone of voice

The fear that I will have no choice
But to stay in there just in case
With you again I find that lovely place.

I continued to have challenges outside of therapy, which Hilary also helped me with. I chose a career in social work and had been in a senior management role for two years. There were times when I was in situations that challenged me professionally and triggered me personally. Report writing was my least favourite thing to do, along with presenting at formal meetings, where I would at times feel intimidated. In those situations, I would be reminded of how, as a child, I didn't fit in and was at odds with the world. Hilary suggested I try and remember that, regardless of who they were, they were human beings and that I try to imagine a particular person, who I had found to be very unpleasant and bullying, naked. I found her approach very amusing and we both laughed. Her words felt empowering, and even though I didn't use that method, just naming how I felt helped me to gain a different perspective.

On another occasion, when I was feeling particularly desperate and experiencing that familiar feeling of wallowing in the shit pit of despair, I managed to phone Hilary, in the moment, on her home phone. She wasn't available but I left a message. I had done what Hilary said and let Little Me knew that she could trust me to find comfort and safety when it was most needed.

The person who answered told me Hilary was working, which I wasn't happy about. I knew Hilary had other clients, but I didn't want her to work with anyone else, especially not when I needed her. I thanked them for taking my message and ended the call!

Whilst I waited with hope that Hilary would be free to call me back, I was in the safety of my bedroom, snuggled under my quilt. I cried with tears that rolled freely and I knew they came from a place of such deep hurt. When Hilary called, she detected the relief in my voice and joked with me, saying, 'I'm coming, I'm coming.' I so wanted to enter her sense of fun, but my fear of being a nuisance overwhelmed me.

Our 'over the phone sessions' had become the agreed time set aside for me and helped me to feel less like I was taking something from Hilary. I knew it stemmed from my mum telling me I had caused her 'breakdown'. I knew I was none of the bad things my mum called me, but I couldn't stop feeling that 'badness' was the very essence of me. I felt Little Me was curled in a ball and I couldn't reach her, and I didn't know what to do. Hilary picked up on the significance of me phoning her, reassuring me and saying, 'She will know you can and do stick up for yourself.'

Hilary then talked about Little Me knowing that my mum was a very unhappy woman and things were tough for her, and Little Me would find it very painful.

I felt unclear over my feelings regarding my mum and struggled to understand where I was with it. If I let her go, I would lose her; if I saw her as a person who was suffering, I wouldn't be able to feel angry with her; if I gave her the badness back, she might break completely. I shared how I felt with Hilary in several messages, saying that I didn't really understand what was happening but that I needed her and that she 'had to be there.'

Hilary was away but messaged me back to say, 'Although I'm away, I'm with you too.'

I knew she was thinking of me, but it remained a challenge for me to hold on to the comfort of her. I would keep myself busy so that I didn't feel, but it didn't work. I sent her further messages. Her responses acknowledged my pain, reminded me she was thinking of me and I would feel less alone for a while. In this way Hilary helped me get through another moment of feeling desperate.

It was easy for me to have a busy life outside my therapy sessions without trying, given I have three daughters, two step-children, two grandchildren and an extended family as well as my career, church life and singing lessons. I was making progress with finding my voice, a voice that was robbed from me because of the abuse. I sang Rachel Lampa's version of 'No Greater Love', which left me feeling close to God and connected with Him in a way I hadn't felt for many months. As I worshipped in prayerful song, I felt lifted as though there was no pain – but these feelings of comfort also didn't last. I wanted God to take away all my hurts, but I still had them. I wanted Hilary to take away all the hard stuff and bring me comfort, and I didn't like it when she went away; it reminded me of how much I needed her and how much I didn't have as a child.

I messaged her to say if she could make it OK for me then I could snuggle in comfort and softness like I did when I was small. Her response was to say, 'I'm not sure if I can make it all ok – I wish I could but I have a feeling that it has to be you who does that – and I really do believe you are doing that.'

I knew she was right, but it really wasn't what I wanted to hear. I felt like I wanted to tell her something but didn't know what it was. I told her I felt angry that she wasn't doing what I wanted her to do, but felt I was withholding something. I didn't know what that something was. I felt like I was on the edge of fading away, like I wasn't being seen, that she wasn't seeing me. At the same time, I felt sorry for feeling angry with Hilary, I was angry that she cared, and I felt I was waiting for her to be like everyone else, for the relationship to turn bad and then it would be just as it was before. Me trusting and being naive, me believing things could be different. I was sick of working so hard and trying so hard just to be left experiencing the pain of it all.

'I am afraid – what if you give up on me just when I let you touch the very core of me,' I said.

> I told you I feared what would happen if I felt the
> sadness
> Of the deep searing loss, the effects of my mother's
> madness
> I fear that I won't be able to breathe
> The grieving and the pain will bring me to my knees
>
> I carry such a burden, it's the legacy of abuse
> Feeling like a dirty rag, a thing of no value, no use
> Sometimes I know your comfort and find that
> lovely place
> Where you have helped me find the feeling of
> being safe
> And I begin to trust that I can know
> It is for me, that love and care you show
>
> But it's so short lived, it doesn't stay Just like
> my mother, it goes away
> No warning, no reason, like a rusty saw
> Ripping at my little self, tearing at my core

I don't know what to do, what else to try
I don't want to exist, I want to feel alive
Why does it have to hurt so much?

Painting by Sezan M. Sansom.

Processing the hard stuff would eventually give way and I would feel more settled, more contained and less burdened. The pain came with little warning but feeling settled was always more gradual. I would often feel bruised from experiencing the trauma I went through as a child; it would feel like I was experiencing it for the first time. I could feel the love and care from Hilary and told her how much I appreciated her. That stubborn belief that I was too much for my mum and not a source of joy for her was so difficult to shift. I believed I had to apologise for being born and wondered how I managed to exist with

175

such a burden for so long. Without Hilary I would not have found the little girl within me. I was being thoughtful, curious about these feelings rather than feeling desperate, which felt good.

There were triggers that helped and hindered with the process in therapy, depending on how I viewed them. My visits to the dentist as an adult were to work on the many fillings which were physical signs of neglect in my childhood, no toothbrush, leaving me with a mouthful of mercury. In later years, as and when I could afford to pay for it, I spent significant hours in the dentist's chair having worn out silver fillings replaced and porcelain crowns in preference to the cheaper option of new fillings or having them pulled out.

On one occasion I had spent three hours with instruments in my mouth, which included impressions being taken. The experience caused me to gag and triggered difficult memories. I shared the experience with Hilary in an email and recalled more details of neglect between the ages of seven and 14. I remembered when I was small, still had milk teeth, I had lumps on my gums that hurt and eventually resulted in a trip to the dentist for teeth to be removed under gas administered via a huge rubber mask. I was adamant that loved and well cared for children didn't have decaying teeth or dirty school uniforms. I remembered being so ashamed, especially at secondary school when the PE teacher pulled out PE kit from lost property and told me to wear it when I arrived at school without any – it was cleaner than my uniform, but it wasn't clean; it smelt of someone else's body odour! Added to that I had no clean underwear and wore my mum's, which fell down as I ran around the field playing hockey. I often didn't have any clean clothes to wear. The humiliation of life at school was nothing compared to the sexual abuse I had suffered or the violence from my mum when she noticed I had taken her underwear, but I still hated being at school.

I felt so sad for the little girl I had been. I wanted to give her recognition and acknowledgement for what she went through, how hard life was for her and how amazing she was to survive and for her strength. I wanted to give her back those child years and take the burden from her. Hilary was the voice for Little Me when I didn't know how to be. She encouraged me when I felt I couldn't keep going. She previously told me, 'If you give up, that little girl won't have what she needs.' As much as I hated Hilary for saying it at the time, in that moment I knew she was right. I told her I wanted to ensure her needs were met but I wasn't sure if I knew what they were or how to do it.

With more patience, with trusting in the processes, I no longer saw or felt like any part of me was in the corner. Little Me had come out to meet big me with Hilary there; but I couldn't seem to reach her. I thought about her and felt an overwhelming desire to love and nurture her. The desperate need for reassurance that Hilary would be there to help me hold, love and nurture Little Me remained. Hilary continued to support me during the breaks regardless of where in the world we happened to be; and when back from those trips she continued to bring the pillow to my sessions. Not being able to reach Little Me was a struggle, but after a discussion about what else Little Me might need to feel safe Hilary brought a blanket and a lamp from home to soften the room and make it more comfortable.

Hilary kept being Hilary and I eventually began to believe that she would be there for me and that she wouldn't come back as someone else after the breaks. I had moved from the empty place of expecting nothing for myself to daring to expect something. I gradually began to know what felt acceptable and stuck up for myself in situations where I previously would not have. A small but significant moment was during a meal out with my partner when I wasn't satisfied with the quality of the food. On these rare occasions neither he nor I would usually have said anything, would pay the bill and give a tip! On this occasion I found myself letting the waiter know I didn't think the food was OK – and to my surprise he accepted what I said, apologised and offered to replace it or remove the cost of it from the bill. I made my choice and he also offered us a drink on the house as a further apology. On another occasion I challenged the way one of the receptionists at my GP surgery spoke to me. She didn't like the challenge, but I was very polite and stuck to my new-found belief that I was a person of value and did not expect to be spoken to in such a way. Without thinking about it or worrying about it, I was beginning to know what felt OK for me and to speak up when I wasn't satisfied with something. I was learning that I mattered.

My missing of Hilary in between sessions and in the breaks remained, but it began to feel OK to acknowledge it rather than it be so painful and a source of desperation and fear. I began to trust and feel the love and sense of belonging, a feeling I knew as a small child before the abuse, before I developed an inner belief that I was bad, that I was wrong, abhorrent to my mother, loathed by her for making her ill. Hilary was offering me something different. I felt like I belonged with her, not as her child but as a person she wanted to love and care about, someone she valued. I wrote in my journal, 'she sees me, she knows me and she values me', and I felt like I had a healthier sense of self. I recognised it as an inner sense of being OK. I couldn't hold on to it all the time and I struggled with it, but it was getting easier and lasting longer. I was beginning to put the responsibility where it belonged.

A few months after Hilary had organised the chairs and made the therapy room safe and warm, she said she had noticed that I lay stiff and in one position, rigid and inhibited, on the chairs for the duration of the session. Her example was that I didn't adjust the covers or myself and it seemed that I 'make do!' I knew exactly what she meant and shared with her that although I was letting her 'in' in a way I hadn't been able to before, I continued to struggle to let go. I shared my frustration of not really being able to let go, and Hilary suggested I cover my head with the blanket to provide me with the privacy I might need. The privacy that worked for me when alone in my front room in the early hours of the morning, with no one else awake; it worked for me when I was alone in the house and had a telephone session with Hilary. I wanted to do as she suggested but couldn't. I felt afraid she would get fed up with me, leave me, walk out of a session and leave me alone. I later sent her a text to tell her how I felt, and she responded, 'I am here, not fed up with you and I am not going to leave you.'

I often wondered where she got her patience from!

Being close, knowing love, taking risks
It is all too much
So tender, so small, a mind so delicate
What could I do, what did I know
I was so little

179

Lost and alone with no one to tell
People around but no one saw
The pain left me numb.

Writing in my journal after sessions with Hilary, after an event, a dream or just because I needed some Little Me time or just Me time, continued to help. At times I would feel a lack of empathy and tenderness towards myself and tired of the internal battle. Hilary suggested I put down the battle, but I didn't know how to. She asked me to think about what it would mean to me to 'put it down.' I didn't understand, so she asked me if I thought by putting it down, I would be giving up on my mum. My instant thought was that if I put it down, I would be giving up on Hilary, and I shared that with her. Hilary suggested that transference might be happening, and I cried. I told her that my most precious and significant relationship had been with my mum but that I felt closer to Hilary than to my mum. At the end of the session she asked me if I felt connected, and I cried as I told her I felt the tenderness and compassion was back. Without realising it, I had let Hilary 'in'. We had reached Little Me together. Knowingly, Hilary said, 'You have been able to cry.'

With that I cried again.

Three years and seven months after the start of my individual therapy with Hilary and by learning to trust her, trust in the process, in our relationship and in myself, I could cry and feel the relief of the tears. I could see that what my mum did to me was about her and not about me. I noticed that I felt more contained.

We were approaching another break, this time for the summer, which was for six long weeks. I knew by this stage that Hilary would be available for me whilst she was away, and, as she would often say, that she would come back 'the same old Hilary although rested and slightly more tanned'! On this occasion I was able to tell her that I feared what would happen if I dumped her with my fears and anger about her going away. I knew from conversations with Hilary that she thought my difficulty with trust was because I wasn't used to a relationship where I could express my emotions without negative consequences. She reminded me to call her if I needed her, and that my need to check she was still there a valid reason to call her, that I didn't need anything bigger. She told me that if she did feel anger about it or demanded upon, that it would be her problem not mine, and she 'will just have to deal with it.'

I wanted to believe her – but I also wanted to punish her for going away. I wanted to go silent on her and not contact her so she would worry about me and miss me and then she would know what it felt like. As I wrote what I wanted to say to Hilary, I imagined her saying, 'Do you think I don't miss you or think about you anyway?'

I imagined saying, 'No, why would you miss a nuisance, a dirty nasty little person with an odour and stench rising from her that would turn your stomach.' I was amused as I imagined Hilary raising her eyebrows the way she did when body language rather than words was the appropriate response.

As I wrote those words, I was struck by the deeply sad perception I had of a child that didn't exist. That child never existed, it was my mother's self-hate, self-loathing that she projected on to me. I carried the belief that I was filth for so long, I had tried to make up for being so bad and repulsive for most of my life, so bad that my mother moved from loving me to hating me because my badness made her ill. As I wrote tears fell naturally and with no effort; there was no shame attached to them this time.

> Mum, I know you were struggling with life
> and feeling sad
> When you screamed at me, called me names,
> said I was bad
> Mum, I know you were hurting and in despair
> When you punched my head as you brushed
> my hair
> Mum, I know you were suffering because of
> what you said
> When you pinched and twisted my vagina for
> wetting the bed
> Mum, I know you were at the end of your
> tether, couldn't take anymore
> When you dug your nails in, broke my skin
> made me so sore
> Mum, I know you were out of control and in a
> seriously bad place
> When you squeezed my neck hard, an
> expression of hate on your face.

I found it empowering to have written how I felt about what my mum did to me and the realisation that it wasn't my fault. But I felt so sad. The acknowledgement didn't stop me hurting. I hated Hilary for going away for so many weeks, but I couldn't tell her that, so I told her I wanted to punish her for leaving me. I wanted to tell her I loved her but all I could say was that I needed her. I wanted to ask her if I could take the pillow and blanket she brought to the session each week home with me, but I couldn't ask her. I sat with the negative feelings of hate and anger and abandonment and considered how I might not be available when she came back. In response to what I did share with her, Hilary suggested I think of some 'nice things' to do on a Tuesday when I didn't see her. I didn't want her suggestions of what I saw as the poor substitute and felt I would rather look after myself than remain dependent on her; it felt safer that way.

By the next day I wondered why I felt so angry with Hilary, which felt over the top for the situation, yet could not feel angry with my mum. I felt insignificant and unimportant to Hilary in my anger, put in my place, and clearly a client or patient and not one of her dearly loved children. I felt stubborn and defiant and was determined not to contact her.

Where are you now Hilary
When I need you the most
With your family, your loved ones
Who you love so much, they are yours
Spending time, swimming, walking
Enjoy them, laughter, sunshine and fun
I'm not a part of that, never will be
That wholeness, special time, it's not for me
The feeling of insignificance, unimportance
Is overwhelming and so familiar
That's what has been given to me
No matter how hard I try to the contrary
My status in life, my mother's legacy
Makes it forever real from infancy
To adulthood there is no change
The facts are real, and they remain
My life, this is it, that's what's for me.

I struggled with the familiar feelings of conflict I was having. I needed Hilary and she said I could contact her, but I was angry with her so didn't want to. I wanted to make her worried about me, but I also didn't want to burden her. She was on holiday after all, and I understood the importance of having a break from work even though I hated being Hilary's 'work' rather than belonging to her. I wanted the pain of needing her to stop, I wanted to stop needing her and weighed up my options of never seeing her again.

Cutting Hilary out of my life wasn't the right thing to do. I had cut people out of my life in the past because the pain of them being in it was too costly. I had cut myself off from myself because the pain of what I was suffering was too costly – but I was no longer a small vulnerable child, and Little Me was relying on me to stay connected and keep us both safe; I didn't want to fall back into old ways.

I entered into an internal self-negotiation of when it would feel acceptable for me to contact Hilary and settled on two weeks after my last contact. Hilary responded the same evening and gave me the phone number of where she was staying. I shared with her about my conflicting feelings and confusion as to why I felt so angry with her yet couldn't feel angry at my mum. Hilary talked about adults not accepting or being able to tolerate my behaviour or expressions of feelings, but that she could and did.

We talked for around 40 minutes, and I initially felt better for having time with her. As often happened, however, I couldn't hold on to feeling better for long and later felt overwhelmed with being in touch with wishing I was dead. I wondered why I felt that way and remembered it was how I felt as a child. I had no one to tell then. I know if I told my mum that I wanted to die she would not have asked what was wrong – she would have said, 'You don't know you are born girl.' I thought about how I might react if one of my daughters said that to me. I would feel dreadful inside and very worried but would come alongside them and ask what was happening for them to feel that way. I felt so sad for the small child that I was, a small child that felt so desperately unhappy that she felt she would rather be dead. I saw myself as a child running, searching and longing for loving arms to envelop me and give me comfort, warmth and love me better, to take away the pain. But there was more abuse, physical, emotional and sexual, lots more emptiness and pain, an ache and a yearning. I wondered if I would find that safe place I so desperately needed. Would I ever be able to cry, cry from the depth of hurt that belonged to such an alone child?

I needed to ask my mum.

Mum, I know you were struggling with life
and feeling sad
When you screamed at me, called me names,
said I was bad
Mum, do you know what your struggles did to me?
When you hurt me, couldn't you see?
Mum, I know you were hurting and in despair
When you punched my head as you brushed my hair
Mum, do you know what your despair did to me?
When you hurt me, couldn't you see?
Mum, I know you were suffering because of
what you said
When you pinched and twisted my vagina for
wetting the bed
Mum, do you know what your suffering did to me?

When you hurt me, couldn't you see?
Mum, I know you were at the end of your
tether, couldn't take anymore
When you dug your nails in, tore my skin
made me so sore
Mum, do you know when you couldn't take
anymore how that affected me?
When you were tearing my skin, couldn't you see?
Mum, I know you were out of control and in a
seriously bad place
When you squeezed my neck hard, an
expression of hate on your face
Mum, do you know where your seriously bad
place put me?
When you blocked my windpipe, couldn't you see?

Mum, a harder press, a longer squeeze and
you would have taken my life from me
You're not here for me to tell that from the
age of seven I was in a living hell
I searched for loving arms to hold me, I
longed for safety, ached for warmth.
It wasn't for me, it didn't come and I was left
so cold, so alone.
Living my life as if I owed you a sorry for
being born, for being so bad
But Mum, I was your little girl, just your little girl
I had no power to stop you and caused you no ill
But you blamed me for your misery, for your pain
And you punished me for it again and again.
Mum, the hate you showed left me in a bleak
and scary place
Those cold, glaring mad eyes, the expression

of hate on your face
I believed I was bad, evil, dirty and nasty at
my very core
I wanted to die, hurt myself, wanted it to end
I couldn't take anymore.
Mum, do you know, can you hear, can you see
What your despair, your struggles, your 'self-
hate' did to me?

Responsibilities and life outside my therapy sessions continued despite how I was feeling. I needed things to remain stable and as normal as I could manage. There were birthday celebrations and social gatherings just to spend time together, which I enjoyed. I also kept on with my singing lessons and had a new teacher, Katie, who I was getting to know. We practiced 'Love Song' by Adele, and it felt like the perfect song for me. Katie encouraged me and praised me for how I sang it and I loved knowing that I was finding my voice. I sang Diana Krall's version of 'The Look of Love' during my 50th birthday celebration, and a voice that I didn't recognize but that was beautiful came from me and all my guests stood up in the restaurant and clapped in delight. I experienced it in that moment and knew it was there, the little girl had risked being seen and heard and she was fabulous. I knew I couldn't get my childhood back or save Little Me from what happened, but I also knew I could love, accept, and keep the child within me safe and I was determined to help her feel safe enough to find that voice again, that fabulousness and hold on to it.

I told her she was fantastic, beautiful, wonderful, precious and delicious and that I loved her. I wanted her to believe it, know it and embrace it.

Feeling angry with Hilary would come and go as part of the process and I questioned the realness of the therapy relationship. It felt like a lie – and then I thought of all the pain my mother had caused me, the pain Ernest caused me and that I felt he was a piece of shit that didn't deserve to live; I was glad he was dead. The news of Tia Sharp, a 12-year-old girl who had been missing but was found dead in her grandmother's attic, hit me hard. I didn't know her or her family, but I felt so sad for what she must have gone through. It triggered memories of my mother squeezing my throat with such hate, such strength and how I believed I would die. I felt so sad that Tia didn't make it to an adult and thought about how we all failed her, how we all fail children that are being abused whilst we get on with our lives. My parents were either working or out drinking with friends, getting their lost teenage years back at my expense. I felt helpless – there will be more Tia's, there will be more Tricia's and I wished we could find a way to stop the abuse and the violence, stop robbing children of their childhood, their lives.

I shared how I felt with Hilary in an email, and she replied with acceptance of my angry feelings and all the contradictions they included. She reassured me that none of my feelings were 'wrong or bad' and said, 'They deserve respect and understanding, particularly the ones that are most uncomfortable.' She suggested we explored them all in more depth when we were back from the break and ended with telling me she was thinking of me. Her words comforted me and helped me to feel more contained.

Within a few months of me asking my daughters to write to me about the good and the hard things in their childhoods they each gave me a letter. I found it interesting that one of my daughters told me in no uncertain terms that she would not be doing that but was the first to write to me. They all said they didn't understand why I seemed to think their childhoods were so bad. I didn't know what to expect from each of them, what their truth would reveal or how we would work through it all. I knew I would find a way with them together just as Hilary was doing with me.

I was challenged and heartened by their letters and proud of them all; they showed such courage. They responded with their truth and generously gave me the opportunity to hear their pain and over time explore how we could improve our communication and strengthen our mother-daughter relationships. I knew I had done my best to provide them with a secure and safe home, but I knew every day was a battle for me and no matter how hard I tried I hadn't managed to protect them from the consequences of some of my poor decisions and some of my pain. I knew I had passed some of my weeds on to them, both directly and indirectly.

It was interesting for me to learn that the things I felt I had most failed them in – material things – was not what caused them hurt. It was the emotional hurt of my actions. I had expected them to complain that I smacked them but to my surprise none of them had a significant memory of being smacked. I smacked them occasionally as a last resort after raising my voice and sometimes shouting at them and warning them on the count of three that if they didn't stop misbehaving, I would smack them.

The last time I smacked them was when they were five, seven and nine. The significance of this day was that they didn't respond to my threat of a smack. I smacked them all but, unusually, it didn't stop them. To my shame, in that moment of anger, I picked up a slipper and hit them with it which incidentally also didn't work. It felt so wrong to inflict physical pain on my children. I withdrew from the situation and shut myself in my room to calm down. I knew this anger was excessive and I didn't want to inflict any further physical pain on them. After calming down I went to them and cuddled them, I told them I was sorry for getting so angry with them and told them I would no longer use the threat of a smack or a smack itself as a means of 'discipline'. I shared ideas with some friends and researched alternatives and came up with withholding treats and positive incentives. It was not an easy decision in a family and culture where smacking children was considered acceptable and the norm, and there were times when I wished I hadn't told them I would never smack them again because it took more effort not to; but I knew it was the right decision

Their hurts related to my inability to connect with them emotionally and see them as individuals with needs of equal importance. I had met their physical and practical needs but being disconnected meant they missed out on some of their emotional needs being seen and met. By opening communication with my daughters about the good and the hard things in their childhoods, with their courage to tell me about their hurts and my acceptance of their truths, we could connect in a deeper and more honest way.

Their generosity extended to an acceptance of my experience of their grandmother. They believed what I shared with them but found it painful because they didn't recognise their loving grandmother and my experience of her as a child as being the same person. Their relationship with Mum was very similar to mine before she became ill. They adored her and loved spending time with her, and she adored them. I found it healing when I saw her love for my children

My relationship with Hilary was benefiting my children and they were encouraging and positive about it. One daughter would affectionately refer to Hilary as 'The Hils', when asking me how my therapy was going. She, like her sisters, could see the change in me and they all generously supported me. My desire to be a good mum to them continues to be as strong as it was when they were small. I grew to be so much more connected with myself and it was wonderful to be able to be connecting with my daughters and spending time with them individually and together, enjoying them as the unique and beautiful young women they are.

Year Four

The beginning of another year of therapy, and I was still feeling angry with Hilary as the day approached for us to return to sessions after the summer break. Hilary and I had agreed that I would email her with what I had entered into my journal so she could read it and think about it before the first session back. We worked on my angry feelings, and I told her I felt as though I had moved from vulnerable child to angry indignant adult. I told her I didn't want to do anything she suggested and that I wanted to cut her off but that would be going back to old ways. Hilary responded saying she thought that was healthy and suggested it was why I went to her in the first place – so I wouldn't carry this pain in my adult years. I knew she was right. I both loved and hated her wisdom!

Not long after the tragic story of Tia in the media there was one about Megan and her teacher, soon followed by the Savile revelations. The subject of abuse was hardly out of the news – and, although very sad, I was glad the public were being saturated with the subject. I wanted to scream out, 'Wake up world – this is happening now!'

I found I didn't need to write in my journal as often and didn't record my sessions with Hilary or how I felt about them in so much detail. We worked on my angry feelings. I was struggling with difficulties in my marriage and on sharing how miserable I had felt about a recent trip with my partner, Hilary expressed frustration with me for 'putting up with it.' I felt like I was just angry and not much else, felt hateful and felt no matter how much I tried I would never get anything right.

I had one of my disturbing dreams and awoke distressed. I dreamt about several children and young adults who all looked the same. They were pale with grazing and bruising to their faces, with short, dark, dirty, oily hair stuck to their heads. They were all dressed in white shirts and could have been male or female. There was no life in them at all and the dream had no colour. The smallest child was about six or seven and had a foot forced into its mouth and toes in its nostrils. The face was stretched and contorted by what was being done and even though the eyes were dark and lifeless there was so much pain from the image. I tried to draw the image but couldn't transfer it to paper and when I shared the dream and distress with Hilary I cried; I knew that small child was me. Hilary said she didn't need a drawing; she could see it vividly from my description.

Over the next few days, I had feelings I couldn't name but I felt distressed and felt so sad for the children. Hilary suggested that Little Me might be feeling more able to show adult me how terrible it was for her and perhaps I was ready to feel it.

As I lay on the chairs, I felt my chest heaving and wanted to sob. I told Hilary that if I was at home under my quilt and didn't have to go anywhere that I would cry. I didn't know how ready I was to feel the pain that Little Me lived with.

As the days passed, I felt that all the children in my dream were me at different ages, and Hilary agreed. I asked her if she had known that earlier and she said she had. I felt comforted by knowing Hilary was so in tune with me; she saw things but waited for me to get there myself.

We had talked about comfort and safety. There had been some noise from one of the other rooms that had distracted me and interrupted my session; Hilary had offered for us to use another room, but I preferred the smaller cosy feel of the room we used so decided to stay there. Interestingly, that conversation was the trigger for me to talk about discomfort and I shared with Hilary how I would often experience a cold feeling, a pain in my bladder when we talked about me being hurt. Hilary suggested I go to the loo if I needed to, so the feeling would be heard and responded to. It felt like we were looking after all of me. As the sessions went on, I was able to tell Hilary that I was afraid that if I let go of my pain, I would wet myself and then I would lose the comfort of her. Hilary asked me what I would do if someone wet themselves and without hesitation, I said, 'I would look after them and help them.' I told Hilary things were OK for me until I wet myself and became disgusting to my mum and that's what made it change. Hilary said that I didn't make anything change but the adults around me caused the change and asked me why I thought she would change towards me. I told her I feared she might find me disgusting like my mum did, but I knew she wouldn't.

I was beginning to see myself as I really was and wondered where I had been all those years. Hiding? Invisible to myself. I had spent my life imprisoned by what others had done to me – locked inside so deep that there was no escape and no way of even knowing there was anyone different to find. I had believed I owed people something because I existed. So sad to have felt that way. So sad that all those years after being traumatised by my mum that I continued to fear wetting myself. I didn't want to allow that to rule me, so I took a change of clothes to my next session, the coldness in my bladder and fear of wetting myself diminished and I began to feel less anxious about it. I told Hilary, who was equally interested in what I had experienced, and we both agreed that I was learning that I could take care of myself when I listened to me!

Several months after my confusion and hurt from the summer break, Hilary and I re-visited the feelings. We had moved on to other feelings and as always had covered a significant amount, but another break was looming, and I knew I needed to talk it through. Hilary asked me about my childhood experiences of my mum going away, and we talked about me at ages seven and 10 when my mum went into hospital. I told Hilary about me coming home from school and Mum not being there, about her taking me to the GP appointment with her and how she hit the doctor because she didn't like what he said in response to her telling him she was at the end of her tether.

He promptly arranged for an ambulance to take her to hospital. I was left to walk home alone in the dark. After we explored that further I realised that I lost my mum emotionally at seven and didn't get her back, that no one nurtured me. When I was seven my great-grandmother moved into the family home to look after us until Mum came home from hospital, but at the age of 10 I was taken to live with my grandparents because my mum had to stay in a psychiatric ward for many months, followed by my dad three months later. I felt so isolated and alone.

I still didn't understand why I found the breaks so difficult and why I felt so confused in the summer. Hilary suggested that she hadn't prepared me for the break, and I knew the feeling of not being seen because my mum stopped seeing me. I cried and told Hilary I didn't feel seen by her leading up to the summer break, and she acknowledged how I felt. It made such a difference to be seen and heard. I noticed that I 'felt colour' and I loved that. I began to experience my life with colour; I found it interesting that not so many weeks before I had dreamt of such a distressing scene with no colour but with, dare I say it, 'trusting in the process', I was starting to experience warmth and colour. I found the breaks less distressing and on the arrival of the Christmas break that year I thanked Hilary for helping me to find colour where there had been grey. She asked me to remember that I should have credit for that too and I knew she was right. We had both worked hard on our relationship and all that came up during the years we had known each other.

There were times when I would feel like something was stirring within me, a feeling that I didn't quite understand but I knew something felt uncomfortable. This stayed with me for a few weeks, but I had learned enough to know that when I was ready, whatever it was would show itself. On this occasion as I tried to sleep, I had the repeated thought of 'he made me do things I didn't want to do.' I wondered what was happening to me but as I lay in the quiet of the night, I realised for the first time that I no longer believed I was responsible for the things I did to Ernest. That it was he who had the power, he who was in control, not me. I knew in that moment that I wasn't bad. I cried with the familiar power of the gut-wrenching pain that came with a realisation and wished that I could call Hilary and be with her. In the moment I remembered she told me that I could hold her in my heart and snuggle with her. It occurred to me that she might not want to get that close to me, but I was aware she would challenge that thought and tell me I was allowing my mum in. I fell asleep feeling Hilary was with me and wanted to be.

Painting by Sezan M. Sansom.

As would happen, the fear that Hilary would get fed up with me would revisit, leaving me feeling desperate. We continued to need to revisit my distress over breaks, my struggle to cry and let go of the tears, my interpretation of what was happening in the moment based on what happened before. I had experienced the revelation of knowing I never was a dirty nasty little girl or a dirty rag, that I wasn't responsible for the physical, emotional or sexual abuse inflicted on me. I had learned that I could call or text Hilary just to check she was still there, and she would tell me or message me back saying, 'I am here Tricia.' I would feel reassured until the next time I needed to hear it.

Life held joy and sadness for me as an adult and I lived through each experience valuing that I could feel what was happening. I was no longer just existing; I was living, and I appreciated it. I felt more confident. My partner and I arranged a trip to South Africa with close friends that would include visiting cousins that I hadn't seen for many years.

We went on a safari in the Shamwari Game Reserve, which was amazing. On one of the trips, I sat in the front seat of a Jeep with our guide, who insisted no one moved as we were approached by a rather large white rhino. There were a few inches between me and his rather long horn. Everyone sat silently, not moving, waiting for him to find interest in something else – which thankfully he did. I felt a joy and excitement I had never known and later that day called Hilary to tell her about it. She was so surprised to hear from me; the 8,000 miles between us didn't stop me sharing my experience with her. I wanted her to share in the significance of how I felt in the moment, and we laughed together. It was such a natural and special moment.

A few weeks later I also had the joy of another grandson. He was born less than an hour after we arrived at the hospital and was as beautifully delicious as the others. It was an eventful experience with several moments of hilarity although I doubt if that is how my daughter would describe it!

As I connected with myself and felt safer, I began to feel what it was like to be the child I was. I felt the hurt, the numbness and the fear. I knew when I was little, I was an observer of everything, looking on whilst others had what I saw as love, laughter, and joy.

In my mind's eye I had a picture of myself looking through the window of a sweet shop watching other children enjoying the sweets, but I never got to touch them, feel their texture or taste the sweetness of their flavour. I knew I was lacking something but didn't know how to find it or how to experience it. My relationship with Hilary enabled me to feel.

The best I could do before was to think something was funny or lovely, but I had learned how to feel the laughter and experience the joy, to feel the lovely. Like the joy of playing with my grandchildren in the paddling pool, spraying each other with water, I loved their laughter and their excitement as I let them soak me and splash me even though I was clothed in shorts and a t-shirt. I entered their fun and the experience felt as exciting as being a few inches from the white rhino on safari. It was real, it was in the moment, and I loved it. I remembered how all those conversations ago I had told Hilary that I wanted to play. Well, I was playing, and it was wonderful.

I think my life needs to be what I want it to be
And not what I think others want of me
The choices I make, the actions I take
Are mine, for me, are real and true
Not governed by pleasing you or you or you.

Hilary had to be away for a procedure, which meant another break, and I had slipped back into survival mode and I felt terrible. I set time aside to spend with Little Me and told her that I was finding life hard. I was soon in touch with how Little Me was feeling and was reminded of how negative the impact of pushing Little Me away could be, how my fragile sense of self seemed all too close to the surface and resulted in Little Me not being seen, heard, nurtured or loved. Given the chance she was able to tell me.

I need you to see me and to put me first
Too much time you have left me to thirst
Left me alone to struggle with the hurts
Of a childhood filled with so much pain
Nothing but existing, every day the same
Lost, alone, empty, numb, cold
There was no colour no warmth
Just me, breathing, existing, surviving
No one noticed I wasn't thriving
No one cared especially not me
I didn't know I was in hiding
In hiding even from me.

As I mentioned earlier my partner is also a survivor of abuse in childhood and our relationship was at times extremely challenging. I was working with Hilary on my relationship with her and with myself, which was providing me with a very different way of being. My partner was caught up in his own pain and had recently embarked on therapy with someone Hilary had recommended and helped him to contact after I had shared some of his struggles with her. It was early days for him, and he wasn't convinced therapy was going to help. He, like me, struggled with his own hurts, but unlike me he wasn't able to contain his pain. Hilary described his behaviour as being 'his shit that he is dumping' and asked me, 'Why are you letting him do that to you?'

I didn't like her asking me why I was letting him do that because I felt as though I had no choice, but she was right; only I could decide what I was willing to put up with. He made his own choices of how to manage his hurts, and at times I felt like an emotional punch bag for him. I could feel myself sinking deeper and deeper into his hurt, and like a sponge soaked up everything he spilled out. It was exhausting but with Hilary's support I began to communicate how I was feeling with him and felt empowered by sharing with him how what he said and how he behaved made me feel. We were both a work in progress and with the help of our individual therapists, both skilled in working on the impact of childhood trauma on adults, I believed we would be OK. Didn't know if we would stay together, but the most important thing is that we were having the therapy we needed.

Soon after returning from a break, Hilary shared the devastating news that she would need to be away for treatment. She knew that every session with her was precious to me and I would feel the loss. Despite what she faced, Hilary kept her word regarding 'being there for the long haul' and she set up some time for us to have telephone sessions during her treatment, when she felt well enough. It was a very difficult time for us both for different reasons. Although I didn't know what type, I knew she was being treated for cancer for the second time since I had known her. I feared that I was too much for her, that she was ill because of me. I didn't want to tell her too much about my pain, I wanted to protect her. But during one of our telephone sessions I found myself consumed with a deep and searing pain that was too great for me to tolerate. I hurt so much I had to stand and pace the floor. I managed to tell her what was happening, and she suggested that when I was a little girl, I had to bear the unbearable and had no one to turn to. She could hear me crying and asked me what it was about. I knew in that moment that my tears related to a comment she had made previously about liking me and caring about me because of, 'Who you are and not because of anything you do.' I didn't need to earn it, Hilary accepted me for me, and it wasn't conditional. She told me if I was angry or in a mood, she would still like me!

This was so different to my experience with my mum. I told Hilary that I tried to be good and love my mum better when I was a child and would help her with household chores and make her cups of coffee just the way she liked it to try and make up for being bad and making her ill. I knew my feelings regarding Hilary being ill were all mixed up with my mum being ill when I was a child. I couldn't get rid of the feeling that I was bad, and my badness made Hilary ill even though I knew I wasn't and hadn't.

Hilary asked me to score the situation out of 10 and I instantly gave it a 10. I wished I hadn't responded because Hilary then asked the obvious question of what the 10 meant to me. I found it hard to say but eventually managed to tell her that I feared she would die, and I would lose her. In true Hilary style she told me I would never lose her and then added that she would be pissed off, if on her death, that was it or that she wouldn't still be in my heart! I didn't know whether to laugh or cry, but I had an overwhelming sense that I would never let her go and that she would always be with me. At the end of the session Hilary reminded me that as a child no one saw but now people see me, and they do know about me. She added that I wouldn't be lost because Maggie knew of me, and she would find a like-minded therapist who would be able to work with me.

A few weeks after her return Hilary was unwell and could not make the session. I felt so disappointed, but I was also worried about her and it hurt. I felt like not seeing her anymore, it was too painful to live with such uncertainty, and then I felt fearful that I might never see her again. I loved her and wanted her to know I was thinking of her, but I was also angry that she had this shit to deal with and because of that, so did I. I was at the point of being able to acknowledge how I felt and accept those feelings and I sent her a text to tell her I was thinking of her. I knew I could call The Woman's Service and ask to see Maggie if I needed support whilst Hilary was off, and although I didn't use it on this occasion it felt good to know the support was there.

Hilary was able to see me again for a few sessions before needing to go off again and as I sat with her in that first session back, I felt heartbroken and so cold. I didn't understand it but Hilary said, 'It was cold when you were a child.' I cried. I felt safe and free to cry and it felt good. I knew I needed to see Hilary and willingly accepted I would take what she could offer when she could offer it.

As April gave way to May Hilary was unable to work and I missed her terribly. Maggie phoned me and left a message to let me know she was aware I might like to talk, that she hadn't forgotten me, and I could call her. I felt so sad that I had missed her call and found myself crying when listening to music or during a daydream where my mind wandered to me as a child. I felt tearful for Little Me who was so hurt and had no one to turn to. No one could see or did see my pain, and I had to hold on to it for fear of being hurt more.

I knew speaking to Maggie would be helpful, but I also knew nothing I could say would come close to describing the enormity of my pain. It felt too hard to find the words to express the pain and too hard for me to say how it felt to be me. There was no going back to reclaim those lost child years. As I wrote I realised that I felt like I was dying inside and felt worthless. I would never hear a 'Sorry' for what they did to me and I would always have been damaged. I had been conditioned to apologise for my very existence and to serve others, to make up for my badness.

These feelings – my hurt of not being seen, of missing out – were triggered by me missing Hilary and missing my mum. I felt a desperate pain and sadness and wanted my mum back, the mum that was loving and kind. I lost her so long ago, when she went away, she never came back as that loving, kind mother. I felt wrong and bad and dirty and not good enough. I was out in the cold with nowhere to go or no one to be with who I felt would love me or accept me.

If you believe you are all bad and
someone offers you a little bit of good
You cannot accept the little bit of good, you
push it away
Cos once you make it yours it just adds to the
bad of you
You cannot feel the good, you just feel a
bigger bad
So how do you break down that self-belief of
all bad
How do you learn how to accept the little bit
of good and
trust it will start to replace a little of the
badness without taking on the rot
How come your goodness hasn't become
bad in me
How come your goodness remains good in me
Because I never was rotten and bad?

If I have enough of you and can internalise
your love and care
If I can hold on to more of you as if you are here
Then I can be free, I can stay living and not return
to existing
Existing is the bleak and scary place with no
colour, with no warmth

It isn't a real place, the bleak and scary
It is where the memory lives
It is the shadows that disappear with light
It is what makes fear thrive
It is when you are not alive
Existing is not living, it is not being

Existing is fighting and surviving, doing
It is exhausting, it is torture and torment
Nothing there, cold yet creates fear
Empty yet full of bleakness.

Maggie and I found a time to talk and I shared how I felt when my mum died, about how my sister and I looked after her for over three years and how we both seemed to know what she needed us to do for her before she asked. We had our loving, kind mother back for those few short years when we were in our mid to late 40s. I told Maggie I wanted to do something for Hilary but that she had told me she didn't need me to and it wasn't my role. All she wanted from me was for me to think of her and wish her well, but I found that so hard. Maggie pointed out that with my mum I could 'do' but with Hilary I can only 'be'. She suggested I try and hold on to what was happening in the here and now so I could experience the difference if I could bear it. She asked me to think about what might help me and we settled on me calling her if I needed to. Maggie also told me that Hilary knew that my thinking of her and wishing her well came from a depth and it was very rewarding for therapists when a person can accept and internalise the goodness of the therapeutic relationship. I felt like Maggie was telling me that Hilary values our relationship and might even be missing me. Before the end of the call Maggie mentioned that when Hilary comes back, she will be the same Hilary returning and there will be benefit to me of having a different and good experience this time round.

I enjoyed feeling contained from my call with Maggie; she helped me to hold on to the good for a little longer. I found fun things to do, spent time with family and booked a massage, which was just what I needed. I carried on with my life as best I could, but the desperation, the missing Hilary, was never far away and it felt unbearable. I thought about how I could feel and hold the comfort of her and wrote how I felt, but it didn't seem to help. I wondered what Hilary would say if I could talk to her. I found myself imagining we were sitting on our bench. I entered into a fantasy of a conversation with Hilary in the way I communicated with Little Me. I could feel Hilary within me. I wrote:

Hi Hilary, how are you?

H: I'm well thank you Tricia. More to the point how have you been?

Not good (as I write tears drop like heavy rain followed by deep searing pain of the then and the now causing me to tremble and wracking sobs erupt, I can't speak).

H: It's ok Tricia, I am here.

I have missed you so much and I needed you. It has been harder than words can describe and I don't know where to start.

H: Did you call Maggie when you needed her, or do you think you held on for too long?

I tried not to be a pest, I tried to bear the pain of the experience and did call Maggie but it was you I wanted, you I needed, you know me and my heart was breaking because you weren't here.

H: Is that how you felt when you were small when your mum went away?

I nodded (then sobbed again, sobbed for the little girl who was so alone, so hurt with no one to turn to, no one saw the pain and no one heard the cry).

H: It is so very hard to be feeling that pain.

I feel like I have been crushed and kept in a place where rubbish is thrown, allowed out for short periods but knowing that I was to go back to the pit. Above the pit was for other people and I just looked on and watched their colour. I had no colour of my own, no warmth of my own. It was only others that had that. They were good and clean and deserved good things. I was dirty and bad and had no right to anything.

H: And now?

I do now but I didn't. I lived that way for so long. Now I know different and I am at a loss as to how I live my life. What I wanted I no longer want. What I was willing to live with I am no longer willing to live with. The people pleaser is going and the pleasing me is coming. I wanted quiet, comfort, peace and time to explore my creativity now that I no longer need to use all my energy to exist and please. I feel like I have reached crisis point and my very life depends on what I do next.

H: Do you think that is real or a fear?

It's a fear. If I do nothing, nothing will happen. If I want to be free, I have to change my life. You said I can be happy in my own life and allow my partner to get on with his, but I cannot because his life and what he does affect me. I don't want to compartmentalise a part of my life and exclude him, surely it is in or out.

H: It doesn't have to be. You can choose not to be miserable. You can choose what you want to do.

It doesn't feel like at the moment. It feels like I am dying inside. I feel like I am losing something, something I valued and loved.

I felt better for having that imaginary conversation with Hilary. She had made herself available to me whenever I needed her for almost five years but now, even though I desperately needed her, picking up the phone or sending her a message wasn't an option. This long unplanned break from Hilary left me feeling the experience of loss for what felt like the first time.

There was talk of Hilary returning, but nothing had been confirmed. I feared I would never see her again and felt abandoned by her. It was only a few weeks from the long summer break and I didn't think I could handle seeing Hilary for a couple of weeks and then have another break. I checked my phone but there were no messages from her. The silence was agony. I sent her a card to say I was thinking of her. Giving her something was giving me something. I wondered when I would see her again, when we would sit together, when would I experience her holding. I missed how she contained my pain, how she challenged me. She had so much courage. I knew I had internalised her but it wasn't enough. I wanted to hear her laughter and see how her eyes lit up when she was being jovial. I even missed how her eyebrow raised when I said something she didn't agree with. Something I would usually avoid. I wanted the Hilary I knew, warts and all.

It felt so hard – there was support and Maggie was there for me when Hilary couldn't be, as was The Woman's Service, but it was Hilary I wanted, Hilary that I missed.

> Where are you Hilary, where are you
> You'll tell me you're here
> and not going anywhere
> That you are out there somewhere
> I don't know how to use Maggie
> She isn't there like you, she isn't you
> When I am distressed, I can phone you
> When I feel alone or cold, I can tell you
> Maggie isn't there in that way, only you are
> This is going on for too long now and I
> need more
> Waiting for you to come back and waiting for
> a call
> It is just too long, and I can't cope with it all.

I heard from Maggie that Hilary would be returning. I had been able to tell Maggie how hard I had found Hilary's absence and she understood. I told her it felt good that Hilary was coming back and Maggie said it was important that I could tell Hilary how it has been and how I felt, which needed to include the Hilary that I could hold on to as well as the Hilary that went away and left me abandoned and alone. I felt Maggie was giving me permission to tell. I wondered how it would feel to see Hilary again. I felt angry that she had been away for so long, but I knew I didn't want to tell her that because it wasn't her fault.

The anticipation of Hilary returning was as hard as the pain of her being away. My feelings ranged from wishing I had never started therapy to being pleased I had. She had been away for 10 long weeks and I was desperate to talk to her but also fearful of how distressed I might be. I wanted to scream, 'Why the fuck didn't you see, why the fuck didn't you even look?' And to Hilary, 'Why the fuck did you leave me for so long?'

I wanted to be back in our room with my pillow and the blanket Hilary brought to the sessions for me. I wanted to tell her how hard it had been and that at times I wanted to die. I wanted to tell her how strong I felt at times and how I could cry freely. How the colour and warmth from her started to fade but how Maggie helped me to hold on to it.

> How do I begin to tell you what is at my core
> In the innermost central part of my being
> When I have no way of naming it,
> describing it
> I feel, feel, feel but cannot tell, tell, tell

Locked in, a slave to my deep, deep hurt
When will I be free, when will I find me
I want to run until there is nowhere to run
I want to scream until there is no sound
I want to cry until there are no tears
I want to find me at my core
I want to know the me before
Before abuse, before the damage
I am in there, somewhere
Is there a key, or a code?
Is there a secret word?
Is there a cost I can't afford

What is it, what can I do
How can I help to free you?
What do you need?
My love is yours
My heart is yours
My soul is yours
All I am is yours
All I have is yours
Please speak to me
I am here, I won't leave you
Remember, no matter how ugly it feels.

I was learning to sing 'Love Song' by Adele and the Eva Cassidy cover of 'True Colours' in my singing lessons. Both songs spoke to me and were for Little Me: 'Love Song' because I was beginning to feel at home with myself, and 'True Colours' because I was starting to live and could see and feel my colour. I was also starting to love myself. I remembered how singing and music had been important to me as a child and I had felt robbed of it.

My singing lessons were like me claiming what was mine. I didn't realise it at the time, at least not consciously, but my singing lessons were an important part of my therapy and my recovery.

It was my 52nd birthday and just a few days to go before Hilary's return. I felt aware of the external appearance of a grown-up me, but inside I felt like a small child hurting. I was feeling so afraid of how I would express myself and what it would be like to return to therapy. After agonising over whether I should make contact with Hilary I shared a newsy email with her, which included me saying, 'I have so wanted to email you and to phone you, to hear your voice, to talk to you. Now you are nearly back I feel apprehensive, unsure, awkward and afraid.' She responded with ideas of how we might start back, saying, 'Coming back is bound to feel uncertain – such difficult circumstances. We'll feel our way and we will get there!'

The uncertainty was really tough. I feared that I would fall apart in the reception area; I wondered if I would feel joy at the sight of Hilary or if I would feel so angry that I wouldn't be able to contain it. I knew and felt that Hilary would accept me and I trusted that we would feel our way and that we would get there!

> 52! How can that be
> Tells the world there's a grown up me.
> No sign of the little girl
> Hurts and secrets with no one to tell.

My first session back with Hilary was a painful and difficult experience. Having my blanket gave me comfort, and I could tell Hilary was treading carefully. She talked about going carefully and that Maggie was impressed with how I had been thinking and had shared some of what I had told her, which Hilary said left her feeling touched. She talked about this being a vulnerable time for our relationship, and I told Hilary that I couldn't show my pain to Maggie or her. She asked me if I thought she didn't know and understand how hard it would have been for me. I said I thought she knew me well enough to know. Hilary told me that Maggie was aware I was hurting from what I had shared with her, so I had been able to express it. I agreed that I had been able to tell her in words but not in tears.

Hilary set out the sessions that she would be able to provide over the next few weeks. She had a hospital appointment for one, wasn't able to give me the extra sessions as she wasn't well enough to return properly but thought it would be better than none before the July break. I agreed that waiting until September would be too hard and that at times, I felt like I was dying, I felt so alone, and I cried. I could hear Hilary telling me, 'You are not alone.'

Towards the end of the session Hilary asked me if we had talked about what I wanted to talk about and wondered whether I would react about the session later. She knew me so well. I didn't know what to say because I felt angry that we had a shorter session, angry that Hilary would not be available for one of my precious sessions before the summer break, but I knew I wouldn't tell her. I felt abandoned and desperate and I wanted her back how I had her before. I wanted to feel cherished and special to her.

I didn't feel I could I tell Hilary of my pain. I felt she was the cause of it even though I knew it was because of an illness she had no control over. I didn't know how to tell her what I was feeling and that was how I felt as a child. How could I tell my mum of my pain when she was the cause? How could I tell Ernest how much I hated what he was doing to me, when he was the cause of my pain? I needed them as a child, I needed Hilary as an adult. The risk of losing Hilary felt too much even though it meant denying the feelings of Little Me. I began to understand the points Hilary had made previously about me, at times, not being mindful of Little Me. In this case it was in understanding how hard my first session back with her was. I felt compassion for Little Me and remembered Hilary telling me she wanted me to feel entitled. I felt angry that although I did feel more entitled, I couldn't just pick up the phone when I needed her because she wasn't available for me and I felt alone.

I thought about what Hilary had said about Maggie being impressed with how I was dealing with being without her, and knew it was the adult me when talking to Maggie but with Hilary it was the child me. The child is not emotionally developed and cannot articulate herself. I couldn't help her because I was too consumed by the child pain. I felt so angry and entitled to justice, but I will never know a 'Sorry' from those who hurt me. I needed to grieve. I didn't know if I could contact Hilary outside of sessions so soon after her return and continued to fear being too much for her. I eventually messaged her to say that I didn't know if contacting her between sessions would be OK but that I needed to ask, 'Are we OK?'

Hilary messaged back, 'I think part of us "getting back" is about us checking that we're ok and it takes time.' I felt OK with her response.

I was able to tell Hilary how I felt about being the child me with her and adult me with Maggie and she asked why I couldn't show Maggie how I was feeling. I felt a feeling of dread within me but with encouragement from Hilary I was able to tell her that it was her that I wanted but I didn't want to tell Maggie that. I also told her how angry I felt that there was no justice or sorry for what my mum or Ernest did to me and feeling entitled would do nothing to help my past. I knew it helped my future but not my past. Hilary asked me in what way, and I told her nothing can take it away. Nothing can change what happened. Hilary acknowledged my pain.

We also talked about the rules in between sessions whilst she was still recovering, which Hilary said, 'Would have to be your call.'

I didn't like that because she was giving me the responsibility for having my needs met but I couldn't tell her. I talked about why I asked her if we were OK and shared that I felt I had done something wrong. She raised the issue of her taking away my Thursday and that it was because she wasn't well enough to be fully back, which is a loss for me. I nodded but couldn't speak because I felt she had given me so much and 'taking away my Thursday' wasn't really a choice for her. She told me that she believed our relationship was solid and that it is important for me to understand that I hadn't done anything wrong, that it was about her and what she could manage and not about me being too much.

She also shared with me that she didn't know how much longer she would continue working because she was nearer 70 than 60, but we would explore what I needed if she could no longer offer to support me. I knew how much better my life was because of her, that I was significantly attached to her and that I loved her. I also knew that I didn't share my level of distress with Maggie because I didn't want Hilary to know. I feared she would be disappointed in me for not holding her in my heart enough!

I realised how much energy I used trying to work out what others wanted of me rather than what I wanted of and for myself! I thought about how I wanted Hilary to hold me in her arms; she did emotionally, but not physically. I knew I needed a relationship with myself that consisted of love and gentleness, of a heart of compassion for my child within, for the child I was. I thought about me at seven and I believed I was an evil, horrible, hateful child. By the time I was 10 I believed I was also dirty and disgusting and felt ashamed and guilty, deserving nothing. From my relationship with Hilary I knew I was a little girl who needed to be loved and nurtured, who needed to be protected, needed someone to love her in all she was and all she would be and 'everything in between.' Thank you Hilary!

With these thoughts in mind, I thought about Hilary saying that phoning her was 'your call'. I needed her so I called her and she sounded bright and cheerful and it was so good to hear her voice. It was a voice that told me I mattered. I actually phoned to tell her that I was wondering how she was and wanted to talk to her, not because I was in distress or desperate but because I felt valued and important and didn't think I was being a nuisance. At last! Hilary asked me what I was wondering and I shared with her that I wanted to know how she was. She told me that it will take some time for her to recover and she will be kept a close eye on and added that when something like her illness happens it makes you think. She added that she would give me plenty of notice if she had to stop working. I shared with her that I found it hard not being able to do something physical to help her. I told her I cared so much

217

for her and she said she thought it was really important that I was not allowed to clean the house for her, which made me laugh, and we both knew she was referring to when I was a child and tried to make my mum better. Hilary also told me she knew I cared about her. I understood that her needs were not mine to meet, and this knowledge helped me in other situations in my life; I was beginning to stand back more and put myself first.

With a greater sense of entitlement came more anger about the abuse in my childhood. I wondered about Ernest and what happened in his childhood and life that lead to him committing such terrible crimes against me and other children. I wished I could point him out in a crowd, expose him for what he was. I knew I would never be able to do that because he was dead and it felt so unfair. I also wanted a photo of him, I wanted to look him in the eyes and hold his stare and challenge him with my new-found strength. I wondered if it would help me if I could – it wouldn't change what happened, but maybe I would feel better for exposing him and challenging him. I felt better for knowing I wasn't here as an apology, nor was I here to make up for the inadequacies of others with their adult vocabulary that blamed and manipulated me. I said to myself ,'I'm not listening. I now have the voice of Hilary who is my positive attachment, she acknowledges me, validates me and appreciates me. I can feel anger and hate towards her and she still cares, acknowledging my feelings and accepting them.' That was new for me!

I needed to hold on to this positive attachment, but with another break looming I felt vulnerable. Yes, I continued to hate the breaks, I wanted to scream out but didn't really know why. When I next saw Hilary, we explored how I felt, the anger and frustration and my desire to have a photo of Ernest to tell him that he couldn't hurt me anymore. I knew I had become who I am in spite of Ernest and my mum and because of my relationship with Hilary. I felt acknowledged and validated by her and knew with all the media coverage of abuse in the Catholic Church and the Savile situation, that society was also waking up to the impact of abuse in childhood. Yet the abuse inflicted on me wasn't institutional, it was familial and by a trusted 'friend'!

We talked about Hilary retiring, and I shared with her that I didn't know what her retiring would mean for our relationship. She asked me what I thought it meant and I told her that I would never talk to her again. As I said it, I felt such deep pain, which she noticed as I gave her eye contact. She responded by saying, 'That doesn't sound very good, we won't do that then.' We both laughed.

The following session was the last until the break and I was dreading it, but I somehow knew I would be OK. I knew she was not leaving me but was taking leave and when she returned, she would be the same old Hilary, just a little more refreshed and hopefully much more recovered.

I wanted to find the words to describe who she was to me and I wanted to be able to tell her, to understand what I felt. Spending time with Little Me continued to help me process those thoughts and feelings.

I feared her, I wanted her approval
I didn't know who I was, I didn't know how to feel
I wanted to cry, my body wouldn't allow it
My fears wouldn't allow it. I wanted to trust
I was numb, I existed, I wanted to live
I looked on whilst others felt and laughed

I wanted to be part of that.
I wanted to know how it felt to feel
I wanted to be on the inside
I wanted to stop apologising for being born,
I wanted to stop justifying my existence,
I wanted to matter
I wanted to stop hurting myself, I wanted to
stop hating myself
I wanted to love myself. I wanted to trust,
I wanted to believe
I wanted to understand why Hilary wanted me
to feel entitled
I wanted to feel it is ok to feel how I feel
I wanted to know how it felt to feel ok about
me.

I feel loved and nurtured by Hilary and
I feel the love of others around me
I feel accepted and valued by Hilary and
I feel that I am acceptable to others.

I knew that I loved Hilary and felt loved by her. I also realised that I still felt ashamed of my feelings, ashamed of everything about me. Nearly five years of working together had been a big commitment from us both. I had mixed feelings about the long summer break and her probable retirement, but because of her I had developed a sense of self and was learning to love and accept the little person I was discovering within and the woman that I was blossoming into. Hilary spoke of my singing lessons being part of my growth, and I was starting to find a greater freedom in expressing my emotions that way.

Feelings of shame would emerge with what felt like little or no warning, and I shared with Hilary that I was ashamed of my feelings. I asked her, 'Why would you, or anyone, would want my dirty guilty love?'

In her strong assertive voice she said, 'Hold on a minute. That is something the abuser would say because of what he did to children. That would be a defensive position.'

'I felt ashamed of how I feel, of my feelings. I was never allowed to express my feelings as a child and was made to feel bad for having needs. I was told I was a dirty, nasty little girl.' I paused and then added, 'I now know that was about my mum, and not me, but that is how I felt.'

Hilary pretended to fall to the side in her chair at this revelation, and we both laughed. I understood that the lies I was told about me by my mum and the old way of believing those lies could still grip me at times and leave me limping and hurting, such is the long-lasting damage of abuse in childhood. That understanding meant I could enjoy the freedom from living with those lies in that moment.

Hilary was late to our last session, which worried me, but when she arrived, I noticed she looked better than the previous week. She told me she was expecting to retire the following December, which would give us around three months after the break to work towards an ending. We talked more about how hard I found it to be in a relationship with her but not be able to do anything for her except wish her well.

Hilary said she was struck by my difficulty in feeling angry with her. I knew I would have such feelings but I couldn't get in touch with them. I felt an overwhelming need to protect her. She asked me if I noticed that she was late to the session and I nodded. She then asked how I felt about it. I told her I didn't like it but I didn't feel angry. She then said she would have to examine why she allowed people to delay her and why she was telling me. She wondered if she was trying to provoke an angry response from me. I told her she would have to try harder than that if she was trying to provoke an angry response. We both laughed. I loved moments like that with her – they were real and in the moment. Hilary said she wanted me to have a different experience of being angry with someone who would accept my anger, and she thought that was why she acted that out by being a bit delayed rather than talk to me about it. I loved her honesty and it helped to reinforce that we are in this together.

A couple of weeks in to the six-week break and I was hurting but feeling stuck and unable to cry. I knew I had to learn to live my life without seeing Hilary, and that felt hard. I felt the sadness of having a mum who couldn't cope and didn't know how to be a mum, who couldn't raise confident secure children. She was out of control and I had to be independent from a young age but with no sense of self-worth. The abuse by Ernest compounded that and I had low expectations for myself but not of myself. I felt like I was carrying the mistakes of my mother, her parents, Ernest, his parents, and having to do all the weeding for all of us. I was driven but I recognised the need to have some me time.

Whilst watching an episode of *Long Lost Families* I cried for the people and the story that was being told, and then I cried for me.

> Existing is a lonely place
> No feelings to embrace

Numbed and stunned
No warmth, no colour
Sensing something's wrong
Numb and out of balance

I was existing, I wasn't living
I wasn't being, it wasn't real
Now I am living, I am being
I am seeing, it is real.

I had an overwhelming feeling of love for Little Me. It felt like it belonged to more than one child, as though I had children within. Six- or seven-year-old me and nine- or 10-year-old me. I thought of what I went through at those times and the feelings of hate and disgust, which were now replaced by so much love. Those little girls were hurting and so unhappy and then nothing, as though I stopped living, stopped being alive and instead existed. I could not recall when I went from feeling unhappy and afraid to nothingness to existing. A child who knew what it felt like to be nurtured and loved to a child who was very unhappy and very afraid to one that was so traumatised that she disconnected, dissociated and existed in a robotic state, lost to herself, looking on as others laughed and cried.

I was existing, I wasn't living
I wasn't being, it was surreal
I was existing, I wasn't living
I wasn't being, I couldn't feel

The bleak and scary place was there
I couldn't see
No colour, no warmth, no love.

Re-connecting was the only way to find myself, and that journey has been agonizing and meant feeling the feelings I disconnected from to survive. It meant moving from invisible and unseen, which was scary because I believed if I was unseen then no one could hurt me. The only thing that has helped is therapy, and I know I am emerging as a strong self-aware woman who, like the pearl, is made of true grit – just like my birthstone!

Although Hilary couldn't be as available for me, she reminded me that I could call if I needed to during the break. I did my usual agonising over that, but I finally got over myself and phoned her. She couldn't talk for long, but we had a quick catch-up and she offered me time the following week. It helped to hear her voice, but it also left me missing her more, which confused me. I experienced the familiar feeling of not being able to breathe and feeling that I would never be able to cry enough to cry all the tears from within away; I feared the cry would end me. I also felt there was no cry big enough to reach and release the deep and searing pain I felt within.

When we talked the following week, I didn't feel satisfied with the session. I felt Hilary was distant from me. We talked a little about me not feeling angry with her. I told her that I had felt I would cry when we spoke but in the moment I couldn't, which felt hard. Hilary suggested I didn't force the feelings and just accepted how I felt. I wished I hadn't called her. Later that evening I felt angry when I heard from my partner about the behaviour of Savile and how he got away with it. In the same evening I watched *Philomena*, which is a film based on the book *The Lost Child of Philomena Lee,* about a woman searching for her son, who was stolen from her by Catholic nuns when she was a teenage mum living in one of their workhouse institutions. I felt so angry about the injustice of it all, of how people knew what was happening and at best were wilfully blind and at worst covered for the perpetrators.

And then came my anger towards Hilary. I didn't want to speak to her or see her again and I wanted to tell her that. I wanted to tell her I didn't want to work with her on me anymore, me and my pain. I was angry that no one would ever say sorry, no one. No one would ever be punished for what they did to me, no one. I hated it that Hilary couldn't be there for me from December 2013 until June 2014 and wouldn't be there properly until September and then just to say goodbye in December. Goodbye because it was what she needed but not goodbye because it was right for me. I felt it was never about me. I felt invisible and it was agony. I wrote how I felt in a letter to Hilary, one that I knew I wouldn't send but I needed to write.

I wrote that I didn't want to see her again, that she couldn't take away my pain so there was no point. I told her the deep and searing pain was so ugly it couldn't surface because it would destroy everything in its path, that there was only hate and violence within it so what good would that do? I also expressed my anger about her being ill, telling her I hated that she was unwell and had been taken from me. I had met her because of the cancer of abuse, and I was losing her because of the cancer in her body. Just as my mum was taken from me by mental illness and I got her back for a few short years just to lose her to cancer. I felt distant from Hilary, and it hurt like hell. I couldn't bear the anticipation of her coming back just to say goodbye; I wanted to say goodbye right then. Having an enforced separation from Hilary was horrible and I didn't feel ready. I felt I'd had to grow up alone over the past few months. I had to do that as a child, and I wasn't ready then either. When I last spoke to Hilary, I wasn't in touch with feeling like that so was left with the difficult feelings. If I could have spoken with her, though, I wouldn't have told her about my angry feelings – they were too raw, and I feared the impact of them on her.

I had a further brief conversation with Hilary towards the end of the break and didn't share how angry I had felt but managed to let her know how deeply I had been hurting and that I had split off from those feelings because they were too much for me. I told her I couldn't do anything about the situation and so had to just get on with it. Hilary said I was part of the decision in how the situation should be managed and that I had someone to tell how hard it was and could be confident that I would be listened to. She also said I needed to talk about how difficult and painful it had all been when we were back after the summer break. I felt so much better, even though the situation remained difficult and she would still be leaving, I felt less distressed and a little more contained.

> Will I ever feel free
> Will I ever find me
> What will it take
> For my soul to make
> Peace with those souls of power
> Souls of the past
> The freeing of my soul comes
> With the pure joy of laughter
> The kind of laugher that leaves one spent.

Year Five

The first session back after six weeks was nearing. I had been away for a week in Spain with my partner along with two of my brothers, our dad, one of my daughters and her friend. We had a great time and I enjoyed my new-found emotional freedom, playing games in the pool like we did as kids and teasing each other.

I missed Hilary and sent her a postcard and an email to let her know I was thinking of her and to tell her I was missing her. She didn't email me back, which was unusual and left me feeling worried and rejected! I wasn't sure about seeing her after such powerfully tough feelings. I felt I was going back for sessions and would need her again, just to lose her again. It wasn't what I wanted, and I felt like I was conforming when I wanted to rebel, and I hated the untouchable life of Hilary. I had bought her a gift I didn't want to give her; I felt my needs were just as important as hers and that she couldn't be the only one who decided when we saw each other. I knew I had a choice too and I thought I might choose not to go or to be late and leave her hanging around wondering what happened and why I wasn't there. That's what it felt like to know I was entitled – I could decide what to do, I could decide to tell Hilary something or nothing and I could decide whether to go to my session and whether to let her know or not!

The first session back didn't go well at all. Hilary asked me lots of questions about my holiday and family, particularly about my relationship with my partner, none of which I wanted to answer. She acknowledged she was asking me lots of questions and that I should say if it wasn't what I wanted to talk about.

I couldn't speak to her. I noticed there was only 15 minutes of the session left and I didn't want to be there. I had wanted to tell her that coming back was just another way of saying goodbye and it was too hard to contemplate, but I couldn't say it. I knew by the questions Hilary was asking that she hadn't received my email, and she suggested I check it was sent to the new address. At the end of the session, I felt I had already lost her, and I didn't see the point in connecting with her again just to lose her again. I couldn't tell her how I was feeling.

When I checked the email address, I could see I had sent it to her old one, so I re-sent it. I also told her that I found returning after the break very difficult and that I felt pissed off. I told her I had failed to assert myself and didn't tell her what I needed, and I felt frustrated with myself and angry with her. I shared how I felt during the break and that being in touch with this anger had enabled me to know that I wasn't responsible for what happened to me. I felt like I was saying goodbye to my mum all over again, but the difference was the rawness that I felt. I felt it at my very core, in the deepest, most delicate part of my inner self, I felt it in my soul. I was no longer disconnected – I was connected, and I was feeling it. When my mum was dying, I denied my own needs completely and focused on her. With Hilary, I was in touch with my own needs and also in touch with what I perceived as being her needs. She had given me so much and helped me 'become', which was amazing. I realised that I felt angry with her in a freer way, which was also amazing; not only did I feel it but I also told her I felt angry with her.

228

Hilary responded to my email by saying, 'I wonder if you're being a bit hard on yourself – and on me too! Perhaps you "didn't do anything" about it because you were feeling your way back – and perhaps so was I … You haven't lost the opportunity to say what you need. It might be more about trusting yourself than trusting in the process in this instance.'

I sent back an amusing comment about Rome not being built in a day, but if I was building it perhaps only a week. I thanked her for her reply. There was so much I wanted to say, and I knew that I wouldn't heal or feel complete in one session, but I would gradually feel more healed and more complete and I would 'bit by bit' make more and more sense of the me I was becoming.

The following morning I woke from a dream where I was a young boy and my father was holding the back of my neck marching me to somewhere. I felt he wanted to teach me something, but I didn't know what or why. I felt afraid and thought about how I felt each time my session ended with Hilary or each time she went away, and I felt as though I couldn't breathe. I didn't want to go back to that place of fear – but when I had that level of dependency on Hilary, I felt that I had her. She was intensively mine and was there for me all the time. She made it clear that I was to phone her whenever I needed her, and every time I called her she would respond as soon as time allowed, and when I texted or emailed her, she would say, 'I am here.' She would remind me I was not alone and say, 'It isn't the same as it was when you were small.'

I loved those times with her – the reassurance, the closeness, my total dependency, with her safe arms holding me emotionally and accepting me for who I was.

I then thought about the fear in my childhood and as before, without consciously thinking, I wrote the following:

'The fear left me feeling as though my body was so completely weak that all my muscles would give way and I would go limp. I would wet myself with the loss of the strength in my body. Then I thought about the fear and the cold and the fear of being beaten, pinched and bitten, having my hair pulled till my skull felt numb and my mother's hands tight around my throat till I thought I would pass out with lack of breath. The fear of what she would do to me was overshadowed by my fear of putting my foot out of the bed on to the floor and feeling the physical cold and the fear of the unknown. At least I knew what would happen to me if I wet my bed but the fear of the unknown, of what was lurking under my bed or behind the door or the attic hatch was so much worse. If my mother, who said she loved me, could hurt me so much and hate me so much what more could an unknown evil do to me? An evil that didn't love me and one that may leave me dead. I remember my legs shaking under the weight of my body and all the energy draining from me. That is what I knew as a little girl when my mummy went away and in her place was her body and her face but not her eyes of love or her hands of holding. Instead, there was a distortion of hate and disgust on her face and in her eyes and hands of violent destruction. In place of her laughter was a gnarl and a growl and with her going away I was lost and alone and

*in the cold. The bleak and scary place was there.
My pain could not be expressed and my distress
and cries were stifled, so my throat closed and all
my pain and hurt sat in my throat like a cold and
jagged rock. When Ernest came along I thought he
was giving me the love I needed, but instead he
violated me and the hard-jagged rock in my throat
became an iceberg. I was so lost to myself and the
devastation left me numb and totally isolated. I
could no longer feel and believed I had no needs
and was nothing.*

*Hilary, until you sat by my side in your
humanness and walked in my pain with me, and
my raw emotion, I was lost. In my adult years I
found Christ and He walked with me and was
living in me with His spirit of love, but He knew I
needed you and He made sure I had you. You have
shown me how to be and how to feel.*

*That morning as I showered, I sang part of 'My
Father's Heart' by Rachel Lampa and it was the
verse that says, 'I never understood how merciful
love could be, until I found his flame light every
part of me.' You, Hilary, are the part – the human
part. As I sang, I cried and I shook and as I cried,
I drew a breath through constricted vocal cords
making the intake of air sound, a sound of sobbing
and inability to breathe freely and I shook my
hands and flexed my thigh muscles as a way of
releasing some of the energy from the grief and
distress. It felt similar to when a child has a
tantrum and thrashes around because they cannot
express enough of their distress, and they cannot*

231

contain the power of it in their body any longer. I thought about my mother strangling me physically and the threat of death if I didn't 'shut my ugly fat mouth' and then of the closing of my throat so that I would only make a squeak noise with my pain. Then I think about the constricting of my throat to stop Ernest's penis choking me, believing that my very life depended on closing my throat. The force and the power of the thrust with sounds of his pleasure telling me with his eyes that I was pleasing him, and he was approving of me. On the brink of death, I was gaining his approval and then he would release his disgusting warm, thick and heavy stuff deep in my throat. Then he would go soft and no longer be threatening my life, I could breathe and he would hold me and be loving and kind. I would feel warm. No longer cold and no longer afraid for I knew there would be no more asked of me for that night. I would sleep.

As I finished typing 'sleep', I cried out unexpected cries with expression from the depth like I have never known. I coughed and retched and took in deep breaths, filling my lungs ready for the next heartbroken sob. I can hardly believe I experienced such depth of release. I was exhausted but I was so relieved that I could at last release the pain – so long after starting therapy, I could release the pain.

I wanted to send it all to Hilary because I knew it was why I was so pissed off in my first session back with her. I couldn't tell my mum when I didn't like what she said or did, and I couldn't tell Ernest when I didn't like what he did, and at 52 years old with Hilary, I couldn't tell her I didn't like what she was asking me even though my relationship and experience with her was not the same as with my mum and Ernest, not the same as when I was small. Hilary was different and I had a healthy relationship with her, one where I was listened to and accepted, but it still felt hard.

Having lived through the recent experience of expressing my deepest pain I knew telling Hilary how I felt wouldn't be as hard, so I messaged her to let her know what had happened and she encouraged me to take what I had written to our next session. I wasn't sure if I could handle what felt like the 'too difficult to look box', but Hilary reassured me by asking if looking at it together would feel more manageable and if waiting until the following day was too much for me. I didn't like to wait but I knew I would have processed some of how I was feeling by the following day and that no matter how terrible I felt, I wouldn't feel that way forever.

For a reason I didn't understand, I felt embarrassed by Hilary's eye contact with me in the next session, which was the following day. I told her I felt awkward and then read through what I had written to her and in my journal. I told her that I believed I had been my mother's world before she was ill, I lost her and then I got her back just to lose her again to cancer, and I felt that was what was happening again with me and Hilary. I cried during the conversation, which was still a rare experience for me.

Hilary commented that she could see I was feeling the pain, not just knowing it, and I felt comforted by the togetherness we shared in that moment. We talked about our relationship and how special she was to me and how special I had felt to her. I told her I missed that feeling of specialness and in that moment, felt my silence the previous week was because I felt like I was back there in my childhood experience, and I wanted her to see my vulnerability and rescue me. I wanted her to see and make it better rather than take responsibility for it myself. Hilary talked about how women are good at reading people, and when we are small our mums do that to help us survive, but as we grow, they do it less because children learn to do it for themselves

I challenged her and said, 'You used to read me.' She asked if it was when I couldn't speak for myself or tell her how I felt and if it was when I needed her to. I realised in that moment that she would read my emotions when I couldn't identify my feelings for myself. I couldn't name them and at times still couldn't, but I was getting there. I had been able to tell Hilary I felt angry with her, I had been able to 'tell' her, and she accepted my feelings and helped me. I felt powerfully how my relationship with her and how she responded, wasn't the same as when I was small.

The subject of Hilary leaving was never far away from my thoughts, and she raised it in our sessions. I felt like I would never be free from the trauma of my childhood, even with the total acceptance and love I felt from Hilary. That feeling of awkwardness would revisit me. Before she told me she was retiring I had wondered about life after therapy, but her announcement had interrupted that wondering. She had suggested we consider what I needed so there would still be someone who would be interested in just me, an important consideration, given that in my personal and work life I was giving out so much. As I allowed myself to just be, to find time to spend with me writing in my journal and trusting in the process, I felt that I was missing lying on the chairs and having the cosy comfort of the dimmed light, the pillow and blanket. I felt less exposed and had become used to snuggling down into the physical comfort of how Hilary made the room. I didn't feel brave enough to allow my feelings to come; I feared it would mean imploding, folding inward or dissolving. Perhaps going without the physical comfort would mean total trust of Hilary?

I look directly into her eyes when I am feeling
brave enough
Most of the time I glance at her, catch her eyes
And look away feeling uncertain, ashamed.
I feel such discomfort and squirm when there
is silence
What is the discomfort, what is that squirm,
I need and want to know.
I no longer want to feel that pain,
Leave my sessions with that sense of shame
I want to believe that she sees good when she
looks at me
I want to look into her eyes and know
She is not seeing dirt in my soul
That there is no dirt in my soul and in my
eyes she will see love
I want to look directly into her eyes and see
her love for me
No more hate and loathing or a wish to
obliterate me from life
Instead I want to believe she approves of me
and loves me
I can't earn it with Hilary but I could with my mum,
I knew how to make her laugh, win her over,
have fun.

If I was lucky and it was a good day
The screaming, hitting and strangling
wouldn't come
I knew what to avoid and what to try
And watched out for the first signs
Of her explosive and angry cry
Knowing it would lead to violence and pain,
Her coming at me again and again.

These words came from such a depth, a depth that belonged to a distressed and frightened child. I knew it was from Little Me, and in my internal conversation with Hilary, I asked her:

Is that why I can't look at you Hilary?
Because when I look into your eyes
You are looking into mine
You will see my vulnerability and I will be
exposed.
You will see the core of me, the agony
The begging, the desperation
What will happen when you do?
Or will you see the wicked, dirty, nasty little girl
And say my mum was right, it is true, all this time
I am wicked, dirty, nasty all through.

I imagined her question: what do you think I will see? I think you will see the pain, the raw unexpressed pain of child hurts. You will see a little person wanting to reach out. You will see a little person wanting to be found and rescued. Seen for the little girl that she was – desperate to be loved and to love. That is what she wanted, that is what she needed but that was not what she knew. Maybe I trust you enough now, Hilary, to let you see my pain, to let you in to that place where the grit is embedded and where the pearl began to develop. Develop from that agony and pain.

> When you look into my eyes Hilary what do
> you see?
> When I look into yours, I don't know what is
> looking back at me
> Is it love and care, is it absolute despair, I
> don't know
> I think I try to be vacant and show no expression
> That way you can't hurt me or see what is there
> I hide my inner pleading and my inner despair
> Can't let anyone see that I don't really want
> to be here
> No longer want to battle with the pain of the past
> The pain of the present that continues to last
> Into my every day, no getting away from it,
> it's here to stay.

The more I followed the process of me writing in my journal, internalising Hilary, spending time with myself, a self that felt less like a separate 'Little Me' and more like all of me, the more I was able to work through my feelings. I found a new confidence in what I felt I could 'tell' Hilary and shared what I had learned about my feelings of discomfort when I was with her, in the moment. Hilary explored with me whether I was trying to recreate a situation similar to that of my mum so that I could keep hold of her – I didn't know, but it didn't feel as though I was. She then asked if I was processing the feelings about it all. I wasn't sure but as Hilary spoke, I thought about how I see, how I look through my eyes that I don't outwardly express a positive feeling but that I look inward and see myself as my mother saw me. I felt as though I was owning my mum's look of hate and disgust as if they were my eyes looking at me. Hilary asked me to clarify what I was saying. It was so hard for me to explain what I meant, but after a moment of silence I told her, 'I feel as if I am in my mum's pupils, as if I am there with her.'

Hilary said, 'Your mum can't have you, she can't take you with her, she can't have you.'

As Hilary spoke and reinforced 'she can't have you, she can't take you with her', I saw myself climbing and jumping out of my mother's eyes. The image of the hate and disgust for me that my mother expressed in her eyes whilst she put her hands around my throat was heartbreaking; no wonder I numbed out as a child!

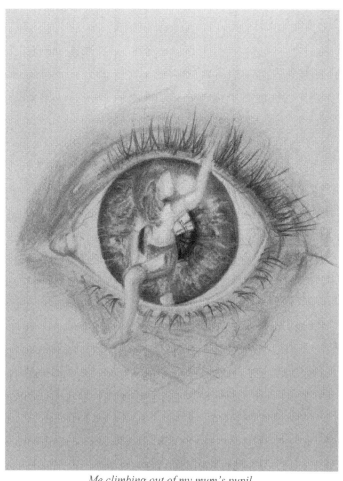

Me climbing out of my mum's pupil.
Artwork by Aileen Churchill.

I knew when my mother was heading for an out-of-control moment and did all I could to distract her and do things for her to stop it from happening. I could sometimes make her 'better', but I didn't feel I could do that with Hilary and shared that with her. She didn't agree. She reminded me of times when I have read her mood and that I knew what made her laugh; she thought I knew her quite well. She told me when she looked at me she saw a warm and caring person and she asked what I see when I look at her. I said I think of her as caring, protective, and nurturing. I also said I thought she was strong and solid. I didn't feel quite brave enough to own up to feeling that I felt she was also stubborn and sometimes stroppy! She asked me if I was feeling uncomfortable in the moment, and I realised I wasn't. I was able to tell her that I missed lying on the chairs, and she said that she also missed the chairs and the longer sessions but knew she couldn't manage them. I felt worried for her but also felt nurtured and contained by her.

I continued to grow in confidence with Hilary, and along with the challenges that life brought for my partner and me – trying to work through our pain with our therapists, make a success of being parents and grandparents and of our careers – there were positive movements within me. I felt good about myself much of the time, had experienced what it felt like to sink into the arms of someone and feel safe, and knew how to play. I was learning to test exposing who I was, to risk being seen and trusting that I might be accepted. Hilary had made that possible.

Hiding the shame, feeling the pain
Living with the drain of a weight with no name
Watching you, watching me
Wondering what it is you see

I called you one day, said I wanted to play
I was grown by that day
But my child was hidden away

When she showed herself
Her bleak and scary was too much for me to bear
You held her for me till I could of her take care

The weight with no name
Was of a child in so much pain
The trauma the dead weight of numb
With your love and care, your hanging on in there
She and I have become.

Feeling able to 'tell' Hilary how I felt in the moment continued to be challenging for me, but I was starting to feel I could say how I felt, if not in the moment then in a later session. I talked more openly about not being able to tell her I had felt punished by not having the chairs and hadn't considered for one moment that she was also missing how we used to work. I wondered why I had assumed not having the chairs was her response to something I had done wrong and that left me wondering what other situations I misinterpreted. Hilary said we had both missed out on sharing something that was important to us by not telling her in the moment, a loss of something we had felt together.

Working towards a December ending continued to feel tough, and with what was happening in my personal life it was all too much not to have the security of her.

Hilary raised the possibility of being able to go on beyond December. We talked about missing out by not being able to share in the moment. She asked me what I was missing in the moment, and I told her it was her blanket; it was soft, and I loved the smell of it. She asked me if I wanted her to bring it with her the following week, and, although embarrassed by my need – it felt like that of a small child – I told her I did. Her strength and solidness had helped me so much. She had previously said, 'With three sessions per week for most of the years we had worked together you have put in a lot of work and your recovering is down to you.'

I knew it was, but it was also down to her and what she gave to me.

I continued to use my journal, which helped me to process my thoughts and feelings, especially when I had one of my 'feeling stuck' moments. I knew I wanted my little girl within to feel safe and know she was entitled to love and care. To know she was precious and beautiful and had the right to fight for herself and what she wanted. She didn't have to sit and take hurt. She didn't have to sit and not be seen or hide away for fear of being hurt by those around her. She could hear Hilary's voice over that of her desperate mother. She knew Hilary's voice like a child knows her mother's voice. It is the voice that she believes and the voice she trusts. It is the voice she takes comfort in and the one that makes her swell with pride about herself. As I wrote these words, I cried. I felt as though I was being loved for the first time; even though I had known the bond of a mother's love in my earlier childhood, I knew I stood in a love and care that was free of cruelty. I had been in a hurry to grow so that I was no longer dependent on my mother, but with Hilary I was in no hurry to grow up and stop being her child.

In the following few sessions we initially agreed that the December ending would be extended until the end of January. This was possible because Hilary had decided she could continue working beyond December. I missed the three sessions each week I had known with Hilary. I had loved having her all to myself, and even though I had considered reducing them of my own volition I found it tough that it was happening because of her being ill. I feared coping with my life without her and questioned if I had enough of her to hold me when I would no longer see her.

As the weeks went by Hilary continued to recover and looked well. I was able to tell her that everything in my life felt hard and I felt like I did when my mum went away and didn't return, and I couldn't talk to her. Hilary wasn't convinced I would be able to talk to my mum if she were to come back because I had protected her and had feared she couldn't bear to hear what I might say. I nodded in acknowledgement and somehow felt I could tell Hilary that although I can talk to her that I felt we had lost something of her already. Hilary insightfully said that although she thought a large part of me was ready to end, there was a part of me screaming out, 'Don't leave me!'

I was amazed at what she said because I felt I had a silent dark place within me that was screaming out with no voice, 'Please don't leave me.' Hilary knew how I felt, she could read me, and we were connected!

I didn't know which part of me didn't want to end, given that Little Me felt so loved and cared for. Hilary reminded me of how I described my feelings towards me in the checked dress, and she thought it was the younger, cute little girl I loved and snuggled with but not the girl in the checked dress. I said that I had felt awkward and lacked confidence because something didn't go so well at work. That I had stopped myself from pinching my face and pulling my hair at the thought of being thick, stupid, pathetic, ugly, dirty, horrible, rubbish. It occurred to me that those negative thoughts were me owning my mother's perception of me. Nothing I got wrong at work or

243

anywhere else could possibly warrant such a violent and over the top reaction. That was my mum's way of doing things and not mine.

I recalled that I had experienced having a dry mouth and had struggled to swallow food. This had happened to me as a child when living with my grandparents. The texture of some food was a problem for me. I would chew meat for what felt like forever but could never swallow it. My mouth would become drier and drier. My grandparents would not allow me to leave food. Sometimes I would manage to spit it in a napkin, but usually everyone was sitting at the table, so I just had to sit there until they gave up and took the plate away. It meant no dessert because I didn't eat my dinner, and I felt punished for having a problem I couldn't help and didn't understand. They disapproved of my refusal to eat the food and I felt bad and naughty. Having a dry mouth was an issue for me too, I wasn't allowed to drink water after dinner, to 'help' with my bed-wetting problem, so even in their attempts to teach me their values and manage my bed-wetting my grandparents were causing me distress. It also happened during traumatic and devastating events leading to my divorce, where not being able to swallow safely resulted in me choking and therefore I was reluctant to eat anything. I lost a worrying amount of weight during that time but gradually found ways to manage it because my children needed me.

To a lesser degree it was happening again. I had noticed it when things didn't go well at work and during my singing lessons. I shared this with Hilary, who asked me how I managed when this happened. I told her I usually had water with me so that I could moisten my mouth, and when eating took smaller mouthfuls of food and drank water to help me swallow. I sometimes gagged and recognised the feeling from when I was being orally raped. I told her, 'There are some foods that I won't eat, some mushrooms and lightly cooked eggs.'

'Slimy food?'

I nodded and felt as though I was back in the room with Ernest, and I knew I was feeling in the moment with Hilary. I could see from her expression that she understood and as I cried, I felt her with me, where I was, in the moment. I shared with her that I had imagined myself sitting with her and crying, no words, no sound just sitting with her in comfort and warmth feeling safe and crying. It was a new feeling, a new experience for me. I asked Hilary what it was. She told me it was reverie.

In that moment I knew I had been able to sink, melt into Hilary's safe arms.

I wrote in my journal and then sent Hilary an email to tell her that I had been thinking about the part of me that isn't ready to end, and that contacting her between sessions would just give me more to miss when we ended, even though at times I just wanted to talk to her, to tell her I felt alone, but wouldn't let myself.

So, me in the checked dress – who, despite having moments of loving her and telling her none of it was her fault – I might still have been blaming. I wrote that I knew me in the checked dress was the part of me that didn't want to end. I hated the dress and I hated wearing it. I was embarrassed and felt humiliated because it wasn't me at all and the white ankle socks and sandals weren't either. I was happier in jeans and trousers then and still am. I felt me in the checked dress was afraid and wanted to say how she felt, and my embarrassment about what she was wearing might also be my feelings about her. She was the child eager to please and the one searching for love. She was the one who was sexually abused and the one who lived the label of dirty and disgusting. So, was I blaming her for what was done to her? Was I punishing her for what my mum and Ernest did to her, holding her to account for being a vulnerable child, unlovable, at fault, guilty? Did I blame her and believe the shame was hers to carry? Had I been kidding myself that I loved her when I really hated her and held her responsible, and so had no empathy for her and wouldn't let her be who she was, wouldn't let her embarrass me with her tears and pain and sobbing because it would be snivelling and ugly and full of self-pity? If that was how I saw me in the checked dress, then that part of me would never be ready to end. If I was that little girl now, I would be afraid of not having Hilary there to stick up for me.

We talked about my email in the next session. Hilary told me she was moved by what I had written because it was honest, and she felt I was looking after Little Me by what I was saying about her. She didn't think it was Little Me who used her to stick up for me because I was doing that for myself. She said she thought it was the big me who needed her.

This was the last session before another break, and I told Hilary I didn't want the break. She acknowledged my dislike of the breaks and asked me if I had thought any more about whether I wanted to end in January. I said, 'I can't see January and don't know how I feel about it.'

We agreed to discuss it after the Christmas break.

I was learning that I didn't just survive during breaks from therapy; I also lived, and the benefits of my relationship with Hilary and how I felt about myself, were also good for those around me. I was able to show the feelings I felt in most situations, I could feel how much I loved my children and grandchildren, and I knew I was expressing my love and approval for them through my eyes. However, I had much work to do on sticking up for myself when I felt my partner was 'dumping the shit of his unhappiness' on me, and it was tough dealing with that and the emotions it raised within me, especially during a break. I knew I needed to talk about those feelings when I next saw Hilary. I felt more willing to talk about my relationship with my partner in my sessions with her by this stage.

I shared the various scenarios I was facing with my partner, the doubts as to whether our marriage would survive all the emotional baggage we both carried, how I was no longer prepared to be hurt by his behaviour but hadn't known what to do about it.

Hilary challenged me, asking why I hadn't stuck up for myself. She used one of the scenarios and asked why I hadn't told my partner that I wasn't prepared to socialise with him because I couldn't pretend not to be hurt. I told Hilary it hadn't occurred to me to say that to him, to tell him in the moment that I didn't want to be in his company; it just hadn't occurred to me that it might be an option. I thought it a good idea and it felt like a tool I could use to stick up for myself and not own the feelings of another.

I discussed how I felt with my partner, and we explored options of selling the house and separating. It was interesting that my change in approach to my partner's way of expressing his pain resulted in him changing how he behaved. The idea of going our separate ways remained an option, but neither of us seriously pursued it.

In my next session with Hilary my indecisiveness about whether therapy would stop at the end of January continued. Given that it was only three weeks away, Hilary said, 'It will not end unless you tell me you want to end.'

We talked about why I hadn't contacted her during the break except for one call where she wasn't home, and I didn't leave a message on her answerphone. I told her that I didn't think I was ready to end, it was difficult to understand how an ending happens in such a unique relationship. Usually if you like someone you don't stop seeing them but in therapy terms the relationship ends and I couldn't imagine that happening.

Hilary talked about the options of 'dipping in and out of therapy as and when you needed it so if you needed to see me again, you could do that in the future.' I knew any future therapy sessions would be under a private arrangement because Hilary was retiring from The Woman's Service, but I was OK with that. I could afford to pay by then and was happy to do that.

I wondered how Hilary felt about us ending given that we had both invested so much into the relationship. On asking her she told me she would feel sad about us ending, saying, 'You are rewarding to work with, and I like to hear about what you are doing and what your life is like.' She shared that she is someone who has a delayed reaction so wasn't sure how she would feel, but said, 'We have achieved good things together and have dealt with some very difficult feelings and been through some hard times.'

I nodded in agreement and felt the mutual respect between us and how we very much appreciated each other; it felt lovely and equal.

So, we didn't talk about when therapy might end for several sessions but spent significant time exploring the difficulties in my marriage. Hilary's knowledge of my partner from our couple work meant that her recommendation for a particular therapist for him had worked well. It was a time when our marriage was at serious risk of breaking down and our therapists independently supported us and made suggestions for us to find the tools to work through our pain and improve our communication. Although more willing to talk about my partner in my sessions, it continued to feel like an intrusion on my time with Hilary. She was never afraid to challenge me, and more than once made it clear that talking about the difficulties in my relationship with my partner was helping me and was focusing on me. A suggestion from his therapist, which Hilary supported, was that we wrote a letter to each other setting out how we felt. I didn't trust him to keep my letter confidential to us and to our therapists, so that wasn't an option for me. Another was that we set time aside to talk to each other when we were not having an angry or painful moment. I felt that would work and we eventually managed to find time to talk and listen to each other. It didn't solve things, but it gave us a starting point to build on, which was better than the end points we both felt we had almost reached.

Another area that I continued to struggle with was expressing myself freely in my singing lessons. I recorded my lessons and listened to them as part of my homework and cringed at the sound of my voice. I knew when I sang alone or in church that I experienced a freedom and enjoyed singing. I remembered how much I loved to sing as a child. I was often chosen to sing at primary school, and I cried for the loss of that innocence and freedom. I wondered whether adult me was stifling Little Me and not allowing her to come through. Was she fighting to get out, and was I stifling her or controlling her? It was something that had bothered me on and off over the years, and at this point it felt too hard to manage on my own. I needed the comfort of Hilary. I told her how I was feeling in an email.

As I wrote, I had a sense that I could hear my mother's voice in mine; she used to sing in the Montague Arms in London with her friend and would often sing at home, practising her performance. I wondered whether that memory had something to do with my struggle. Hilary responded to my question about Little Me by asking, 'Is there perhaps still some shame of her, affirmed by your mother's voice? But she is not shameful – she is brave and beautiful – always has been – always will be. Sounds as if she needs to sing with you. Exciting stuff! Love Hilary.' I felt overwhelmed by her words and basked in the warmth and colour I felt from the comfort of her.

Working through these feelings was difficult and I didn't always understand the process I was going through, but I continued to feel the benefit of being more able to tell Hilary how I felt in the moment. The experience of the warmth and colour, the comfort from Hilary, enabled me to tell my singing teacher how I felt when I played back my lesson. It was so good to feel able to tell her of my disappointment in my singing and to share with her that I was in therapy working on the impact of trauma as a child. I didn't go into detail, but my teacher was attentive and talked about muscle memory. She believed, from working with me over the months, that my struggles to sing freely were psychological. She continued to encourage me to sign up for the performance night, where I would sing in front of the other students and their families, and although I knew I didn't want to do that, the time we talked made a huge difference to how I felt. I was hiding less and allowing myself to be seen a little.

With all this pain I needed Hilary, and at 00:54 am the following morning I emailed her to tell her '… I had been so close to letting go of what felt like a lifetime of pain, but I was afraid. When I'm not with you I think I can express how I'm feeling but can't when I see you and I'm feeling stuck. It's not how I want to feel and I'm hoping talking will help me with it. Love, Tricia.'

I knew I wouldn't hear back for many hours but as usually happened, I felt better for knowing she would read it at some point and be thinking of me. It didn't help me sleep, though, and as I lay, I imagined myself spewing out all the loneliness, fear and hurt, leaving me exhausted. It reminded me of the scene in the 1997 film *No Child of Mine* where a young teenage girl, who was sexually abused, vomits after being held by a safe adult in a safe place.

> The burden of shame of being numb of
> feeling separated, dissociated
> The shock of the pain coming again and again
> becoming integrated
> The burden of shame replaced by the pain of
> the abuse inflicted
> The trust restored the safe person adored by
> the woman so wounded
> The growth of the child inside becoming the
> woman now depicted

Later that day Hilary responded, saying '… it would be fine to have a quick hello but I do believe that the tears, and everything they express, need to be shed without shame when we're together. I think closeness on the phone can unintentionally collude with the secrecy and the shame of being "seen". What do you think?'

I didn't like Hilary's response initially, and knew a quick chat wouldn't work for me, but had learned over time that I needed to allow myself time to absorb what she was saying rather than interpret it as disapproval or rejection. As I re-read her words, I knew talking over the phone was an important lifeline but at that point I knew it was a way of me hiding with feelings of shame. I wanted to be able to face the feelings of shame with Hilary. I felt those shame feelings were gradually being replaced by a feeling of the deepest, most profound hurt and I had not quite reached the point where I could let go. It felt like the critical mother voice was gradually being replaced by the voice and actions of the love and acceptance from Hilary. I wanted to find a way of letting go of all that pain and I knew Hilary wanted it for me, too. I emailed her to let her know I agreed and that I would wait until our face to face session.

I was able to cry in the following session after sharing how I had been feeling since our email exchange. As we came towards the end of my session, Hilary shared with me that she required more surgery and follow-up treatment so would be off for a few months. She told me Maggie would support me whilst she was away, and she hoped it wouldn't be for a few weeks to give us time and allow for her to have her planned holiday.

As she talked, I felt so sad and cried; I knew I was crying for us both. Hilary had been looking so well and feeling better so had delayed her retirement. We had agreed a later ending for May or June, so I wasn't expecting to stop seeing her so soon. I didn't feel ready, and I didn't want her to be ill again. The session was ending and with the heaviest of hearts I folded my blanket and began to pack my things, getting ready to take the pain away with me. Hilary said she had a feeling I wanted to say something, and I told her I did but that we were out of time. She said if we needed longer, we could have it and in that moment I cried freely. I told her I had feared making her ill with my shit, reminded her of when I believed I was a dirty rag and that I would cause her to be ill. Hilary looked straight at me and said, 'You ain't that powerful,' and I laughed. I laughed through the pain and the tears, saying, 'I know!' Hilary's knowledge of me and her ability to know when to use humour to bring home a point was an amazing and beautiful connection; it was ours.

It was the biggest 'ouch' feeling for me, I shared in an email, along with my thoughts about a plan I had for an ending therapy with her on her return in May or June.

Hilary replied that it was a big ouch and it was a good way to describe it. She asked if she could run my ideas past Maggie. I felt fearful when Hilary wanted to check things with Maggie and understood it as fearing she would think me ungrateful or demanding when I had been given so much.

In a later email Hilary, sensing my distress and saying something didn't sit right with her, offered me a phone session, which I accepted. 'The word "ungrateful" is not one I would ever associate with you,' she said.

As we spoke it occurred to me that I had thought of Maggie as the grandparent and that I hated it when my mum said she would tell my gran about something I had done wrong.

In our next session we talked about me seeing Maggie for support whilst Hilary was away, and I promised I would phone Maggie if I needed her. Hilary told me her operation had been brought forward, so we were in our last session – an even bigger ouch. I shared my fears of something happening to her and me not knowing about it. She said that she was expected to survive the surgery and had been told by the consultant that she wasn't going to die.

'I fear that I will never see you again, but rather *that* than you dying.'

'I will text you after the operation so that you know I am OK.'

I wasn't expecting that and felt moved by her kind gesture. I shared with her how much I had benefited from her, Maggie and The Woman's Service and felt I had been given so much from them.

'After what you have been through it is a good stroke of luck that we were both in the right place at the right time. You have a right to be receiving support from The Woman's Service and every right to have therapy.'

I knew she meant it.

As promised, I received a text message from Hilary after her operation saying that all was well. I felt so good hearing she was OK and being able to wish her well. I felt weak yet strong, fragile yet robust, fearful for Hilary, fearful for myself but more secure in myself about myself.

I looked through the cards Hilary had given me over the years and chose the one with 'our bench'. It continued to help me reconnect with her during the breaks. I imagined myself sitting with her on our bench; I felt as though I could smell the beautiful scent of the flowers, feel the warmth and love from the colours, it helped me to feel held, give me hope. Hilary knew what that meant to me, and I wanted to share it with her, for her. I searched the internet for the print on the card but couldn't find it so contacted the company who had the copyright. They told me it was out of print, but to my delight they agreed to print me two copies as a one-off. It meant I could send Hilary the warmth, colour and love that I had because of her and wanted to give to her. When Hilary had been away previously, I hadn't sent her a card or letter and decided that I would send her newsy letters and cards from time to time which she could choose to open if she felt up to it; she knew my handwriting and I trusted it would be OK. I sent a card to her saying I hoped each day brought her more strength until she was fully recovered and that I was thinking of her.

I missed her so much and continued to have quiet 'me time' and use my journal to help me manage my feelings. I wrote as if I was talking to Hilary in the same way as when I spoke to Little Me and how I spoke to God. They were positive connections created from the relationships I had formed.

Colours are brighter, and they touch my senses. The brightness of the flowers brings sweet scent and warmth. I see and feel them. I didn't know them before you introduced me, and I didn't know it was possible to feel colour as if absorbing the delight of it into my very being. Now that I know it I cannot unknow or un-feel its brightness, beauty and warmth.

I used to look out through eyes projecting my inner belief of badness, sense of grey. Sense of evil, a dirty rag, a stench of a rotting soul dwelling within. I would sleep a deep sleep escaping from myself for those hours, waking to find the same person with all the burdens and all the feelings of bad returning with a speed that left me feeling the sleeping respite had brought no relief.

You helped me to shed the cape of shame as bit by agonising bit we worked on every experience and exposed every facet until the route was exposed and neutralised by truth. The truth will set you free! I am free of the cape of shame, of the burden of guilt and the annihilation of self. I am me who carries the responsibility for my actions and not of others.

This helped contain me for a while, but my sense of myself with warmth, colour and acceptance where I felt I was walking proudly in my own skin, feeling good about me, would be revisited by the fragile, insecure self and would at times leave me feeling lost and alone. The difference was that I knew I didn't have to manage on my own, and as agreed with Hilary I contacted Maggie.

Maggie arranged to see me a week later. I shared with her my fears about Hilary, checking out how she was with her.

I talked about my gran looking after me whilst my mum was ill and shared with Maggie that it was how I felt about her with Hilary being ill. I told her that Hilary had talked about the situation being a different experience for me and my telling Maggie was me facing my fears instead of hiding from her. I knew I had done that the last time Hilary was away. Maggie expressed interest in what I had said and asked, 'So I am the matriarch?'

This made me smile – she was softer than my gran, with a soothing voice, and I felt that title didn't really fit her! Telling her about feelings that had felt so scary and her accepting those feelings took away the power of a fear that had left me feeling I needed to hide.

I went on to share what was happening in my life, how I felt and how much she, Hilary, and The Woman's Service had helped me and my partner. Maggie referred to the article in the *Oxleas NHS Trust Exchange Magazine* (issue 24, 2011) about the award given to The Woman's Service and the letter I wrote to her back in September 2010. She talked about how special I was to the service and how important my letter had been in helping The Woman's Service stay open, and I felt so good. This many years on I was better able to understand the importance of my letter, the significance of Maggie's letter to me in that moment. I knew I had given something back. We explored what I felt I needed whilst Hilary was away and agreed on a session each month during April, May, and June.

Over the next few weeks, I began to feel so alone without Hilary. I missed her so much and feared I was losing her just like I had lost my mother. There was no further news other than it was taking her longer to recover and I found it all so distressing. Maggie had agreed with Hilary that she would let me know how she was as and when news was received, which felt good to know, but it was still hard to tolerate the silence.

Feeling so alone in this busy life
No one stops to say hello
People all around, none at my side
Maybe now is time to go
Silence from Hilary is hard to bear
So much with her I want to share
So used to her being there
For me to tell my hopes and fears
So, what shall I do with my life?
Stay where I am and see how it goes?

Go off and set up another home?

Jack in my job and do something new?

Find a different life with different things to do?

Unusually, I couldn't seem to find comfort in writing and my May appointment with Maggie felt so far away. I had been so used to exchanging text messages with Hilary, leaving messages on her answerphone and hearing her voice when I needed to, and speaking to her in addition to weekly sessions; even though I had felt ready to end, this felt too hard, this wasn't planned, and it wasn't my choice or Hilary's. I hated it.

I still had the print of 'our bench' and decided it was the right time to send it to her. I worked on the words I would use, and wrote the following:

Dear Hilary,

I have wanted to send you a copy of the card you gave me that became our bench, our place to be when I need you. It has worked so well for me every time I have asked if you will join me there and when I look at the picture, I remember the comfort and warmth I feel when I imagine us there together. I feel warmth and comfort, I feel safe, and I feel free. It is a place of wellbeing!

I know it is for me, but I also know it is something we share, and I hope you will know something of the love and care I am sending you with the picture.

Maggie told me you will need to be away longer than you thought, and I know you will not

be happy about that. Thinking of you and hoping
you are fully recovered very soon.

Love, Tricia

I sent the letter and framed print to Hilary, not knowing how long it would be before she would be able to return. This somehow freed me up and I was able to write how I had been feeling and the details about some recent dreams. I had distressing dreams about not being able to bring life to the lifeless body of my grandson, and in the same dream a friend left me feeling completely powerless. A few days later I awoke from a completely different dream. I was in a beautiful calm place that I didn't recognise. I could hear Hilary's voice and feel her presence but didn't know who she was.

Another voice said, 'Hilary has been amazing in all this, she was in a nearby hospital when it happened.'

I didn't know what had happened, but I felt calm and then I heard Hilary's voice say, 'People sometimes hide until they are ready to come out.'

I talked to her and experienced her body language and presence as so loving and accepting and I felt completely safe. As I woke, I felt as though I had seen Hilary and as if she had held me in her arms like a mother would hold an infant. It was healing. I wanted to go back to sleep to find her again, to capture the beauty and specialness of that moment in its entirety.

I knew I couldn't wait any longer to know how Hilary was, so called Maggie to see if there was any news. She had recently seen Hilary but was waiting to talk to me about it in our next session. I told Maggie not knowing was the hardest thing for me. She told me that Hilary wouldn't be able to return to work until the following September but that I was in her thoughts, and she was happy for news of how she was to be shared with me.

I knew Hilary wouldn't be happy about not being well enough to return to work and this was much longer than I had imagined. Hilary wouldn't have received my letter or framed print because she was in hospital, but Maggie said she was sure Hilary would be pleased to receive the gift and I knew she was right. Maggie also said she thought it important that I knew what was happening because honesty and trust was missing from my life as a child, and I must have it now. I very much appreciated Maggie's care of me and thanked her.

In our next session we talked in more detail about what was happening for Hilary and how I was feeling about the sadness I felt for her being so ill and the pain of the long silence resulting from it. Maggie acknowledged how difficult it was, given that Hilary and I had been in a relationship with regular contact for so many years. She said that she had known Hilary for a long time and had frequent contact with her over the years but since her illness all contact was through her husband. Maggie acknowledged the silence was hard and said she missed her too. She talked about her relationship with Hilary being different to mine but that she knew for a therapist the relationship is personal and asked if I understood that. I did understand, but with Maggie's honesty and openness it somehow meant more to me. I told her that knowing how Hilary was doing helped me, as the silence had been too painful.

Maggie also said that Hilary wouldn't be returning to The Woman's Service. I had hoped to have an ending with her there, for her and me to meet in June.

Maggie said, 'Although I am not Hilary, I am here for you now and in the future if you need me.'

I continued to feel amazed at how much Maggie was willing to give me. Saying 'thank you' didn't feel enough.

My life continued to be very busy with work, family, and voluntary work. I was a social butterfly and liked spending time with family and friends, and kept up my singing lessons, so there was plenty to occupy me. Being busy was also a way of not feeling the pain of missing Hilary and at times I would allow myself to become busier than was good for me.

In my next session with Maggie we talked about some of the other things in my life that I was struggling with, and it felt good to share those with her. She updated me about Hilary and how poorly she was with a disease that, although it would not kill her, could not be cured and that she might not be recovered enough to return to work in September.

I knew I would not see Hilary again at The Woman's Service and in that moment wondered whether I would ever see her again, wondered if our agreed private arrangement would ever happen. I didn't feel I could express how terrible I felt, but Maggie acknowledged things were tough and said, 'Hilary cares deeply for you and will be missing you too.' In a moment of such sadness, I found those words so comforting. Maggie offered me a date for July, which I accepted.

So, four months into Hilary being off sick and with Maggie's support, I was finding ways to manage myself, my emotions, and my life without contact with her. I often felt as though I was surviving again rather than living, but I managed not to sink back into being numb and found lots of fun things to do in an attempt to balance the hard things

I faced and the emotional pain I felt. I knew I was holding on to the experience of my relationship with Hilary and all she had given me, and to Maggie during her absence.

My July session felt like a long time coming, and I needed Maggie. She told me Hilary was on the mend and hoped to return to private practice in September. She told me that Hilary thinks about me and wanted to continue to work with me because I had moved on so much and had used therapy so well. I liked hearing that, but it didn't feel enough. July meant there would be a break of several weeks from support, but I had prepared myself for that.

Maggie asked me if she could offer me anything more and reminded me that I could return to the Service if I needed to. I thanked her and told her I had decided to see Hilary privately when she returned, which was the plan before her last surgery. Maggie advised me that she would update my GP and would recommend further psychotherapy in case I wanted to return to The Woman's Service in the future.

The subject of abuse seemed to be in the media on a daily basis with headline stories and people coming forward for help, but the services were not there to meet that need. It meant people who needed talking therapy tended to be referred for CBT, a valuable therapy in its own right but not something to replace what The Woman's Service offered. Maggie informed me that the service was going to be moved to another site. I had written a letter to the Local Health Authority many years earlier about the poor environment of the original mental health centre that stood on the same site as the current building.

I felt so sad when I left Maggie that day. I had been going to The Woman's Service since 2007, and nine years later I was leaving there for the last time. I felt angry that such a lovely environment was being taken away for those who needed it. I wrote a letter to the CEO of Oxleas asking them not to relocate to the new site. Unfortunately, it didn't stop the relocation, but the Service continues in its new home and that's the main thing. I sent Maggie a copy of the letter along with a card expressing my appreciation for all she had given to me.

In the weeks between ending with Maggie and waiting for Hilary to return I experienced the whole gamut of feelings from loneliness, distress, sadness, misery, unhappiness, no colour, cold to indifferent, resentful, sorry, OK, happy, joyful, warm and colourful! It was tough but I was feeling, which was so different from how I had been before. Sending Hilary updates of how I was and what I was doing helped me feel connected to her, and I knew she would be pleased to know how things were for me. I didn't expect to hear from her, but I missed her so much. I also felt so angry that she left me for so long.

It was approaching the end of August and I had had no word from her. I didn't know when or if she would be back and I feared for her and for me; it was so, so hard.

Year Six

Hilary's long-awaited email came in the first week of September, and I was surprised at how mixed my feelings were about it. I had imagined I would jump for joy at the news of her coming back – but instead I felt overwhelmed and comforted all at the same time. We talked about how she was and the unpleasantness of what she had been through, then talked about what might be helpful to me and her fees. It was quite strange talking about what times would suit me, when she would be free and what her fees were.

Her return came at such a good time. I had recently learned that my stepfather had advanced cancer of the oesophagus and the prognosis was very poor because of his other health problems. He had told me he didn't care because he missed my mum so much and just wanted to be with her since her death nine years earlier. I knew he meant it and I felt very sad. I told Hilary about it and she was her lovely self. Talking to her brought me comfort, but I also felt a little reserved, which she picked up on. She said, 'Just because I am ready to come back doesn't mean you are, and it is perfectly OK if you decide not to see me.' It felt so good to talk to her.

I thought about what I wanted to do and emailed Hilary to let her know that along with it being lovely to talk to her it also felt a little odd. That we were moving into something new. I told her I had missed her so much and at times it felt unbearable, and I knew I would find it extremely challenging to express the negative feelings of not being able to see her for so long. I shared my concerns that we were solid and familiar before the break but that it felt different and although I was trying to be curious about it, I felt fearful.

I added the following quote I heard at the end of the well-known American crime series *Criminal Minds* and said I would like to live by it.

> *'Scars remind us of where we've been but they don't have to dictate where we're going.'*

Hilary responded, agreeing a day and time, and asked if I would like to talk to her to go through some of the things I had mentioned. We talked and she opened the conversation, offering me a few free sessions because she didn't think it was fair that I hadn't been able to end with her at The Woman's Service and it would give us some time to explore what would work. I wasn't expecting her to offer me any free sessions, but she said she wanted to. I accepted her offer. I felt as though Hilary was giving me a 'sorry' even though she couldn't have done anything about being ill and absent for so long!

The session was still a couple of weeks away, and I was very busy with my stepfather and his hospital appointments as well as with the grandchildren who were the light in the darkness of it all. I had allowed little time for me or to think about my upcoming session with Hilary.

I arrived at Hilary's with half an hour to spare, so waited in a side road before parking on her drive. I was aware of feeling nervous, and as I rang on her bell I regretted being there and wanted to escape. I kept telling myself not to be daft and that it was 'only Hilary'. We had shared so much intimate pain and emotion over the years, including the births of my grandsons! Yet this felt different, like unknown territory, a road never trodden by us.

When she opened the door, I was struck by how different she looked; she had lost so much weight, but she looked well. It felt odd to be sitting in her consulting room in her home. I had often teased her about coming to live with her and had long wished I could be with her in her home and there I was. I felt I had no right to be there and was itching to get out, but I also wanted to stay forever and didn't want the session to end.

She had a comfortable chair with a footstool in her consulting room, and I settled into telling her how her love and care had replaced the abusive feelings and how I no longer owned all that my mum and Ernest did to me. I told her I was the strength for Little Me because of what she had given me. At the end of the session Hilary said she thought I was together and that I looked well. I agreed with her but said I still wanted to climb in somewhere and feel safe. She nodded and smiled and then I said, 'My suitcase is in the car,' and asked, 'Where are you putting the tent?' and we both laughed.

Seeing Hilary again brought up so much turmoil. One moment I wanted to leave, thinking I didn't miss her and didn't need her; the next, I wished I could have cried with her and told her I was afraid. I wanted to thank her, resist her, fight her. I felt the rawness of what it felt like to be without her for all those months. I felt I was in chaos, in hell and feared I would be like a swarm of bees for her.

I sent her a text. 'I hope you are ready for a flood, well OK, a few tears!'

'Am ready for tears, floods and all the stations in between!'

Interesting that I couldn't share the enormity of how I felt with her even though a large part of me knew her response would have been the same if I had. I felt so calm and settled after exchanging those few words with her.

Over the weeks we talked about how hard it was being without her, the long silence, and the agony I felt at times. How I needed to cry and express all that pain but couldn't. She asked me what I thought might help but I couldn't tell her, nor could I tell her that in the first session after her return I felt she had moved away from how I was feeling when I told her about it. Interestingly, she asked me in a later session if she had moved me away from those feelings. I didn't want to own up to feeling that way because I knew she had been through such a terrible time, and I knew she would not have found it easy to accept that she couldn't work or that we had to stop our sessions.

I missed Hilary and I knew she also missed me. She had made sure I was supported in her absence, and I had felt heard and cared for by Maggie but also appreciated by her. They had managed to give me a different experience to that of my childhood. It felt hard to express feelings that I felt were negative and selfish when they had given me so much. I managed to tell Hilary that at times I wanted to die rather than feel the pain I was in but that I couldn't tell Maggie for fear of being seen as ungrateful and if I said those words out loud, they would be out there and real.

Tears fell as I found myself telling Hilary the enormity of the distress I felt. She reminded me that I had been so sure I would be punished for my feelings and that would have made it hard to tell Maggie and her. I knew these feelings belonged to the child me, feelings that gripped me with fear and paralysed my emotions causing me to stay silent. Learning to tell was scary, but with the skill and support of Hilary and Maggie and my determination not to allow the abuse to continue to govern me – and my very brave little girl within – I was gradually finding the courage to do it.

Soon after my return to Hilary, I was so moved by the letter Maggie sent me in response to my letter of support and thank you card.

Dear Trish,

I have been taking in the words of your lovely card, thank you.

I am so impressed at what you have achieved and also with the way you use words poetically to communicate the real and lived experience of an alive and ongoing psychotherapy relationship. You demonstrate that a relationship can form and may begin to challenge the predominance of internal abusive connections. It's really inspirational ... Whatever the future hold for any of us I shall always keep you in mind as someone who has never stopped trying to survive, to create, to love, move on, and to make sense of all that life has thrown at her. You give me hope.

Best wishes

Maggie Schaedel

I didn't share Maggie's letter with Hilary in the next session – not sure why. I talked about the impact of Hilary's influence on me, and how our relationship benefited me and those around me, particularly my children, grandchildren and partner. The acceptance and love I felt from Hilary and from Maggie was deeper and more containing than I felt as a small child even before my mum became ill. It was a beautiful experience; they were beautiful connections.

Another break was upon Hilary and me, but this time for a few weeks for a holiday. A much better reason to be having a break, but still not easy for me. In the second week of the break, I had a disturbing dream. It was my mother's face on mine. I was looking at myself as if in a mirror – evil angry eyes and a contorted mouth spitting out hate looked back at me, but I was also observing it as though looking on – I clawed at it to get her off me. It made me think about a comment Hilary had made in one of our sessions about me telling my mother that, if she looks at me with disapproval, I should tell her to go away. This was more than disapproval – it was hate; but I knew it didn't belong to me. It felt so significant, and by the time Hilary and I were due to meet I didn't feel a single session would be enough to work through the enormity of what I felt. I contacted Hilary and asked if we could have an additional session. She offered me an additional day the following week and acknowledged the difficulty of returning from a traumatic break and then having another quite long one.

When we met, I thanked her for the additional session and said that I had managed without her for so long yet found the prospect of not seeing her for a few weeks so hard. I told her about the dream and that I knew I was clawing at the face to get it off me because I knew it wasn't me. I said that the distress I felt whilst dreaming caused me to cry out, awakening my partner. As he called my name and took me in this arms I woke up and the feeling of distress left me. I understood what my mum did to me was terrible, that I knew at my core that it wasn't my fault, and I wasn't responsible for making her ill.

Hilary nodded and said that she must have been desperate, and I said I remembered her being a good mum when I was small. Hilary asked if I could try and hold the face of my mum gently when I experience those dreams rather than claw at it. I wasn't expecting her to say that; it gave me something to think about. I told her I knew I linked her and my mum, but they were very different.

Hilary said when my mum went away it was very traumatic for me and she was different when she came back. Hilary had been away and had been very ill, which had also been traumatic for me. She said we needed time to connect and for me to trust that she wasn't different. She would often remind me whenever she went away that she would be back as 'the same old Hilary' and she was. I didn't want the session to end, and I didn't want to leave.

The feelings of desperation for Hilary and the distressing dreams, along with the feeling of that rock in my throat and pain in my gut, had revisited me. I told Hilary of my dream of Little Me afraid and in a distressed state; I had a sense of Hilary being around, but she wasn't visible. She asked if Little Me felt comforted. I told her she didn't and that usually my partner would wake me during a distressing dream, but on this occasion my partner didn't hear me. I was stuck in the dream until I woke myself up from it. Hilary talked about the different feelings I have when we meet and that they are all OK. I expressed the struggle I had with holding on to the solidness and security I felt with her and that I would sometimes lose it. That at times I felt fearful and desperate. Hilary said because I am in tune with her that I

270

might well be picking up some of her fear and desperation. We spoke of my mum, and I told Hilary, 'I know at times I feel back in the dark place of my childhood where I felt lost in that bleak place and felt bad.' She acknowledged my feelings.

The following night another distressing dream visited me. I was in a train station and there were problems with the trains, which meant I was at risk of being late for my appointment with Hilary. I tried to get a message to her, but the text and phone icon wouldn't reveal themselves, nor would the email. I asked for help, but none came, I tried to get a bus but couldn't and I knew I had no way of letting Hilary know I wouldn't be able to get there, but worst of all I wouldn't be able to see her. No comfort, no Hilary, no help. I was so alone. I woke from the dream feeling tense; my body ached, my jaw ached from the efforts I had made to reach Hilary. As I lay in bed in the early hours with sleep as unreachable as Hilary had been in my dream, I imagined sitting with her in her room telling her about the dream and saying, 'I have to have you in my life, you have to be there, I need you.' I imagined her saying, 'I am here, and you have me, it was your mum you needed when you were small.' I knew there were deep sobs within me for that terrible situation. I was so lost, so alone. That alone was enormous!

I thought about how for so many years I had existed, that wasn't good enough for me any longer. I wanted to live, I wanted to feel the 'beautiful in the moment connections' that I experienced when I was with my grandchildren. I recalled a lovely moment with my granddaughter snuggling up with me, chatting away with her sparkling happy eyes and joyfully free voice, giggling as she spoke and laughing at the film we were watching. I felt so protective of her. As I recalled that special moment with her, I realised she had reached the age I was when Ernest sexually abused me. I knew she would not be able to protect herself from something like that. The beauty of her freedom, her sense of self, would be destroyed in a moment – it didn't bear thinking about, it was too horrible.

I felt a rush of sadness for Little Me, how small and vulnerable I had been with no one to protect me or look out for me. I had known this but not felt it in such a deep way. Hilary had told me over the years that Little Me was a heroine, was beautiful, and I had experienced moments when I felt that, but this new level of understanding of how vulnerable I was as a child went deeper. This knowing was of mind, body and soul.

The struggle with crying with Hilary and my habit of holding back continued to plague me. I questioned why it felt so hard, why I didn't feel as though I had enough of Hilary even though she had given and continued to give me so much. I told her how desperate I felt when I had no way of seeing her or talking to her when she was ill. She told me it was no surprise I felt that way given what had happened to me as a child. That my mum had gone away when I was young, and when I was an adult she died of cancer, and then Hilary went away, and she has cancer. She asked me what my worst fear was, and I told her that she might die or have to retire, and I would never see her again. I talked about how much our relationship had helped me, but Hilary put it back to me, saying, 'Our relationship worked because of what you put into it.'

I knew I had, but so had she. I talked about how she had made the journey to The Woman's Service every week through the snow, the rain and the heavy traffic to see me. Hilary said she did the journey because she wanted to work with Maggie and be part of The Woman's Service and was there for me because she wanted to be. I cried!

We had a few sessions left before Christmas, and Hilary talked about needing a long break so I wouldn't see her for a few weeks. We talked about how I coped when she was away and whether emailing her with what I was doing and how I was feeling helped. I told her it did and reading my journal also helped. She asked me how; I shared with her how I had drawn strength from our relationship, and just as sadness would sometimes wash over me, a sense of feeling so secure would, too. I told her I would walk tall with confidence, feeling good about myself as though I had no burdens to carry, I would feel free and light. I liked feeling that way, but it didn't stay with me all the time and would give way to me feeling so terrible that I wanted to die. The longer I didn't see her, the harder it became to hold on to the sense of good and I would be afraid.

I so wanted the abuse I suffered in my childhood to impact on me less, to feel less burdened. I told Hilary that I knew I could never change what had happened, but I didn't want it to have so much power over my thoughts and feelings. I managed to tell her that I couldn't let go of the pain I was feeling and had pain in my chest and neck because I was holding back the tears. Hilary asked why I was doing that, and I said, 'I'm afraid you will see the person my mum saw. The "ugly, snivelling, miserable little girl, the hateful, nasty little girl with the ugly fat mouth who was filthy and disgusting".'

Hilary said she had never thought of anyone in those terms and that she cared about me and didn't see me that way. I knew what she was saying was true but I wasn't quite able to feel it. I thought about the years we had been meeting and how Hilary had reiterated that to me so often over that time.

My relationship with Hilary continued to feel very much like mother and child. I told her I felt she had emotionally nurtured me from the abused, traumatised little girl and I had noticed a more equal relationship emerging where I felt like an adult with my little girl within me. As though I was somehow able to understand the link I made between my mum and Hilary on a different level. I felt I was separating Hilary from my mum, separating myself from what my mum used to say I was. My relationship with Hilary had been with me in child, the vulnerable Little Me who was so hurt and damaged existing in the bleakness of the cold bleak place. I felt different, I no longer saw Little Me as a separate person; I felt like the little girl was me and I was starting to like myself.

Hilary nodded. 'There may be times when the little girl might come separately and that would be OK.'

A photograph I took of Kelsy Park Lake, symbolising my life – a cold, bleak place but now with a touch of colour.

I told Hilary how moved I felt when thinking about my granddaughter who had reached the age I was when the sexual abuse began. I couldn't imagine being free and happy when I was nine years old. I was so different to her at that age. Hilary asked me what I thought my granddaughter would do if someone tried to abuse her. If a person touched her and tickled her genitals doing things that felt nice so that she didn't recognise it as abuse.

I felt a strike of pain go through me, like a stab in my soul, as I heard those words, 'I don't know, but I hope she would know it wasn't normal to be touched that way and she would tell her mummy.' My feelings went deep, so deep and I felt Hilary was being realistic about the risks to children now and also helping me see that I was not responsible for what was done to me. No child can ever be responsible for the actions of an adult, no matter the circumstances and regardless of what they are told.

In our last session before the Christmas break, I took a gift for Hilary. I had done so since early in our relationship as a thank you. She would always ask if she could open her gift in the session, and I would always say yes. She expressed delight at her gifts, saying she loved dark chocolate and commented on how beautifully I wrapped her gift, asking if I did that for everyone. I laughed and said, 'Not to that standard.'

'Just for important people,' she said and we both laughed.

We talked about the break and how I felt a sadness at Christmas time that I didn't understand. I told Hilary how hard my mum worked to make Christmas special and how tired she would be, resulting in her screaming and shouting at the slightest thing that didn't go right on the day. I talked about how unhappy I had been for most of my life and that Christmas brought that to the fore. Giving gifts brought me pleasure and I put a lot of thought into what to buy people, what I thought they would like.

I talked to Hilary about how I could feel less burdened, and she suggested I left those feelings with her, and she would look after them for me. She said I didn't have to take them away with me. I smiled at her and acknowledged that I didn't have to. She asked me if there was a particular time over Christmas that was difficult for me. After some thought I said, 'After it is all over, I feel down and sad.'

Hilary suggested I call her after Christmas when I feel that way. I was so grateful for her offer but felt worried that I would experience that terrible yearning and pain of loss during the break, that I would feel lost and wandering in that bleak and cold place. It felt horrible when I thought about it but I somehow knew it would be different this time. The break wasn't because of illness or because I wasn't wanted or loved or cared about. As I thought about my session with Hilary I felt as though I had moved from something completely traumatic to something manageable – I knew I wasn't the bad, dirty or horrible child but the decent and important human being that I had always been. I couldn't see that before because of the damage and hurt. The label of shame I carried because of what people did to me. It was never me; it was never mine. I know that now because of all the hard work both Hilary and I have done.

I felt more contained during this break and that helped me to feel free in a way I hadn't before. There was much happening in my life, and Christmas was always a very busy time, with family gatherings and last-minute preparations. This year brought with it added pressure for our family because cancer would drastically reduce the life expectancy of my stepfather, a life he hadn't wanted to live since my mother died. We hoped he would eventually embrace life as a widower, but he had little interest in treatment. He fought the medical professionals when they suggested anything that would prolong his life; and had asked me to arrange a trip to Zurich so he could choose how and when he died. It wasn't something I felt I could arrange but believed he had the right to choose. I helped him find the details he needed so that he could arrange it for himself and agreed to travel with him. His relationship with my younger brother was strained, but he was very fond of his teenage grandson and to my relief seemed to change his mind about Zurich after a visit from him.

So, an eventful Christmas, but one where, although much sadness was around, I didn't feel burdened with the pain and hurt that I would usually have felt.

I missed Hilary over those weeks with a fondness rather than a desperation. I tried to call her but unusually her answerphone wasn't working so I couldn't leave her a message. She had told me her availability and mentioned that she would be away for a family wedding but would be free after Christmas. I eventually managed to speak to her. We had a brief chat and exchanged some of what we had done over the break which all felt light-hearted and good. I didn't want to talk about anything heavy. In a moment of silence towards the end of those few minutes, Hilary said, 'I'm still here Tricia,' and I enjoyed the comfort and warmth of knowing that she knew me so well.

In the following sessions I managed to talk to her about my feelings of rejection when I couldn't reach her, which opened up the conversation about feeling abandoned and alone when she was off sick. Hilary acknowledged my feelings and told me that she had abandoned me due to illness, which was similar to that of my mum. Her acceptance of how I felt made such a difference to me; it seemed to help me accept myself. I gradually became more and more aware of feeling the comfort and safety when I was with her, and I loved feeling that way. As often happened, it would soon be met with feeling insecure and I didn't understand why. I had learned enough to know the feeling would pass, but it felt horrible whilst it lasted.

I messaged Hilary to let her know how I had been feeling, saying '… Having sat on it, I still don't understand it? Think I just want you to know, I feel comfort in telling you.'

She replied, 'I'm glad you've told me and perhaps you're feeling a bit better. I wonder if it's the vulnerability thing – we were talking about things you have no or little control over – illness, your stepdad, me, your mum?'

It helped me to hear from her; I loved her wisdom, I loved how she knew me, was so tuned in to me. I loved our relationship. I responded with, 'Thank you, Hilary, I'm taking some me time this morning with my journal and will see what comes. Think I might be learning to be curious – with the proviso that I don't end up like the cat!'

Between holding on to Hilary, contacting her when I couldn't hold her enough to feel safe and secure and using my journal, I would usually manage to process my feelings and there was comfort in both methods. Some might think aspects of the latter a type of madness, but it worked for me.

My conversation with Hilary about my granddaughter came to mind and I wondered if that was how Ernest started on me. I had no recollection of anything so subtle but hated the feeling of vulnerability, of being exploited. I experienced a sensation across my chest, felt anger and fury for the betrayal of trust. It felt powerful and horrible, and I feared for my grandchildren. I questioned how we could protect my grandchildren when abuse was so subtle and so easy.

I talked about it in my next session with Hilary and told her about the horrible feeling I had at the mention of my granddaughter being abused and how I'd felt fearful for my grandchildren. I shared with her that I had no recollection of any of the abuse I experienced being so subtle. Hilary told me children wouldn't be suspicious of being touched, particularly not back when I was a child. She then said children can learn to protect themselves, and if they are safe and secure, they may be able to tell someone.

Towards the end of January Hilary was unwell with a bug and had to miss a session. I noticed my first reaction was to feel responsible. She recovered quickly, though, and offered me an appointment a day later, which I jumped at. I shared with her how much I feared for her and for me whenever she was ill. Hilary reminded me to reassure Little Me and let her know she is safe. I told Hilary that I felt cared for by her, that I still felt she was careful with my feelings, which meant I felt she planned for me and considered me like a parent does. I shared with Hilary how much I loved to play and giggle with the grandchildren, with such beautiful freedom, a freedom that was robbed from me at such a young age. Hilary remembered me saying, "I want to come out to play," in the early days of therapy and I was continuing to 'come out to play' with my grandchildren. I was beginning to know what it felt like to be present. I had previously felt like I was on the outside looking in but that was changing; most of the time I was on the inside.

At the end of January Hilary sent me a text message to ask if I could arrive for my appointment a little earlier. I immediately worried; she had offered me longer sessions, but I knew arriving 10 minutes early wouldn't be for that.

On arrival I avoided the news I dreaded, but Hilary asked me if I wondered why she asked me to come earlier, and I had no choice but to hear her tell me the cancer was back and she was going to retire. She told me she knew she needed to stop work to be fair to people.

I would have weathered the storm with her, I would have accepted cancelled appointments at short notice if it meant I could continue seeing her, but I knew that wasn't going to happen. I told her, 'I couldn't want this to be happening less if it were happening to me.'

Hilary told me she was so sorry that I was going through this again with her. I felt terrible and couldn't imagine how she was feeling. She said, 'I have lots of people who love me, including you.'

I cried, saying I was so sorry she had to go through this again, 'Sorry for you and sorry for me,' I said. 'Cancer is a cunt.' I was shocked at my words.

Hilary appeared unphased by my comment, and with a thoughtful look on her face said, 'The word cunt means vagina and it is a shame to use it so negatively.'

I laughed at her response and told her that word isn't one I ever used, that it was a taboo in my childhood, a forbidden word. I told her I didn't know what to say and I cried again.

This news must have devastated Hilary, but somehow she managed to hold herself together during the session, keeping me at the centre. We talked about what support I might want. I had set enough money aside to see Hilary for around a year, to give me time to end when I was ready. I wanted to end my sessions on my terms, and although I knew she would retire at some point I couldn't imagine her out of my life.

Hilary told me she would be 70 the following year, and laughingly said, 'I am an old biddy.'

She managed to make me laugh again – but I felt so robbed. I couldn't find the words to describe how I was feeling. I felt she was my life source, that she had raised me emotionally from that hurt little six-year-old girl and I had become a connected person, with such depth, because of her. She had given of herself, and I loved her for it.

For a reason I didn't understand, I felt uncomfortable in my next session with Hilary. We exchanged looks that I couldn't read and didn't understand. I talked about my frustration of not being able to let go of my pain and cry with her in the way I felt I needed to. I asked her why I couldn't. She asked me why I was asking her that and I said, 'Because I don't know!'

'Why do you think you do it?' She seemed quite firm in her response.

'I think it is because of how my mum treated me but that is in the past.'

Hilary said, 'At times you speak and appear childlike, and I believe you are trying to manipulate me to draw out the child in you. I won't do that because it wouldn't be fair, I won't be here to look after her, but you will be.'

I was shocked at what she said but as she spoke those words our eyes met, and my tears began to fall.

I talked about how I didn't bond with her when we were meeting for the couple therapy but that I saw how she dealt with my partner's behaviour, how she accepted him and worked with his pain, and I thought she was strong, and I trusted her. I talked about when I told her I wanted to

281

come out to play and how I remembered her saying to me, 'You are great.' I told her I didn't know colour until she showed me.

I could no longer talk but I could cry, I cried in a way I could cry when I was alone, but I felt comfort when crying with her. As the tears began to slow, I wiped them on my blanket and Hilary said, 'There are tissues for that,' and I laughed. I used the tissues and dried my face, but I felt too embarrassed to blow my nose properly so just wiped it.

Hilary looked at me knowingly, she knew how self-conscious and awkward I felt and said, 'Why don't you give your nose a good blow – crying is about tears and snot and it is OK.' I laughed again and then cried again. It was something I had needed to do for so long. I felt exhausted by all the crying, delicate.

I felt such sadness. Hilary was a healthy attachment for me. I feared I would fall apart without her. I thought about all the times I needed her but wouldn't call her for fear of being too much for her, fear of making her ill. I lost count of how many times she would tell me in her lovely, firm, assertive, and at times frustrated, voice to 'pick up the phone' if I needed her. She told me it was her responsibility to decide if I was too much for her and not mine, and if she couldn't talk or it wasn't a good time for her, she would say so and arrange a time when she could. She told me she was there for me because she wanted to be. I knew all that she said was true, but it felt so hard to hold on to that truth.

With only a few weeks left before her retirement I knew I needed to make the most of every moment available with Hilary, and I didn't want my insecurities about contacting her between sessions to stand in the way. I left a message on her answerphone asking if we could talk before the next session. I loved hearing her voice; I felt soothed by it.

We talked about all the challenges I was facing. My daughter was struggling with a life-changing health condition, my partner had been diagnosed with diabetes, my stepfather was in a hospice for end-of-life care, and Hilary was retiring and also had cancer. It was all too much. We talked about my fears.

'Are you afraid that I will die?'

'I know you will die one day. My fear is that you and I will not see each other anymore; you have been in my life for so long.' I told her that her retiring felt so final, and the relational approach has meant we have both invested so much.

Hilary said that she questioned whether she had told me too much about her reason for retiring and then felt it was important to be honest with me, reiterating what she and Maggie had said before about honesty being missing from most of my life. She was right; knowing was painful but it was honest, and I wanted to know.

'I wouldn't change anything about our relationship,' Hilary said.

I was so moved by her words and knew it was hard for her too. I cried as I said, 'Nor me.' I told her that she settles and soothes me and there wasn't anyone else who did that for me.

'You know Tricia, there may be something exciting and lovely out there.'

I looked at her, unusually unafraid to hold her gaze, and said, 'There is something exciting and lovely for me in here.' We didn't speak but shared a lovely moment of being moved and amused.

My stepfather died on 21 February 2016 after several days of wonderful care from the nurses and doctors at St Christopher's Hospice. It was where my mother had died nine years earlier and where he wanted to be. Various members of the family had been by his side as he made the journey of departing from this world, and on the day of his death those of us closest to him stayed by his side. My younger brother was with us too, and I felt a peace within me which I hoped he felt. We talked as if he was awake, joked and laughed about things that he had said and done until we could recall no more.

As the early hours arrived, he gradually slipped away, and we all sat in silent respect for his passing until the silence was deafening and, one by one, we left his side. He looked so peaceful in death; no more grieving for the woman he had married 40 years earlier, and, although he didn't believe in God, he longed for death to be with her.

In the session with Hilary following my stepfather's death she said she was so sorry and asked if I was expecting it to happen so quickly. I wasn't and shared the experience with her. She listened as I recounted the story of what happened and how I felt. I told her about the visit my sister and I made to the Chapel of Rest a couple of days later, how young and peaceful he looked and that I had cried, I had cried freely without pain in my neck or throat and thought how easy it was to cry! I told Hilary that I felt time was slipping away from me; she asked whether I meant generally or with her and me. I cried as I nodded and said I wanted extra sessions with her, and as I said those words I cried some more. I would no longer see Hilary after 24 March, and we were at the end of February. We agreed on two sessions each week, which left me feeling so much better.

My remaining sessions were mostly used to talk about our relationship, recapping on what I had learned, things we had shared. We talked about how I had moved from living in a bleak and scary place to colour and warmth, from feeling fearful to being curious, and I reminded Hilary about the emotional 'high street' and how helpful I had found it.

Hilary was amused and said that Woolworths was her 'angry shop', and we both laughed. I talked to her about a holiday we had planned to Vietnam and Cambodia, and she said it was an amazing place to go and shared details of the scooters and her visit there. I loved sharing with her; it felt safe, warm and colourful.

I struggled to write in my journal during some of this time, which left me feeling stuck and unhappy. I had learned over the years that eventually something would shift but not until I was ready for it to happen, I couldn't force it. Not ever a good feeling, but horrible when I had only a few sessions left with Hilary.

After a few days I managed to write again, and as I did, I realised that I no longer felt an inner burden. I was aware of the external pressures and events that burdened me, but the inner burden of feeling worthless like a dirty rag, not being good enough, were no longer sitting within and causing a pain in my gut that weighed so heavily on me. I felt like there was no longer a bleak and scary place, but I knew it was there. I shared this with Hilary and how good it felt when I experienced the freedom and when I could stick up for myself, and she said she hoped I could hold on to both when we were no longer meeting.

We talked about how difficult it was for me to express my anger in my sessions, and it was something Hilary was concerned about. I had always struggled to 'be' angry with

Hilary – and with the cancer back and her having to retire, there was no way I was going to 'be' angry with her. I knew it was one of the undealt with areas that I needed to work on at some point.

Hilary encouraged me to think about the support I wanted before we had to end. I said that I would like to see Maggie when I felt the need for more therapy, and she was supportive of my decision. We both knew Maggie would support me to find someone suitable if she couldn't see me herself.

Those last few sessions were hard but amazing. I asked Hilary if she remembered me saying that I had written in my journal that I wanted to sink into the arms of someone safe and sob, sob and sob? She remembered, and I told her I had found that person in her. She was my safe haven, somewhere I could run to. She told me that working with me had been a wonderful experience because I had the ability to grasp hold of something and work on it and grow. She said she couldn't tell me how much she would miss me. I couldn't say anything when she said that, but I kept eye contact with her and nodded. I eventually told her that I couldn't find the words to express how much she and our relationship meant to me. I knew my journal and poetry would be a way of my doing that and used it.

> I didn't know how to laugh
> I didn't know how to cry
> Knowing how to feel or being alive
> Had passed me by.

I felt the fear of crying melt away, and in our penultimate session I made myself comfortable with my blanket and we sat in an easy silence. I cried in gentle sobs with no throat or gut pain, no sign of the jerking body movements. They weren't angry tears. I knew Hilary was with me in those tears; I knew this was hard for her too. I told her that seeing her for those few months meant so much to me, an opportunity for us to work on some of the things we couldn't previously because of how abrupt the previous ending had to be. Hilary said it meant a lot to her, too. I shared with her how my closest friends had described her as 'a lovely lady' because of how she had helped me. Hilary laughed and said, 'I suppose I can be a lady some of the time,' and we both laughed. She had that glint in her eye and told me, 'I believe the child in me is what the child in you reacted to ... we are very similar, and our little girls are fun and mischievous, and we have a connection there.' I felt so complete with her in that moment, so connected.

We planned for tea and cakes for our last session. I wanted to celebrate with Hilary. Celebrate us, me, her, and our futures – whatever they would hold. I chose a variety of cream cakes; we had shared cakes in the past, so I knew what she liked. I had chosen some gifts for her, a purple scarf because I thought it would suit her and keep her warm. Although I am not sure if I ever told Hilary, her character reminded me of the poem, 'When I am an old woman, I shall wear purple'! I also chose her a small pack of dark chocolate eggs from Hotel Chocolate and a retirement card with a woman celebrating, balancing on a man's head with a glass of wine in her hand.

For the third gift, I copied and framed a photo I had taken of fireworks on New Year's Eve. I had managed to capture the most beautiful explosion of colour with my camera, where a floral firework blossomed lighting up the dark winter sky in front of the Millennium Wheel, and I felt it was a visual description of how I felt because of her. I had learned to see and feel colour out of so much darkness.

I knew Hilary would ask if she could open all the gifts with me and I was looking forward to her reaction, her sensitivity and her sense of fun that I had come to know and love.

I wanted the last session to be for her as much as I could. I gave myself some quiet time and thought about our relationship and all we had worked on over the years. As I thought about our relationship, all Hilary was to me, a poem gradually emerged.

The day of our last session arrived, and I wondered whether I would have the courage to go. A part of me wanted to take a break from therapy, but a bigger part didn't; again, the decision was taken from me, and I had to stop seeing Hilary whether I was ready or not.

I wished I could make the world spin back in time but knew it would be unhelpful to disconnect. I knew I had to face this, but I wasn't facing it alone – Hilary was facing this with me – with her own sadness. We chatted as we ate cakes and drank tea, but I could sense that our hearts were heavy. I asked Hilary how she was feeling, and she said she didn't want to think about it and asked me how I was feeling. Always the therapist! I told her I didn't want to say goodbye and that I didn't feel I had been able to show acknowledgement for the lovely things she had said in recent sessions. I told her I loved it that she was looking forward to retiring, that she would miss me and that she thought our little girls within had connected. Hilary said she could see it meant a lot to me and that I didn't need to say something for her to know. I nodded and acknowledged that words aren't always needed!

I talked about how Hilary had looked after Little Me with the Russian dolls, and cried, saying, 'What if I can't look after Little Me without you, Hilary?'

'I will always be here for her and for you Tricia, but it is you she needs.'

I knew she would always be with me; the love, the care, the challenges, the heartbreak and the laughter would always be with me.

I gave her a copy of the poem I had written.

Early in our relationship you asked me
What I felt about the little girl I used to be
I couldn't feel much, you knew there was more
And with photos to help we began to explore
When we looked back what did we see
A wounded shame-filled little me
Filled with fear numbed by the pain
Inflicted on her again and again
The little girl trapped within
Could do nothing more than withdraw
And there she stayed hidden unseen
Believing she was rotten, dirty, unclean

In moments of panic, in moments of fear
At the thought of ending what we've had for years
I cry out in total despair
What will I do when I see you no more
Will I feel the dread, the cold at my core
I've been in that place before
Hurting, desperate feeling insecure
Filled with self-hate, riddled with shame
Believing I deserve nothing but pain
That dreadful feeling of being alone again

Then I remember in that panic and fear
Your words, 'can you be curious' so I ask myself
Does it belong to the here and now
It was how the child I now hold so dear
Felt existing in that bleak and scary place
No colour, no warmth, no love
I didn't know how to reach her
Didn't care to know she was there
You knew she was there, listening, watching
Waiting till I could show her love and care

The difference you make will always be ours
The love you give, the care you show
An acceptance and appreciation I had never known
Thank you for walking every step of the way
Through so much darkness, so much pain
For caring, for loving, for staying, for being
For helping me understand and accept my feelings
Because of you and all you have given
I know how to play and how to be me
I've moved from existing to living and loving
I live with colour, with warmth, it's so freeing
Hilary, you, our relationship will forever be
The most precious gift ever given to me.

I had intended on reading it to her, but I didn't feel brave
enough in the moment. I could see it was hard for her to
read; she didn't need to say anything and nor did I, which
was just as well because I couldn't have spoken! The
poem did that for me.

I gave her the scarf and chocolates, which she loved. She was delighted with the framed photo and amazed that I had taken it, saying it looked so professional.

My photograph of the fireworks; I gave a copy of this photo to Hilary.

I told her it represented my growth from darkness to bright colour and I wanted her to have a copy because it represented how I had grown because of her. With gifts all given and the loveliest feeling I sat back in the chair with my blanket, and we looked at each other in recognition of our beautiful connection.

The moment came for the session to end. Hilary said, 'We have to finish.' She didn't say, 'It is time,' which was how we usually ended the session.

I couldn't say goodbye – it felt too hard. Hilary thanked me for making her retirement so special. As I stood up, I said, 'We have worked so well together, haven't we?'

She nodded. 'Is this a moment for a hug?'

'Yes, I think so.'

We hugged and Hilary kissed my cheek and then said, 'Oh sorry – I hope that wasn't a wet one!' We laughed and held hands before parting. As she saw me to the door, she affectionately rubbed my arm, saying, 'Take care Tricia.'

'I will – and you.'

Leaving Hilary that evening was so tough. I held her and all she was to me within me and believed nothing, not illness or even death, could take the love I felt inside away from me. I also knew feelings change and my strong sense of self, of goodness, could still be fragile, which would at times make it hard to hold on to that love. I knew those times would leave me feeling lost and alone, but I had learned to be curious about how I felt, and I was emotionally connected. I knew refusing to say goodbye and the pain and hurt of no longer seeing Hilary would need a safe place to be explored, understood, accepted, cried for and healed from, in a way I couldn't with Hilary.

I also knew those feelings were complex and tangled with the wounds and damage from childhood trauma, and I had more work to do, such is the long-lasting and devasting impact of abuse in childhood. I had much support from family and friends and, unlike in my childhood, I didn't have to face this pain alone. I knew I would need more therapy and that Maggie would be there for me when I was ready.

I contacted Maggie three months after Hilary retired. I needed more therapy which helped me to move on and is another story.

Printed in Great Britain
by Amazon

87214550R00176